Faces of Love, Death and Transformation:
A Spiritual Memoir

by
Connie Marshall

Faces of Love, Death and Transformation: A Spiritual Memoir
Copyright© 2008 by Connie Marshall. All rights reserved.

No part of this book may be reproduced or transmitted in any form or by any means, graphic, electronic, or mechanical, including photocopying, recording, taping or by any information storage or retrieval system, without permission in writing from the publisher.

MAYFAIR BOOK PROMOTION, INC.
PROFESSIONAL PUBLISHING SOLUTIONS

For information contact the publisher:

Mayfair Book Promotion, Inc.
P.O. Box 91
Foresthill, CA 95631

www.mayfairbooks.com
prospct1@foothill.net

ISBN: 978-1-934588-34-5

Printed in the United States of America.
Distributed by Reality Press for Mayfair Book Promotion, Inc.

Dedication

To my husband Byrne in humble gratitude

for his grace, humanity, humor

and the eternal love that blesses my soul.

Contents

Acknowledgements vi
Foreword by Chris Hedlund viii
Introduction xii
Chapter 1 1
Chapter 2 15
Chapter 3 29
Chapter 4 31
Chapter 5 41
Chapter 6 59
Chapter 7 69
Chapter 8 79
Chapter 9 101
Chapter 10 111
Chapter 11 119
Chapter 12 127
Chapter 13 143
Chapter 14 149
Chapter 15 165
Chapter 16 173
Chapter 17 183
Chapter 18 187
Chapter 19 191
Chapter 20 199
Chapter 21 205
Chapter 22 219
Chapter 23 227
Chapter 24 239
About the Author 283

Acknowledgments

I have immense respect for the contribution editors make to a work. I had the good fortune to work with two talented professionals:

Thanks to Lesley K. Payne for her support, unlimited patience and insight in helping me create a strong structure and form, integrating the bones of astrology, past lives and ordinary reality so that they move together with grace and harmony—no small feat.

Thanks to Kyle Roderick for inspiring me to dig ever deeper into the motivations and connections of the main characters and encouraging me to mine the story for those rich nuggets of truth that make it shine ever brighter. I would not have had as much courage to plumb the depths without her support.

Thanks to astrologer Chris Hedlund who generously shared his knowledge while diligently researching and analyzing the charts of the main characters. His culling of important connections and transits added validation, purpose and meaning to the story.

Foreword

When Connie Marshall came to me in the late summer/early fall of 2002 and asked me to give her astrological input on a book she was writing, I was deeply intrigued. She said she was attempting to weave a biographical story with past life experiences and astrology into the narrative, something I hadn't seen done before.

I understood the challenge of trying to integrate different layers of reality in a narrative; I had just completed a novel of my own, Jaguar, which interwove the initiatory altered states of shamanic mysticism with a spy thriller. Connie was going to integrate three layers of reality, and the challenge excited me.

At the time I had been a professional astrologer for 31 years, and previously a Teacher-in-Residence at Esalen Institute in Big Sur, California, specializing in transits, the ongoing patterns of planets in the heavens and how they parallel world events and the developments in people's lives. My view is very adamantly non-fatalistic; I do not believe people are controlled or defined by planetary patterns, but they do exert powerful energies that we must navigate wisely.

I suggested to Connie that we examine the astrological patterns that occurred during the various events and developments in the story, and also how they influenced various characters in the story's personal horoscopes when those characters were actively involved in Connie's tale.

Connie diligently performed an archaeological excavation of her life, digging up the dates of scores of key events and developments as well as most of the characters' personal birth data. I studied the planetary patterns of the various time periods of Connie's story and how those patterns interfaced with the personal charts of the characters involved in the events. Over and over the planetary patterns at play during various dramas, turning points, and developments in Connie's story related closely with the astrological energies and made perfect sense.

As a professional astrologer, it was a juicy opportunity to go through a well-chronicled life and examine the many planetary patterns at play. I examined three basic kinds of the astrological patterns at work in the various developments of the story. First, there were the 'fun' patterns, brief periods that occurred during the romance, play, parties, or vacations in the story. Second, there were the very somber, often challenging planetary patterns that tend to hit us with tough issues, tests, ordeals, major life questions that we have to respond to successfully if we are to continue growing and progressing as individuals. Third, there were the life-cycle influences, indicated by the slower planets moving through the various houses of the individual charts and demarcating key developmental stages of life. Over and over again I found those themes matched the kinds of events and developments they were connected to.

In the process of doing this work I have gotten to know Connie's life quite well as I poured through all the key events of her story and through several drafts of the book. I've become intimately familiar with the characters and have developed a deep bond with several of them even though I've never met them.

Some of the things that happen in the story are quite amazing, especially one point in the story where Connie and her husband Byrne experience a shared past life during separate regression sessions and recount precisely the same story in vivid detail.

Connie's story is a fascinating tale, very rich and full of inspiration for people on the spiritual journey and especially for younger women in search of a female role model. Connie's life is no cakewalk and has been filled with severe trials and ordeals, but she finds her spiritual path while thriving professionally and building a deeply fulfilling long-term love relationship with a man who participates in her spiritual journey. While the tale is bittersweet at the end, Connie again triumphs as she digs into her deepest spiritual strengths, abiding in love and creating profound meaning throughout her final, heart-wrenching journey with Byrne, her great love of many lives.

Past lives and astrology aside, this story is a rich and inspirational tale of how one woman continuously finds a way to rise to the challenges of life and become a bigger person with each test. This is the kind of story everybody can gain something from reading.

—Chris Hedlund

Introduction

I was not born to lead an ordinary life. It's written in the stars of my natal astrological chart. Pluto, the planet of transformation, in my 8th house of sex, death and the deep psyche decrees I must face my demons, find my heart and know my soul.

I have come to write this book; it's what I'm supposed to do. It's part of the agreement I made before reincarnating. I'm determined this will be my last tour on this planet—old soul walking, one last ride on the karmic wheel. I'm not doing this anymore. I talked the powers-to-be into letting me jam the karma of several lives into this last one. To go for it, run the gauntlet and be done with it. This life requires I pull myself from the abyss and soar to heights I never considered possible.

I have three projects penciled on my cosmic dance card: to realize I have a higher purpose, to find out what it is and to do it. Fate helps me choose the roads leading to my destiny, bringing the opportunities and challenges through the people I draw into my life and the experiences I need. Fate is the journey, destiny my ultimate goal.

My soul's journey through past lives and the karma of lessons unlearned comes with me into this life. I came to embrace these concepts in my forties after I had my first astrological reading. This triggered a hunger in me to find depth and meaning to my existence that went way beyond my current understanding. Astrology helped me connect the dots from my self to my soul, like a compass for seeing the road map of my life. Astrology gave meaning and purpose to my experiences and the desire to live a more conscious life.

I have learned to appreciate the complex dance of energies among my Sun, Moon, rising sign and the planets, all acting as teachers and agents of change as they move through the different houses of my chart. The positions they occupied at my birth powerfully impact my life, as does their movement through the twelve astrological houses, pushing me to grow, teaching me my gifts, my challenges and clues to my inner being. My astrological chart is a blueprint I can alter with my creative intelligence. The planets offer many ways to express their energy from light to dark, as do the astrological signs. I always have choices. I'm not bound to any particular fate or way of being. There are many potential forks in the road of fate on the path to destiny.

I found great comfort in the realization that in a seemingly chaotic, serendipitous world, there is divine order. My Higher Self collaborates with the planets to keep me on track with my destiny. At various junctures in my life, the planets form powerful energies to keep me on the right road or stop me in my tracks as they did in 1974, wanting me to get serious about my journey through this lifetime.

I believe that my destiny in this life is a journey of the heart. My karma has to do with lessons of love. In a previous life, I had love and didn't appreciate it. In this life I have to experience what it's like to want love, not have it, to find it, and to cherish it. I've known the isolation of a closed heart, the pain of a broken heart and the ecstasy of a healed one—the light and the dark between those points.

In this memoir, four loves return from my previous lives to help me learn my lessons of the heart: My friend Bobby taught me the meaning of unconditional love; Richard and I shared profound passion; Eddie showed me the dark side of love and what it should never be. Byrne, my hero, showed me the meaning of eternal love and its power to transcend time and space, opening my heart and the door to my soul.

I believe the human spirit always reaches higher, and my heart yearned for the bliss of connecting to the divine love. When I was ready, shamanism came into my life and helped me make that connection in powerful and dramatic ways. I have come to experience things most people only dream about.

This memoir of a soul encompasses the tapestry of my karma, my past lives, and my astrological linkages and the lessons of romantic sexual love that led me to the deep love and connection to Spirit—the higher consciousness, that oneness that knows my soul and loves me.

I've heard it said that young souls create karma and old souls resolve karma. I'm an old soul with some loose ends. Successful resolution of the old without creating any new karma is my ticket out of this dimension to new worlds and a higher level of consciousness; I'm graduating; this life is my final exam. Join me on my journey as I work through my karma. Buckle your seat belt, it's going to be a wild ride.

Faces of Love, Death and Transformation:

Chapter 1

Saturn, the inspector general of the planetary cosmos, has been in my 8th house of sex, deep relationships and death since September of 1973, evaluating the foundation and structure of the life I've built over the previous eight years. He finds them weak and crumbling like a house riddled with termites; my life prepares to collapse around me. During the two and a half year renovation, walls tumble and Saturn clears large spaces, eliminating the weak areas and demanding I rebuild on a stronger foundation. Saturn never fools around.

And neither does Pluto, a powerful planet of transformation. Pluto prowls the lair of my subconscious, and deep psyche; he knows the treasures of my soul, gatekeeper to my past lives, ruler of sex and death. Pluto takes me to the dark places in my soul and just when I'm afraid I won't find my way back, he lets me stand on his shoulders of transformation to see the light. He readies to alter my life in ways I never thought possible.

Two other planets of change, Neptune and Uranus, team up to move the process along. Neptune in my 1st house of personal interests and new beginnings raises questions regarding my life and the choices I've made. Her androgynous, mystical shape shifter shrouds me in a web of fantasy, confusion and illusion one moment and gifts me with clarity and enlightenment the next. Neptune gives me my dreams and dissolves my illusions. She traverses the roads in my deep psyche, moving through the dark to light, offering soul connections and transformation. Neptune is magic, transcendence, and nirvana to the few.

Uranus, lord of chaos, holds court in my 11th house of friendships, goals, hopes and wishes, conjuring painful change. Uranus has a direct line to my Higher Self. He knows who I am, holding the mirror to my soul, wanting me to be true to myself and my purpose. When I'm off track as I am now, he brings shock, disruption and even trauma to get my attention. He means business. Uranus seeds visions of what I must do to be a more whole and loving being.

Uranus and Neptune as change agents stir the cauldron of my restlessness and frustration—like the witches from Macbeth.

San Diego, California
September 13, 1974

I can't or I won't cry; I don't know which. Probably both. I numbly wait in the quiet shadows of Pluto's domain—death and transformation. Pluto isn't here for me; he's here for the man I love deeply. Not my husband, or even my lover, but a longtime friend who I love for his kind spirit, innocence and humanity.

I sit in the metal chair at Bobby's bedside, wondering how I can feel so numb and still ache with pain that runs so deep and strong that it feels endless. I keep my tears hostage inside me as I've done since I was a small child.

It was a contest: If I cried, my mother won; if I didn't cry, it proved she couldn't hurt me.

Our battle of wills began at my conception. My teenaged mother thought of me like a cancer killing her dreams, feeling her life would end if mine continued. She lost her battle to abort me, surrendered and married my father at seventeen.

I don't think she ever meant to be a bad mother; she loved me as much as her emotional wounds allowed. My grandmother killed herself when my mother was three. This devastating abandonment left a big hole in my mother's heart and soul. Mom filled it with her lost dreams and the manic depressive illness she inherited from her mother. My existence constantly reminded my mother that she lived a life that she didn't want or consciously choose. I never made it easy for her. That willful tomboy energy of my 1st house with its assertive Mars in Sagittarius rising personality and smart mouth endlessly enraged and frustrated my mother.

I can still see the tiny dining room in the doll-like, one bedroom house in West Sacramento and the violent scene we reenacted on a daily basis.

Mom reaches for me, holding my wrist tightly as we dance our own perverted version of Ring Around the Rosy. Panic compels me to run. We whirl around and around and she slaps and hits me wherever she can. I view this from outside my body in a kind of slow motion. I scream, "You can't hurt me; you can't. You can't make me cry." I say it even as I sob.

To survive, I choose a classic Venus in Capricorn coping mechanism: I erect an impenetrable wall. I will myself not to cry and bury my feelings so deeply that I almost stop having any. I have them now, sitting at Bobby's bedside waiting for him to die and reflecting on our love and friendship.

I'm dying, too, just not in the same way as Bobby. The last time Saturn inspected my 8th house, I'd started first grade at St. Joseph's Academy. My mother, the atheist, hoped the nuns could tame what she experienced as my stubborn, rebellious personality. My Aquarian Sun and I lived a spontaneous, unfettered life while my Dad served in the Navy aboard a cargo ship in the South Pacific during WWII. My mother had her hands full with two small kids and working as a cocktail waitress.

With my strong Mars energy, I was the ultimate tomboy with bruises all over my body from fights and falls. Each morning, I would wake early while my mother and baby sister slept. At four years of age, I quietly dressed in my overalls and T-shirt, strapping my six guns on my small hips. I stuffed my hand-made slingshot in my back pocket, carefully placed my prized marbles in my left front pocket, my pocketknife in the right pocket. My cowboy hat hung from my neck, falling down my back with my long, dark blond braids, tendrils of hair flying around my face. No shoes, I preferred to be barefoot.

At that age, I saw each day as a glorious new adventure awaiting me, along with the breakfast of tortillas and beans I begged each morning from our elderly Mexican neighbors. I preferred those soft, fragrant pillows of delight and rich, dark beans to the cold cereal I would have had to fix for myself. Lunch would be fruit from one of the many trees on our block, or carrots and radishes pilfered from Mrs. Marriot's Victory Garden. It wasn't unusual for me to be gone until dusk when my friend's parents called them inside and I had to go home at last.

I'm not sure what pushed my mother over the edge. I think it was the day my friends and I were playing pirates and we needed treasure to bury. I volunteered my new shoes my mother bought with her carefully saved ration stamps. We never found them. When she put me in first grade at age five, my carefree life abruptly changed course. The Universe pushed me along, with Saturn's help.

Faces of Love, Death and Transformation:

St. Joseph's Academy
September 1946

I stand in line before class that first day, looking in disgust at my navy blue skirt, white middy blouse and navy blue tie; I feel ridiculous. I wear jeans and play with boys. Here classes are co-ed, but during recess the nuns strictly segregate boys from girls with a line down the middle of the playground. I don't know how to play with girls. I'm totally lost.

Bebe Cervantes stands in front of me, smiles, kicks me in the shins and runs off, giving me a preview of more painful experiences to come.

When school ends that first day, I wait in the empty schoolyard for my mother to come and get me. Two hours pass. I sit alone in the deserted yard on the bench and cry, thinking she's finally gotten rid of me. As I work myself into a crescendo of hysteria, a nun finds me, takes me to the principal's office and calls my mother. I bury my face in her voluminous black robe; my body convulses in sobs that make me feel like I will break into pieces. The nun says my mother hasn't abandoned me, just forgotten where I am.

I protest my incarceration at St. Joseph's and refuse to learn anything. I didn't know at the time that my Sun opposite Pluto destines me for major power struggles in my life. My stubborn intelligence rebels against the strict program of discipline and structure imposed by the nuns. Sister Mary Christopher and I engage in fierce battles of will.

I spend my days in passive resistance, drawing Christmas trees to comfort me. I plan to be so uncooperative I'll be sent home never to return.

Alone during recess, I crouch against a wall with my coat wrapped around me against the cold, grieving for the carefree life that's been torn from me. Fun loving Venus hunkers down behind my protective Capricorn wall in survival mode.

Saturn, in the authoritarian guise of Sister Mary Christopher, beats the crap out of me on a daily basis for a full year before I concede defeat. Her favored punishments for me include yanking my braids, slapping my hands with a ruler until she sees tears in my defiant eyes, grabbing the large collar of my sailor's middy blouse, twisting it into a knot and choking me before hurling me like a guided missile against the hissing radiator on the wall. She slaps my head like my mother. I endure the physical abuse; I'm almost desensitized to it. But her ultimate weapon—humiliation—brings me to my knees. Not even my mother called me stupid and lazy, ridiculing me in front of everyone. I'm emotionally paralyzed.

In one of the defining moments of my life, I stand in a circle for reading. I recognize a word for the first time—daddy. I'm so excited I raise my hand and blurt it out. Sister Mary Christopher waits for me to continue. When she realizes that's all I've got, she slaps me and calls me an idiot. My traumatized five-year-old bows before the relentless Sister of Mercy, who never shows me any. Like a good solider, I learn to keep quiet and never stick my head up out of the foxhole.

At the end of the year, I get all F's on my report card; a job well done. But Saturn refuses to cut me any slack.

Sister Mary Christopher confers with my frustrated mother, consoling her with the certainty I can do the work; I just refuse to do it. She promotes me and announces she will be teaching second grade the coming year.

That autumn, I surrender unconditionally by learning to read and write the first month of second grade and do what is expected of me. I escape into books, devouring stories of lone dogs abandoned in the wild north, struggling to survive and overcoming all obstacles. I strongly identify with the lonely journey of each one. Saturn pushes me to be strong and develop the discipline I need to put my world together in a way that will stand the test of time. He's a formidable ally and a stern taskmaster—not much fun, but he keeps me on track, insisting I go the distance when I don't think I can. Saturn makes me stronger each step of the way and rewards me for my hard work when I earn it.

It's impossible to rationalize child abuse, but I realize now that my experiences at home and with the nun toughened and prepared me for the times ahead. That's Saturn's job as cosmic drill instructor. My tendency to endure and drift in my rich fantasy life required a wake-up call to get me on track—just like now, as I wait for Bobby to die.

I feel a surreal kind of comfort in the hospital room. I'm a nurse; I move confidently in this world. My rational left-brain focuses on the technology. My right brain plays hide and seek with the emotional pain trying to connect. I don't touch it; I don't want it to touch me. My wall holds steady. I sit and wait.

The life support machines in the cramped room buzz and beep, making familiar noises, comforting in their predictability.

The respirator pushes air in and sucks it back out twenty-two times a minute. An intravenous line drips drugs to maintain blood pressure. A catheter snakes from under the covers, draining scant amounts of dark urine into a bag hanging from the bed frame. A cardiac monitor traces Bobby's heart rhythm on a screen jutting from the wall overhead.

I spend hours watching Bobby's normal sinus rhythm repeat over and over. I want this pain to be over, his and mine; I wait for the arrhythmia that signals the end. I pray for it. I watch for it until my vision blurs, but it isn't time yet.

I stare at the walls and wonder where in the hell they found this vile yellow green paint. I envision the hospital administrator calling maintenance, "Hey guys, they're having a sale on puke green paint, pick up about 500 gallons and we'll spiff the place up. I know it's a terrible color, but these people are dying; they don't care."

I maintain an uneasy truce with the ICU nurses. They're an uptight bunch: efficient, unfriendly, detached. One of the day nurses checks the IV. Annoyingly officious, she lectures me. "You have to wear a mask when you're in here. You wouldn't want him to get an infection would you?"

I stare back at her with defiance. We both know that's a whole truckload of bullshit. He's dying, and no mask can protect him from that. She turns and leaves without a word of comfort or caring. I understand her detachment. I have the same ability to distance myself from pain, death and anguish. It's a defense mechanism I've used my whole life. I don't know how else to cope.

I stand by the bed, take Bobby's flushed hand in mine, smooth the hair back from his forehead and put my cheek next to his. "I love you, Bobby. It's Constance; I'm here." He's beyond responding.

I don't know if he's still here or not. I wonder if his spirit roams out there somewhere checking things out before he shuffles off this mortal coil. I don't know what Bobby's spiritual beliefs are. The closest we ever came to discussing God happened when I cooked ham for dinner one Sunday. Bobby protested, telling me he was a Seventh Day Adventist. I told him it was ham or nothing. He ate the ham.

I disowned any notion of a Higher Power when my father died eleven years ago at age forty-three. He was my hero, the force that kept my tenuous life together. I thought God—the mean old shit—let my father die for no reason. I haven't forgiven him or the Catholic Church who denied my father entrance to their heaven for not being baptized.

My vigil for Bobby unleashes those same helpless feelings. The anger isn't there like it was then. Instead, I feel the emptiness of inevitability, like a chicken waiting to get its head chopped off.

Bobby looks so different now. Three years of chemotherapy takes an insidious toll. His hair lies in damp wisps of dark blond. His face is bloated beyond recognition from the fluids his failing kidneys can't excrete. Closed lids hide the mischievous blue eyes I love. His slim, six-foot frame sprawls across the narrow bed, a starched, white sheet covering him from the waist down.

Stress and sleep deprivation mess with my mind. I stare at his crotch, smiling inexplicably. I wrestle with the urge to look under the covers. I stare hard, trying to see through the sheet. Bobby would love this. It's my last chance to see it—the legendary member that earned him the nickname Horsecock Hansen. I resist the urge, leaving it to legend and imagination. The male organ holds no fascination for me. It's like a samurai's sword, only as good as the mind wielding it.

I struggle with guilt for not having had sex with Bobby. He loves me and would have wanted to make love to me. I couldn't do it. I've never been attracted to Bobby sexually. He never ignited the passion in me that Richard did.

My love for Bobby resides on a higher plane. I didn't want sex defiling that love, although I'm sure—if I'd offered that option—he'd have definitely gone for being defiled. He took whatever I gave him and cherished it. He taught me the meaning of unconditional love; it makes sitting here waiting for him to die all the more painful.

Only one other person ever loved me the way Bobby does—my Gramma, the childless aunt who took in my mother at age twelve. I loved Gramma even after she stuck her head in a bucket of lye when I was six. My insensitive, manic-depressive mother said Gramma killed herself because I wasn't affectionate enough. The guilt crawled into my gut like a condemned prisoner to live in solitary confinement for forty years before I could release it. I think that's when I closed my heart to keep the pain out, not understanding I'd locked it in with me.

During the day and evening, I sit with Bobby. At night, I sleep on the floor of the ICU. We're all here, our close-knit group of friends that love him. Holly, Bobby's mother, sits silently on the other side of the room from everyone, like an untouchable. We ignore her, denying her the compassion due a mother whose son lays dying. But we have our reasons.

I'd rather be home with my little girls, waiting. Bobby has a wife. But I'm compelled to be here. I'm not conscious of it yet, but this death-watch is a past life debt I'm settling.

My ability to recall past lives varies. Some I see as vividly as a Picasso painting etched into my soul. I recall them in riotous color, richly evocative with detail and meaning. Other lives reveal little to me, like a black and white sketch, but enough to give a sense of the meaning behind it—like this one that I shared with Bobby. I have no sense of a time period. I'm a Mayan living in Tulum in some distant past. The details aren't important, only the lesson.

Tulum, Mexico

I hid in the dense forest, thick with vines clutching tall, ancient trees that reached to embrace the sky. The humidity suffocated me, but sheer terror held me there, silent and motionless. As a medicine woman, I healed people. I didn't abandon them the way I had my beloved husband. My fear of death, stronger than my love for him, shamed me to my core.

The village chose Bobby and me to marry during the annual fertility rites. We spent our first year together, as was custom, in relative seclusion. The villagers fed us, and we made love in the hut built especially for us. Our year didn't produce a baby, and our relationship was compatible if not passionate. We lived happily together in a companionable, intellectual way, our world tranquil and fulfilling until a warring tribe came.

Bobby lay sick with fever, unable to move. I left him and fled into the jungle where I ultimately died of starvation. The guilt of abandoning him locked into my soul and lives in my DNA, waiting to be released.

That cellular memory tugs at me now with no conscious awareness of it; I just know I have to be here for Bobby. I can't let him die without me.

I hold Bobby's hand and stroke it compulsively. I think how different he is from my other friends. He has an immense capacity to love, the courage to feel the joy and the pain of it, a vulnerability that the other men in my life don't have. I realize how much I've taken his love for granted, and now I'm losing it.

Richard comes back into the room and takes the seat next to me. We don't speak but instinctively reach for each other's hand, and hold tightly. These last three years have been especially difficult for Richard. Beneath his sometimes gruff and tough exterior, his tender heart and kind soul weep when anyone suffers. He's been an almost constant companion to Bobby, driving him to his chemotherapy sessions and having to witness the havoc it's wrought on Bobby's body and psyche.

Bobby continued to work doggedly as a narcotic agent, making undercover heroin buys after chemotherapy sessions. He made a convincing doper with his ravaged body, puking in the gutter, looking to score. Bobby held onto the thought that the horror of Hodgkin's would disappear one day like a bad dream if he kept going. Richard covered for him at work when Bobby made mistakes his weakened body and mind inevitably missed. Richard's caring friendship helped Bobby and his wife, Liz, keep it together, cheering them on through this whole ordeal. No man has a better friend.

I think how handsome Richard is with his chocolate-colored, curly hair and hypnotic dark eyes. His Leo rising, magnetic sexuality still holds me captive. We share a profound, persistent passion that neither one of us can ever forget, or let go.

But it isn't only the passion that draws me. Richard shares the same emotional makeup as my father—remote and unattainable, irresistible. My Daddy issues hook me as strongly as the passion.

I have a picture of me sitting on my father's shoulders. I'm one or two years old. He looks joyful holding onto my tiny arms, handsome in a Gary Cooper way. His languid gray-green eyes innocently flirt with the camera; the sight of his easy smile still stops my heart. He's tall, a strapping six foot three. He's strong, loyal, emotionally aloof. The picture shows me that there were times when he was loving and affectionate. I don't remember when that changed. Maybe it was the war and being away for three years. Time and trauma change the heart in mysterious ways.

Growing up, I knew my father loved me even though he couldn't show it or say it. I felt it. I loved him, but I couldn't say it, either. Gestures of affection or love were nonexistent in our family. I didn't know how to express what I felt.

His Capricorn Sun and Virgo Moon gave him a strong desire for structure and order. Plumbing the depths of his emotions threatened to cast him into chaotic waters that might sink his ordered life. He opted for safety on the shallow shore. We each carried a strong fear of rejection. Neither one of us had the courage to breach the other's wall.

I loved him, but my mother didn't. The doctors told us he died of a fulminating hepatitis, but I know he died of a broken heart from never being loved by the only woman he ever loved.

I won't forgive my mother for that. I'm not yet able to forgive myself for not being able to tell him how much I loved him before he died. I sat by my father's bedside in so much pain that I could barely breathe. As he lay dying, before he slipped into a coma, he asked my mother to get me to take him home to die in his own bed. He told her I would know what to do. She didn't tell me until after he died. Even if she had told me, I didn't have the emotional strength to do it. My father was the weighted base of our family gyroscope. No matter how wildly my mother's emotional storms pitched and tumbled us, my father kept us steady. When he died, my life tipped over, spinning off its axis.

My parents mirrored the opposite ends of the emotional spectrum for me. My mother constantly seethed with emotion, like an active volcano, erupting unexpectedly, causing chaos and psychological destruction. My father's emotions lay deep as an Arctic glacier—solid and impenetrable. I watched, learned and lived with the pain of those extremes.

As it happens, I have no water in my natal astrological chart. People with no water generally do one of two things: they go off the deep end with their emotions, spewing them like water from a broken fire hydrant, or they turn them off tightly, as I do.

The absence of water creates a formidable obstacle to my soul's destiny. I purposely chose a difficult life. I picked my parents, as I believe we all do, and helped design the blueprint for this life. I picked my birth date and time to orchestrate the planetary energies in a delicate dance of synchronicity designed to bring the opportunities and challenges I need to promote my growth on a soul level.

I'm not yet aware that before I die, my soul wants me to walk through the door of the 8th house into the mystery of the unknown, to plunge into the realm of the deep psyche, explore the mystical and the psychic, see and know the light and dark places of my self. I need to experience the breadth and depth of love and passion found in the 8th house, to know the bliss of transcendence, the ultimate love. It's why I was born with Pluto in my 8th house; this is my destiny. Bobby dying is the catalyst, opening that door to my deep psyche

Before I can plumb the depths of my being, I have to find the courage to feel my feelings. The wall I erected in childhood has to come down and allow love access to my heart again. Until then, I experience feelings through the people I pull into my life, like my parents who taught me that love means sacrifice, rejection and the inescapable pain from not feeling loved.

Richard shifts in his chair, and lets go of my hand. "How long do you think this can go on?"

I shake my head. "I don't know. No one knows. It happens when it happens. Have you talked to Eddie? How are the girls doing?"

"The kids are fine. Ed's mother is with them."

It's better that Eddie isn't here. As his father says, "That boy is as useless as two tits on a boar hog." The father of my two girls doesn't do well with crisis, or much of anything else, for that matter.

When Eddie told me Hodgkin's tumors riddled Bobby's body, I plunged into despair, sobbing like a small child locked in a dark closet. My Capricorn control deserted me. I needed comfort and hope. Eddie responded, "You might as well get used to the fact that Hansen's gonna croak." Eddie presents me with tough and important lessons of love, like my mother.

Instead of Bobby dying in '71' when he was diagnosed, my mother did. A month before her forty-eighth birthday she made good on the threat she'd lodged my whole life.

I found her in the backyard, lying in the dark green Elephant Ear plants with her head under the exhaust pipe of her car. Her face, shiny and tight, told me that death had come hours before. I looked with horror at the macabre smile on her lips, as if she were enjoying the ultimate practical joke. She left a note instructing my sister, brother and me not to take it personally; it was just time. I had two emotions: relief and deep anger. My sister Joan shared my feelings. Our experiences with our mother were much the same.

Our twenty-year-old brother, Graydon, felt lost and abandoned, guilt-ridden he'd disappointed her somehow and drove her to end her life. Nothing could have been further from the truth. Of the three of us, Mom loved him best. As soon as he was old enough to drive, he became Mom's chauffeur, driving her home from various bars when she was too drunk to drive herself. She rewarded him at age eighteen by having him arrested for possession of the marijuana she found in his room. The reluctant judge told her these situations were usually resolved out of the courts, but she insisted the judge give him the choice of joining the Army or going to jail. My brother wisely chose the Army, scoring highly on their exams. He qualified for Officer Candidate School, but the felony arrest Mom insisted on for the marijuana precluded that option. The damage was done.

Joan and I didn't have the emotional energy to comfort our little brother as we should have when Mom died. We were too mired in our anger and resentment. We repeated the pattern of when our father died, unable to reach out to him when he needed us. I cry thinking about the anguished twelve year old who crawled into bed with Joan and me the night Dad died, desperate for comfort. I held him while he cried, but I didn't have the emotional reserves to give him more.

Mom came to me that night after she killed herself as I slept fitfully; her hand grasped my arm, pulling at me. She was lost and wanted me to show her where to go. I angrily pushed her hand away, and I told her to go and leave me alone. I wasn't responsible for her anymore.

Her death freed me from the immense burden I'd felt for her all my life. The anger stayed with me for a long time. It took nearly a lifetime for me to understand the pain her demons caused her, to find compassion for the three year old whose mother left her alone, but it didn't absolve her of the pain she caused to those who loved her. I still wonder if she found her way out of this life to the place where our souls go when we die.

The women in my family have a predisposition to killing themselves. It's like some mutant genetic programming. Menopause or having a bad day can set it off. My sister Joan and I are the only two grown women left in the family. Manic depression wiped out our grandmother, two aunts and our mother. Joan and I don't talk about it much, but we both wonder if we have the family curse. We wonder if we've passed it on to our daughters. But at least we know what it is now and that there is help if we should ever need it. We aren't doomed to repeat the pattern of destruction.

"How's Liz doing?" I ask Richard.

"She hanging in, but she still doesn't want to believe he's going to die."

Bobby's wife and I aren't close. She's never been comfortable with her husband's feelings for me. I understand that. I'm not comfortable with her. Her barely disguised air of superiority grates on me. She reminds me of Sally Wimmer from high school. Sally generated the same kind of cognitive dissonance in me because her words and her vibes didn't match. She would approach me in the hall between periods, smile, and make polite conversation while picking imaginary lint off my sweater and adjusting my white dickey that didn't need straightening. I always felt her inspections found me wanting in some disturbing way. I've watched Liz watch me these last three years. I get the same feeling from her, but it doesn't disturb me as much as it amuses me. I forgive her for not liking me because of the way she's loved and cared for Bobby. She's truly been a gift to him. Nothing else matters to me.

Bobby and Liz became a couple by default. Her short-lived affair with Richard left her with a broken heart and a badly bruised ego—she and a legion of other women. She found solace in dating Bobby. We're a fairly incestuous group of friends.

Bobby proposed to Liz in typical Hansen fashion: "Let's face it. You would have been happy being married to Richard, and I would have been happy married to Constance, but what the hell—I think we'd make a good couple. You wanna get married?"

I kiss Bobby's cheek. I want to remember the good times, to hold onto them like an amulet to comfort me.

Faces of Love, Death and Transformation:

Chapter 2

Jupiter the cockeyed optimist, cheerleader and life coach in my 4th house of new beginnings, wants me to live my life large, go for it, do it, have fun. Mystical, soul connecting Neptune joins transformative Pluto angles to my Venus to bring a new group of friends who will be with me the rest of my life. Sexually charged Pluto angling my aggressive Mars bestows upon me an intense relationship filled with desire, frustration and passion.

Sacramento, California
November, 1963

I sit alone at a table in the large party room of College Fair, the apartment complex my roommates and I moved into the week before. At 22, I'm taking tentative steps down the path of my new life from the hell of a brief, disastrous marriage and the loss of a baby born too soon to survive. I'm still emotionally raw from my father's death two months before.

Large gatherings make me uncomfortable. I think myself shy, but I'm not. My social skills are merely unpolished, like tarnished silver. I think I'm attractive, but not entirely convinced. Our parents had attached labels to my sister Joan and me long ago, and we've never removed them, like the warnings on bedding that declare a severe penalty for doing so. She's the beautiful one; I'm the smart one. We didn't think we're allowed to be both.

I have my Dad's bedroom eyes, Mom's big breasts and long, skinny legs like a newborn colt; Joan has Mom's blue eyes, small breasts, and long shapely legs that start at her neck. Our parent's physical attributes are divided evenly between us. I got the boobs; Joan got the legs.

My roommate and co-worker, Jennie, enthusiastically cruises the room, beating the bushes like a hunter flushing out the best of the big game. I admire her fearlessness in the face of potential rejection. Petite and cute, she flaunts her seductiveness with bravado.

Here in the party room, Bobby walks over to my table—a tall, sun bleached blonde with the face of a fallen cherub. His crisp blue eyes crinkle at the corners. His body looks soft, like an unbaked baguette. I like white teeth; the three packs of unfiltered Camels he smokes every day have dulled his, but his smile is warm and inviting. He cocks his head slightly to one side and opens his mouth, but nothing comes out. His stuttering doesn't seem to embarrass him or dampen his enthusiasm for asking me to dance.

Bobby has rhythm and some good moves, twirling and dipping me. I love that. We exchange data quickly. He and his roommates are Criminal Justice majors at Sac State. We live in the same building. They're on the first floor in 105; we're upstairs in 212. Jennie and I work as nurses at Mercy General in labor and delivery. Then he asks the question, "Is it true what they say about doctors and nurses?"

"What's that?"

"All doctors are queers and all nurses are nymphomaniacs?"

He dips me back; my head almost touches the floor. I try to decide if I heard him right—if he's serious or being a smart ass. I look into his eyes and see nothing but innocent curiosity. I shake my head and walk away.

I wonder how nurses morphed in the male psyche from angels of mercy to whores of Babylon. Who created that dumb-assed mystique that we're perpetually horny and know more about sex than ordinary mortals. It's a curse.

Over the course of several months, I meet the others who, with Bobby, come to form the core of our group of friends: charming, magnetic Richard; classically handsome, enigmatic Patrick; red-haired, gangly, gregarious, proudly Irish Filben; goofy, free spirit, womanizing Gary; and funny, self-deprecating, outrageous Eddie. We drink $1.49 a gallon jugs of Red Mountain wine, hold raunchy conversations about sex, Bobby's legendary organ and the politically incorrect behavior of our resident shock jock Mr. Ed, who streaks through the parking lot naked at odd hours to the delight of his friends. Eddie reveres Bobby's male member, swearing if he were so blessed he'd never wear clothes. He claims it's so big Bobby has to pee with his back against the wall so the backpressure doesn't knock him down.

Jennie and I patiently listen to their hilarious but reverent tales of Big Kay the bespectacled, six-foot, nymphomaniac nutritionist next door to us who fills her medicine cabinet with colored condoms and her bedroom with one hundred candles she ritualistically burns during sex like a temple priestess. Eddie, Bobby and Gary eagerly worship at the altar of her generous charms.

We don't do the drugs popular in the sixties. Our conservative upbringing and their chosen profession of law enforcement preclude that kind of experimentation. We pay homage to the god of cheap spirits in all of its forms from ABC beer to the bathtub gin Richard brings from Garberville.

I delight in how alcohol makes me feel: light, happy, free and fearless. Just like I did as a kid when I would fly as high as I could on my swing, taking flight at the pinnacle of the swing's arc. The euphoria I felt flying through the air more than made up for the crash landing. It's the same with alcohol for me.

I didn't drink before I connected with this group, but now I plunge into excess, testing my limits and feeling for my boundaries with the beast currently wrestling my mother for her soul. I'm unafraid. I'm a tomboy again, one of the boys trying to prove myself. Over indulging in alcohol is a transient phase in my life.

At work, I'm the "kid." My more mature co-workers and the doctors I work with, settled into their responsible lives, implicitly and overtly encourage my life style, telling me to have fun, party, enjoy life before joining them in what they see as their more ordinary lives. They envy me mine, imagining the endless, boundless adventures of youth awaiting me. No one told me on the occasions I showed up for work hung over I was drinking too much. Instead, they bundled me up in the coffee room with warm blankets and a tank of oxygen, clucking over me like mother hens while I clutched the oxygen mask to my face and breathed deeply.

The guys drink for more complex reasons relating to nature and nurture. Each of them has a past life where they abused alcohol and/or drugs; it's part of their karma, and for Eddie and Filben, it's in their genes. In this life, they've chosen to channel part of that karma into a career in law enforcement, a more socially acceptable way of dealing with those old issues from other lives. But they still have to deal with it on a personal level. In their chosen profession, alcoholism is epidemic and considered an occupational hazard, where divorce and suicide rates are well above average.

We don't talk about the part alcohol played in our childhoods with emotionally absent and/or alcoholic parents. We're too immature yet to consider such deep issues. We're young with all the hubris of thinking we're immortal and indestructible. The potential long-range emotional and physical effects of excessive drinking don't concern us.

Faces of Love, Death and Transformation:

Neither does the politics of Vietnam. We live in a cloistered consciousness of sex, booze, the Beach Boys and the Beatles. We hover in that void before the gathering storm of political and social upheaval born of a potent Uranus/Pluto conjunction that will scatter us about like autumn leaves. This group will be important in my life for years to come. I have important karma with three of them: Bobby, Richard and Eddie.

We all know Bobby isn't a mere mortal, rather a modern Don Quixote, haplessly lurching through life, battling his way toward the unreachable dream, scarred but undeterred, a romantic idealist, devoted and loyal. He believes in love—the old fashioned, romantic kind—and he never gives up the impossible dream of making it his. True to the heart of his Aquarian Sun, he reveres authenticity as the ultimate value and lives his life accordingly. To Bobby, plastic is the ultimate epithet. He's honest to a fault, blurting out whatever truth just burst in his brain and exited through his mouth. You either love his honesty or hate his unintended insensitivity.

Bobby's consuming curiosity about people is more intellectual than emotional. He maintains a certain Aquarian detachment that allows him to ask probing, personal questions minutes after meeting anyone. Whoever meets him, never forgets him for good or ill.

Bobby loves spending weekends traveling all over California in George his beloved, grey Volkswagen Beetle. George looks like a World War II relic, proudly bearing dents and scrapes from Bobby's notoriously inattentive driving, covered in mud and bird shit. Bobby loves this scarred wreck like Quixote loved Sancho Panza. The running joke in the group is to give Bobby the name of a remote little town in California and he'll know someone there. And he invariably does.

We watch over him with a mixture of awe, admiration and fear for the wearer of the Brown Helmet. We imagine it like the one Snoopy wears as the Red Baron when he flies on his missions—more symbolic than functional. Bobby's helmet is brown from all the shit the blue bird of happiness dumps on him, which is about as often as it rains in Seattle. His life lurches through a Uranian minefield of unexpected changes, windfalls wiped out by quirks of fate and surprises around every corner.

College Fair Apartments
May 1964

The spring semester ends with a thud at Bobby's feet. He flunked Life Science. He's depressed. Richard and Gary burst into the apartment in post semester euphoria to find Bobby aimlessly swirling peanut butter over two pieces of bread. The look of desolation in his eyes shifts their mood.

"We heard, Bobby. Sorry." Richard offers. "You okay?"

"I'm fine; I'm going to kill myself, going to jump off the Golden Gate Bridge."

"Why are you making sandwiches?" Richard inquires.

"Because, I might get hungry on the way." He licks the knife.

"Well, hell," Richard declares, moving to Bobby's side, putting an arm around him. "If you're going to kill yourself, we are, too. What do you say, Gary?"

"Sure, I'm game. How are we going to do it?"

"We have to get a jug and think about this. Bobby, get the Red Mountain," Richard instructs.

Bobby brightens. "Yeah. We need to be shit-faced to do this right."

South seas music on the radio delivers inspiration: they will build a yacht and sail into oblivion. Richard orders the crew to erect sails from sheets. They christen her the "*Shit House Mouse.*" The jug of Red Mountain disappears and they start on beer.

The next morning, Richard wakes to the smell of vomit, sour wine and stale beer. White sheets blanket the living room. Bobby curls on the floor in the fetal position, clutching the main sail under his chin like a small child with a blankie. Gary lays prone in the hallway, vomit dried on his shirt. Richard's head feels heavier than a fallen redwood. A smile cracks across his aching face: It was a hell of a drunk. His mouth tastes like bird shit. He stumbles to the bathroom and brushes his teeth. Bobby joins him and vomits in the toilet.

"Thanks, man."

Faces of Love, Death and Transformation:

"No problem. That's what roomies are for." Richard grins at Bobby. He has a soft spot for anyone in need. It's one of the things I love about Richard.

February 1965

Bobby and I, as fellow Aquarians, fall into a comfortable friendship reminiscent of our Mayan life in Tulum. We accept and celebrate each other's eccentricities. We feel emotionally safe with each other. He makes me laugh. Our times together nurture us in ways we don't experience with the others in our group. We understand and love each other. We also love foreign movies.

On Sundays, we have an unspoken contract to immerse ourselves in an intellectually stimulating film. We love them fraught with psychological undertones, and liberally laced with symbolism and subtext, the kind of film shown at the Guild theatre on 35th Street in Oak Park. The Guild features arty little films by French New Wave directors and visionary Japanese filmmakers. We feel intellectually superior reading subtitles.

Sundays belong to us, and I carefully leave Richard out of our conversations. My love affair with Bobby's close friend and roommate interjects awkwardness into our otherwise comfortable relationship; we avoid the subject. I know it pains him. I suspect why, but I don't want to open that door.

"Woman in the Dunes," directed by Akira Kurosawa, plays this Sunday, a darkly erotic work about two people trapped in a hovel dug deep in the dunes, continually threatened by shifting sands. We watch the movie intently not wanting to miss any important themes or concepts worth dissecting later. The movie ends, the audience stands and pauses for a moment before beginning the exodus from the darkened theater.

Bobby stretches; his loud voice booms, "Wonder what Old Goody would think of this movie. Probably wouldn't like it, didn't have enough phallic symbols to keep the old pervert happy." His sniggering, dirty laugh crackles through the air.

Two rows in front of us, a dignified looking man turns toward the sound of the voice. Old Goody, Bobby's professor of abnormal psychology, fixes a contemptuous gaze upon him and says, "Good evening, Mr. Hansen," his voice icy enough to freeze vodka, his exit worthy of a Prussian prince.

Bobby looks like he's been flash frozen. Goody's frosty greeting promises hideous, inevitable retribution.

"Geez! Oh, God! It's Goody. Shit!" He throws his arms over his head in his familiar gesture of frustrated helplessness and falls back into his seat; he rests his forehead on the seat before him, banging it rhythmically. "The old pervert will flunk me for sure. All I need is another class like Life Science to curse me." He wipes his hands across his head in a frustrated frenzy. "Why do these things always happen to me?"

"What are you doing?"

"I'm wiping the shit off my Brown Helmet."

Within moments Bobby decides he'll survive. So what if Goody slaps a bad jacket on him. A glimmer returns to his blue eyes; his cheeks flush with familiar color. "There's only one thing left to do—get a drink!" He assures me this isn't anything a few martinis can't fix.

After our Sunday movie, we usually retire to our favorite watering hole, the Fireside on H Street, a dark, smoky den of serious drinkers enduring the invasion of their hallowed space by raucous college students. The tiny restaurant off the bar area serves the best steaks in town, and when we can afford it, we share one.

"What is it with you and Life Science?" He'd just flunked it for the second time. The pained look on his face makes me sorry I brought it up, his humiliation palpable.

"I don't know. I guess I just don't give a rat's ass how frogs fuck."

San Francisco, California
February 13, 1965

Bobby marked his twenty-second birthday two days before. He invites me to a belated birthday dinner with his parents. I've never met Holly and his stepfather Jack, but their reputation precedes them. A nervous flutter skitters around in my stomach, but Bobby's broken heart requires my attention.

Bobby's love affair with a blonde cutie named Ruth fueled his dreams of love ever after. The life insurance money he'd inherited last year from his biological father went to romancing her, buying her gifts and taking her on expensive weekends to Monterey. The beautiful romance turned ugly when she dumped him. Last week he stood in the parking lot of our apartment building, screaming in vain for her to come out and talk to him at 3 A.M. Jennie, roused from sleep, ordered me to shut him the hell up. I went downstairs and led my broken hearted friend upstairs. He told me he'd really loved her—the bitch. He cried and I settled him on the couch and cradled him until he fell asleep. Bobby brings out the mother in me. I'm helpless to stop the rejection he encounters with women, but I can console him. At least he knows he has one woman in his life he can count on.

I love his parent's house on Filbert Street, a quintessential Victorian. As we climb the stairs to the living room, I inhale the aromas of fifty plus years of food, spices, sweat and perfume that cling to the walls and hang in the musty air. The smell of roast beef beckons on the comfortably warm air. Loud voices from above mingle with the sound of ice clinking in glasses.

Holly and Jack reverently nurture a major sauce problem. Growing up, Bobby didn't know it wasn't normal to sleep in the car parked outside a bar while his parents drank until 2 A.M. every night.

More surprises. Last year he found out his biological father wasn't the deceased war hero Holly made him out to be, making the flag she gave him a cruel hoax. His father's file at the State Department of Criminal Investigation and Identification where Bobby works the 3-11 shift remains open. Bobby came across the file accidentally. The shock sent him on a two-day bender, ending in an emotional firefight with Holly, wounding Bobby further, but he got the truth.

Bobby's father liked robbing banks, and his long rap sheet suggested he wasn't very good at it. Richard related the tale to me: During WWII, a judge gave Bobby's dad the choice of the Army or jail. The Army sent him to Europe and he promptly deserted. He holed up in a wine cellar somewhere in France, posed as a downed fighter pilot and stayed drunker than shit for a year. The Army trussed him up like a runaway slave and shipped him home. Legend has it he deserted again and disappeared forever, but the certifiable truth remains murky at best. Holly declared him dead and went on with her life. When Bobby found out the truth, he took the flag out of the plastic bag where he'd reverently kept it for years. Since that day he uses it as a bedspread, in silent testament to his disillusionment.

"Ma! I'm home." Bobby yells up the stairs.

A plump woman with bowl cut, gray-blondish hair waits for us. Holly starts when she sees me. "I didn't know you were bringing someone home, Bobby." An insincere half smile slashes across her face.

"Ma, this is Connie."

Bobby doesn't offer Holly any more information regarding the nature of our relationship.

"How do you do?" She looks at me from tip to toe, not offering her hand, sizing me up like a prison matron inspecting a new inmate.

I meet Jack, a red faced, boisterous man of about fifty. Cocktail time must have started at least an hour before I surmise by Holly's flushed cheeks and Jack's red nose.

"Well, Bobby," Jack asks, "How's Life Science? I hear you're taking that sucker again!" He laughs and slaps Bobby on the shoulder. Bobby winces but doesn't respond.

Holly demands, "You think you'll ever get out of school? What kind of a dummy flunks the same class twice? I keep telling Jack maybe you shouldn't be in college. Maybe you should get a job."

"Ma, I'll graduate, I'll graduate!" The tension in the room gathers like cumulus clouds before a storm. "Constance, you want a drink?"

"Martini sounds good." I need something to get me through this evening.

Three martinis later, Holly serves dinner. Jack falls asleep with his head in his plate. Holly eats, never taking her eyes off me. She asks no questions and makes no attempt at polite discourse. She studies me like an arachnophobe peering at a black widow. I pointedly ignore her. Bobby seems to be enjoying his mother's evident displeasure. It's obvious to me they have a complicated relationship.

Bobby wants me to see the Chinese New Year parade. Holly seems relieved we won't be staying, but not half as relieved as I am. We go to Chinatown and watch the parade wind down Broadway to Grant Street. Blocks of colorful dragons and thundering drums weave through the streets; firecrackers pop everywhere, dispersing evil spirits. The drums and paper dragons chase the fog away, making the night unusually clear in The City. I've never seen anything like it. I love this colorful cultural celebration, the drama and romance of it.

Faces of Love, Death and Transformation:

San Francisco is Bobby's city. He knows every nook and cranny. He spent his formative years exploring the diverse neighborhoods, sampling the cuisine from each and always meeting people. He tells me as a kid he sang in the Children's Opera or Choir, I can't remember which, and delights me with a spontaneous aria, displaying his deep, rich baritone. He's full of surprises.

After the parade, Bobby takes me to La Rocca's Corner, a small tavern nestled at the point where Columbus and Taylor converge in North Beach. Leo and Rose La Rocca built a successful business. Bobby tells me they're famous for their Irish coffee and immaculate restrooms.

La Rocca's caters to a diverse clientele: cops, movie stars, felons, ex-cons, blue-collar workers and residents of the Italian neighborhood, all of whom mix happily within these walls. Filben will meet his wife Diane, affectionately known as Babycakes, here. Friday and Saturday nights rock out like an old world Italian wedding. Leo plays the guitar, son Jack the accordion; son Vince tends bar. Buy three drinks and you get the fourth one free. Everyone wants that free drink.

I feel immediately at home amidst the raucous, joyful energy. The small dance floor jams with patrons spilling out onto the streets, everyone drinking and talking animatedly. Everybody knows Bobby; they greet him warmly, slap his back and hug him. He introduces me to his extended family, and they clearly love him. The earlier tension fades from his face; his eyes sparkle again as he greets everyone with, "Hi! How ya doin'?" He's home.

We don't say much on the drive back, riding on the crest of the energy and excitement of La Rocca's. We'd danced until we were dizzy. I think how happy he makes me and how special our time together is.

I don't know when Bobby decided he loved me. He didn't tell me until after I'd married Eddie.

Sacramento, California
August 27, 1966

The 19th Hole dangles at the end of a strip mall on Arden Way. The patrons don't know the difference between the front or back nine of a golf course, and none of them ever swung anything heavier than a whiskey glass.

Bobby loves this kind of bar, filled with interesting characters whose lives somehow ended up in the ditch. Ordinarily, he'd spend hours getting the stories of each one of them, but tonight he has something else on his mind.

Heads turn as we walk in. Our formal clothes make us conspicuously overdressed, having just come from Patrick's wedding. We look like Ken and Barbie slumming. We sit at the end of the bar away from everyone else.

Bobby orders drinks: "We'll have two martinis. We just got married."

The bartender lights up, "Hey, we got newlyweds here."

"What are you doing?"

"Cool it, somebody will buy us a drink."

I get it. I nod to the bartender. "We're on our way to Monterey for our honeymoon, but we wanted to stop here because this is where we first met." I work it, looking at Bobby lovingly, stroking his cheek for effect.

"Buy the newlyweds a drink on me," intones a romantic drunk at the other end of the bar. The bartender promises two more rounds on the house.

I contentedly sip my martini, savoring the crisp bite of the gin, the cold ice against my teeth. I eat my olive with relish and stir my drink with the naked toothpick. The Army took Eddie, the only one of the group to get drafted, and he waits for me in Germany; I am to join him in October. Life seems good.

"I'm going into the Army."

Instant panic fills me. "Why? You don't have to go. You're the sole surviving son of a deceased war veteran." No one ever explained how Holly convinced the government to make that designation. "They can't take you."

"I insisted."

"Is Holly behind this?" It would be just like her to use Bobby to expiate the sins of his father. She never stopped telling him he was a loser like his father.

"Sort of—not really. It's just something I have to do."

I sigh in resignation. "I'll bet those little old ladies at the draft board love you."

"They baked me brownies." Bobby grins. "They think I'm very patriotic."

"Aren't you afraid of getting killed?" I search his face.

He shrugs. "If I die, I die."

"When do you leave?"

"October."

"I need another drink."

Bobby signals the bartender for reinforcements. I stare into the depths of my martini and think about the possible consequences of Bobby going to war. The Brown Helmet won't protect him from getting killed.

"Why didn't you marry *me*?"

Old pain, still sharp, rakes Bobby's face, the same look he had when I told him I planned to marry Eddie. Our gazes lock. My heart sinks. I hadn't expected this.

"You never asked me."

The simplicity of my answer touches him. His eyes shimmer with tears. I will my eyes to stay open to hold mine back.

"I never thought you'd marry anybody but Richard."

"Me either. But that wasn't to be, so it was a toss up between you and Eddie. He asked."

I'm not forthcoming with the real reason. How could I explain to Bobby that I loved him as much as I could without being "in" love with him? He wouldn't settle for less from me like Eddie. Bobby wants more emotionally than I can give him. He deserves more.

He tries to smile, but the corners of his mouth quiver, "I love you, Constance." Tears flow unchecked down his cheeks.

I reach out and wipe a tear away with my finger, tracing it gently to his chin. "I love you, too. I'm sorry. I didn't know."

Bobby throws his arms up in that familiar gesture of furious surrender. "That's because I'm a dumb shit!"

We burst into relieved laughter.

"If you get to Germany and Eddie doesn't treat you right, or you're not happy, call me and I'll send you the money for you to come home, okay? Promise?"

"I promise."

I throw my arms around Bobby and kiss his wet, salty cheek. I love him so much. Maybe I should have married him. Maybe I'm the dumb shit.

I'm doing the right thing, but not for the reasons I think. I have important lessons to learn about different types of love and won't learn them married to Bobby. We'd be like we were in Tulum, content and comfortable. I have some serious growing to do, and I need more intense experiences, like the ones coming—soon.

Faces of Love, Death and Transformation:

Chapter 3

Saturn in my 8th house of deep emotion decrees my wall has to come down, releasing the emotional issues I've suppressed. Saturn opposing my Venus makes the situation especially sad, bringing home the immensity of my loss.

San Diego, California
September 14, 1974

At 6:30 A.M. something compels me to wake up. I've spent another night on the floor of the ICU waiting room with Filben, curled into his back for warmth. I stretch my stiff muscles and go back into Bobby's room. Liz stands by the bedside, staring down at Bobby, clutching his hand to her heart.

It's shift change. The monitor beeps an erratic heart rate; Bobby's pulse slows and then the flat line crosses the screen. His life doesn't ebb quietly; it explodes in a fury before yielding to death. Fluids erupt from every opening in Bobby's body. The stench fills the room. A nurse dabs at the vomit. I wave him away and hold Bobby's hand tightly to my cheek. "Let him be."

Liz stands immobile, grief etched on her haggard face. He's gone. I let go of Bobby's hand, turn and walk through the door to the waiting room. I stand there dazed. The naked pain on my face tells everyone it's over. I see Patrick's, outstretched arms and stumble toward him. My emotional wall cracks. With each sob, it shudders and shakes; my feelings surge as it crumbles. My tears flow unchecked. I feel like I did when my Gramma died: alone, frightened, vulnerable.

Patrick holds me silently, my knight in shining armor—Sir Patrick. I feel safe wrapped in his strong Scorpio energy. I'm thankful he could be here. He's currently working for Centac, an elite, secret unit of the Drug Enforcement Agency devoted to international drug conspiracies, highly dangerous work his Scorpio Sun loves.

Richard watches us. "It doesn't make any difference now, but did you two have sex at Eddie's birthday party in '64'? Remember? You and Patrick disappeared into the bedroom for a couple of minutes."

Patrick flashes a confused smile. We made out a couple of times in the early years, cuddled in his bed on many a lonely night, even ended up in the shower together one tequila soaked night, but we didn't have sex on Eddie's birthday.

I shake my head. How like Richard to carry that pain around for ten years. A Moon in Virgo can carry hurts for a long time, like a camel with a belly full of water. I remember his anger that night; I hadn't a clue what upset him and he refused to tell me. We have a long history of hurt feelings and hot sex.

Chapter 4

Sacramento, California
January 1964

Richard and I first met at a Halloween party. It's our first date. He's taking me to see the Smothers Brothers at Sac State. He shyly holds my hand during the concert. His full, unbounded laughter warms me. Afterward, we go to the IHOP on El Camino. It's there I meet the sweet, attentive side of his Virgo Moon and the adventurous dreamer of his Gemini Sun. He beams, telling me his dream to own a boat and sail to exotic places around the world. My Aquarian Sun finds the dreamer in him immensely attractive. He'd actually had such a boat but sold it to go back to school to avoid the draft.

I like that he has dreams but a practical side to him, too. I don't realize how complicated that combination of Gemini Sun and Virgo Moon is for him, how much it affects him. Gemini and Virgo are an odd couple in astrology. Gemini soars to heights of fantasy and exploration like a kite bobbing on the winds of high adventure. Virgo ties a 20 ton boulder of reality and responsibility to Gemini's tail, rendering it earthbound. Finding a working balance between the two is challenging, especially for Richard.

College Fair Apartments
February 22, 1964

> Jupiter infuses my 5th house of romance with opportunity this Saturday night. Mars connects with Venus, adding fuel to an erotic fire with passionate Pluto in my natal 8th house, the place of intense sexual experiences and profound intimacy that can be healing on a deep level, making erotic nirvana possible.
>
> With forceful Mars in Richard's house of sex, we run nose-to-nose with the hot to trots for each other. Mars in his 8th house makes sex hotter; My Venus makes it better. A formidable

> attraction, like cosmic catnip, magnetizes us. Neither of us knows where our passion will take us.

Richard kisses me passionately. "I have to have you."

The reality of spending another night on the cold, vinyl couch helps make the decision to say yes. One of my roommates, Betty, and her boyfriend have the bedroom again; I need a good night's sleep, so what the hell.

Richard's sweetness, patience and amazing persistence over the last six weeks has won me over. I admire his rugged good looks and he kisses better than anyone I've locked lips with since my high school steady. I love his warm smile, his perfect white teeth, and he doesn't smoke like the others.

"Okay."

He freezes in place, his lips still on my neck. He hadn't expected that answer.

"We have to go to your place, if that's all right?"

A wide grin breaks across his face; his dark eyes glitter with excitement. Wordlessly, he pulls me off the sofa, sprints for the door and lopes down the stairs like a young gazelle in heat, not wanting to give me time to change my mind. His enthusiasm flatters me.

He hurries me through the empty apartment to the back bedroom where his twin bed rests against the wall. He kisses me, undresses quickly; I unbutton my jeans and sit on the bed, stretching my long legs toward him. He pulls my jeans off. I remove my sweatshirt and bra.

He drops to his knees in a reverent gesture, as if he's in the presence of something holy. He stares at my breasts, definitely one of my best features: full, firm 34 C's. My nipples stand at full attention.

Tenderly he brushes his lips over my tingling nipples. A storm of heat moves through me. I put my hands to his head and pull him to me, kissing him with a surging passion that surprises me.

He moves me down on the bed, hypnotizing me with new sensations. As if making the Fourteen Stations of the Cross during Lent, he takes an erotic pilgrimage to every part of my body, paying loving homage at each stop. I've never experienced this kind of passion. Before tonight, I'd experienced sex in a detached way. Now, I whirl in the vortex of the powerful energy surrounding us.

I arch my back and lift my hips to him; I draw in a sharp breath as he enters. He groans. His Mars and my Venus plug into each other like a 220-volt connection. The frenzied thrusting lasts three strokes:

"Oh, God. No! Oh, God." He groans in horror.

Oh, shit! I knew this was too good to be true.

"I'm sorry. I swear to God, that's never happened to me before." He collapses helplessly in my arms, unwilling to look at me. The anticipation was too much for him.

"It's okay. Don't worry." I stroke his hair as he buries his face in my neck. I can feel the heat of his humiliation. I kiss him consolingly and turn over to sleep. He pulls me back. We make love again. The only sounds are the rain beating on the window, the rustling of the sheets and the creaking of the bed as we move together. I lose all sense of time and space. Insistent passion envelops us. Our bodies dance to music our conscious minds can't hear, instinctively knowing each other's moves, everything flowing effortlessly in perfect rhythm.

Utterly spent, my body glows like a dying coal. A thin coat of perspiration covers us. We smile at each other. He reaches out and touches my long, blonde hair, damp and tangled, clinging to my face. The pungent smell of sex hangs heavy. Richard's eyes mist with spent passion. I remember how those eyes startled me with their intensity the first time I met him. Sitting up in bed, I pull my hair back to let the air cool my neck. I gaze at him, entranced by the passion we just shared.

He brings me water; I stand at the bedroom window in his blue, terry cloth robe, staring into the dark night. I love the soft rain and the mist that hangs on the air like wisps of wet smoke. Cold stars shimmer from another world. Peace and contentment embrace me.

Richard stands behind me with his arms around my waist; his lips nuzzle my ear. I close my eyes and settle against his warm, naked body, covering his arms with mine. We keep the silence between us, holding each other—the night magical, surreal. We make love again and again.

We've unknowingly triggered cellular memories from an important past life. Our passion didn't begin this night.

Faces of Love, Death and Transformation:

**Kyoto, Japan
October 1600**

This life is quite vivid for me. In this one, I not only see the scenes, my body remembers the passion.

My aunt watched me prepare the tea for her. We shared this ritual whenever business slowed in the brothel. She observed approvingly as my supple, tapered fingers whipped the steaming water and tea into the desired froth.

Her face looked sad, edged with regret. She thought I should have been a "Castle Toppler," the kind of courtesan a daimyo or shogun would give up his castle and wealth to possess. She felt there wasn't a Tayu, a top courtesan, in the entire Pleasure Quarter who equaled me.

Hair, thick and lustrous, cascaded down my back, touching the base of my spine. I'd loosely tied it with a broad, satin ribbon of scarlet that matched the obi sash I wore to hold my blue kimono closed. My nineteen-year-old face glowed with unadorned youth and natural beauty, unlike in later years when white makeup and elaborate hairdos would become the fashion among geishas. Large, almond shaped eyes and close-set eyebrows set off my face, shaped like a delicate melon seed. My nose blended in perfect harmony with my other faultless features. My small waist gave way to slim hips and long legs, adding a regal bearing to a near perfect body. I sensed a keen intelligence and a natural grace.

Two things deprived me of attaining geisha status: eyes the dark blue of a winter sunset and hair the color of golden forsythia. What a shock for my mother to see that yellow hair and those blue eyes for the first time. Inspired, she named me Amaterasu after the Sun Goddess; the name fit me well.

My widowed mother bore me ten months after she took in a Dutch born, Jesuit priest as a boarder to keep from starving after the death of her husband. The Jesuit, highly embarrassed by the obvious evidence of his indiscretion, left my mother's house in her sixth month of pregnancy before the head of the order in Osaka found out. He never saw me. He had a higher calling, saving souls in the name of his God, the deity called Christ.

My mother turned to the only profession open to women of all classes in Japan at the time: prostitution. She worked off of one of the boats that traveled the river between Edo and Kyoto, a hard life. On my eighth birthday, my mother sold me to her sister the supervisor of a house of prostitution. My mother offered gratitude to her sister for my care, feeding and training to become a professional prostitute. She wanted her daughter to have a profession and a future, not be forced to work off the boats as she did.

As is customary at age 14 in the house, I became a working prostitute. I'd prepared for this eventuality and accepted my duty. The structured, restricted life of the brothel suited me well: I knew nothing else, expected nothing else.

My exotic looks limited my building a steady clientele, no matter how talented I was. My aunt reasoned that even though I would never attain high rank as a geisha, or make sufficient money as a prostitute to earn my way in the house, I could still be of service, fulfill my duty and feel a sense of honor. I eagerly engaged in learning those arts that I would teach when I retired from prostitution at the customary age of 26. I would then train a whole new generation of geishas. I made a reasonable investment of time, my aunt concluded.

Life in the house fulfilled me. The other prostitutes, from the highest ranking to the lowest, doted on me. Because of my handicap, I presented no competition. They told me their secrets and taught me the arts of being a successful courtesan for the time when I would pass on those lessons. I fell heir to their garments, outdated but still attractive.

Although content with my destiny, one desire lurked within me: to be a dancer, a shirobyoshi. I spent my free time perfecting my grace and skill. I frequented the small stages around the Pleasure Quarter and watched the shirobyoshi perform. Closed to me in that life, that unfulfilled desire followed me to a life as a ballerina in London in the 1700s.

I lived vicariously through the other prostitutes in the house, preferring it to the pain and suffering I saw among my peers when they inevitably succumbed to passion and even love. The faces changed, but the stories and their outcomes remained constant. Some prostitutes, fortunate to have their contracts bought by an impassioned client, retired to respectability and marriage. They were the exceptions.

Being a practical woman, I knew I wasn't destined to be a wife or mother. I felt no regret. My life would remain within the walls of the Pleasure Quarter. I needed nothing else until Sakon.

Sakon lived to die. He began every morning in the same way. He bathed, groomed his thick forelock of black hair into the mitsu-ori style. He oiled his hair, tied the fore-

Faces of Love, Death and Transformation:

lock into a queue, folded it forward then backward and tied it in place. He dressed, meditated, thought about death, the many ways a man could die. It was the Way of the Samurai.

Sakon embodied the highest ideals of a samurai: courage, honor and a willingness to die for one's master, comrades or a worthy cause. His ambition and passion made him a superb warrior.

Samurai revered the bonds of the warrior, needed only each other. Many preferred to love only each other. Older samurai introduced young pages to man/boy love, an accepted, even honored practice. Many samurai believed sex with a woman depleted a warrior's energy and effeminized him, ruining him for battle. They considered young boys with slim muscled bodies and long black hair not yet shaved on top the pinnacle of beauty. Sakon was indeed beautiful.

Unlike his young friend Tonomo, Sakon never acquired a fondness or preference for man-on-man sex, but he accepted the sexual attentions of the older samurai with respect.

As with many samurai of the time, Sakon, fascinated by the potential of meditation to hone his focus during battle, studied the teachings of the samurai masters in order to attain the state of the "no mind."

> "The undisturbed mind is like the calm body water
> reflecting the brilliance of the moon.
> Empty the mind and you will realize the undisturbed mind."
> —Togo Shigekata

He cultivated the undisturbed mind, his meditations so powerful he tapped into a consciousness he didn't intend. Unwittingly, he triggered the latent power of the Moon in his 8th house of sex and mystical/psychic experiences, his undoing.

Sekigahara, Japan
21 October 1600

On that misty, cold morning, the two armies of a 100,000 men faced each other in the narrow valley west of the village of Sekigahara. The troops of the shoguns, Tokugawa from the east and Ishida from the west, engaged each other in the last great, decisive battle for control of Japan. Sakon fought with Tokugawa. That battle forever changed the country, the future of the samurai, and Sakon.

A Spiritual Memoir

As the fighting commenced that morning, Sakon willed himself to the "no mind" and plunged into battle. As he raised his sword for a kill, a thing most curious happened: an image of his head severed from his body and a bloody sword held aloft by his friend Tonomo flashed through his mind. The vision retreated instantly; he recovered to meet the challenge at hand.

Victory came to Tokugawa, and 60,000 heads of the vanquished fell. Sakon took no joy in the victory. Still in shock, his thoughts fixated on the vision of his severed head. What could it mean? It was not a good omen—of that he was certain.

Life in the house unfolded quietly until the winter came and the snow blew little mountains of white onto the thin branches of bare trees. The hibachi in my small room warmed me sufficiently as long as I wore an extra kimono. I blew wisps of warm air on my cold fingertips and watched my breath billow thin streamers of smoke.

Restless for some time, I sensed a change in the space around me, like a void waiting to be filled. It puzzled me because I lacked nothing.

The water boiled for tea. The shoji door opened with a great force. I lifted my head. A man stood in the doorway, legs straddled apart; his short sword hung from his left side. He stared hard at me, his eyes fierce and cold as the snow clinging to his hair. Their intensity startled me.

I bowed without speaking. The young man silently studied me, his eyes glazed from too much sake. I saw something else: sadness, a hunger, an unknown horror in his eyes. Familiar with the fear and weariness in a soldier's eyes, I knew this was different.

His dress told me he was a foot soldier, probably a swordsman, judging by his well-developed forearms. He wore a heavy, winter kimono and traditional sandals. We faced each other without speaking. He didn't move; his gaze fixed on my neck. I untied my obi and let my gown hang slightly open so he could see something of what awaited him; I moved to the sleeping mat. I didn't have all day.

Sakon kneeled in front of me and gently brushed the tips of his fingers down my neck, then to rest at the hollow in my throat. He seemed to yearn for that softness like a frightened child craves his mother's breast. He sat next to me and gently lifted my hair away from my neck and closed his eyes; his lips tentatively grazed the delicate curve at the back of my neck. His fingers explored my body with tenderness foreign to me. I sat motionless, feeling the warmth of his lips on my skin; the rhythm of his breath increased. Then he made love to me.

I had heard the other girls describe something like this. I'd been having sex since I was 14, but I'd never experienced this before. A new sensation ran through my being, opening a place within me I found frightening, seductive and futile to resist.

I felt Sakon melt into the dark blue of my eyes. He touched my hair. Instead of being repelled by the strangeness of my features, he seemed magnetized.

As a seasoned prostitute, I knew how to behave with a customer, but now I moved instinctively in this dance of passion, following the cues his body gave me. I offered him a part of me I didn't know existed. I surrendered my carefully constructed life of detachment and fell headlong into the passion of my waiting soul. I plunged into the void. He waited for me there.

We came together: not in a white heat, but with a soul healing sweetness that forever changed our lives then and in the ones to come. We merged into the energy of the mystical 8th house and experienced profound sexual union. The waiting ended, the void filled. I fell in love.

Over the winter months, Sakon visited me when his regiment sat idle, not engaged in business for Lord Tokugawa, his master. In spite of weeks between visits, he always came.

Spring filled Kyoto with the blossoms and fragrance of cherry, plum, and jasmine. Loving me created a major life crisis for Sakon. The mystical, sexual connection we shared became his new passion, an addiction he willingly embraced. He told me heaven could not be more ecstatic. As lovers, we experimented and explored all that sexual pleasure offered. I delighted him with my inventiveness and versatility. He especially loved the times we combined meditation with lovemaking.

In a sitting position, I straddled his crossed legs and wrapped my legs around his waist. I placed his growing organ inside me. My right hand rested on his heart, his on mine. We looked into each other's eyes; our faces close but not touching. We breathed. As I breathed in, he breathed out. Our breath created a circle of energy around us of giving and receiving. We didn't move, only breathed, concentrating on the flow of energy and the love between us. The restricted movement only heightened our desire, creating exquisite agony. Our energies blended; we became as one. I clenched and relaxed my vaginal muscles alternately, holding him in a vice of heat and exquisite softness. The unbearable pleasure brought release with no effort. Sakon told me I was truly gifted.

My aunt, keenly aware of our love affair, encouraged me to be happy. Sakon paid for the time he spent with me, but she knew it couldn't last. Sakon would never have the money to buy my contract. It wasn't meant to be.

My lover's close friend Tonomo thought the romance a disaster for Sakon, that it ruined a potentially great samurai. He loved Sakon and the thought of him making love to a woman proved unbearable. He hoped his friend would eventually come to his senses.

No great battles were waged after Sekigahara, and Sakon's taste for war vanished. He contented himself with a more peaceful life, happy in our love.

In 1603, Tokugawa announced his plans to move the capital from Kyoto to Edo and build a castle. He decreed that all samurai directly in his employ would reside full time in Edo. A married samurai with enough money could stay six months in Kyoto and six months in Edo. Tokugawa instituted heavy taxes from his samurai to pay for the expenses of the new capital.

The news devastated Sakon. He'd have to stay in Edo, never to see me again. He protested the unfair decree by committing seppuku, appealing to his master's conscience and intelligence. Without me, life held nothing for him. He instructed Tonomo to tell me what happened and that he loved me.

Sakon kneeled on the raised platform cross-legged, his kimono loosed to his waist, his chest bare. He tucked the sleeves of his garment under him, assuring his fall forward in death, as proper for a samurai. Tonomo kneeled to his friend's left side.

On the tray in front of Sakon rested a 12-inch dirk. He lifted it reverently, his thoughts of me: memories of our times together, our lovemaking. He smiled at the joy we brought to each other. Abruptly, he plunged the dirk into the left side of his exposed abdomen. Agony swept over his face as he jerked the blade to the right, turned it over and cut upward. He removed the dirk.

Tonomo lurched to his feet, raised his sword and struck the final blow to sever the head of his friend and end his agony. It was done.

Sakon had last visited me two months before. He'd never been away this long before. A heavy anxiety held my heart.

Tonomo came to visit. He told me Sakon lived in Edo now. He wouldn't visit me ever again. It was over. He found the courtesans of Edo far more talented.

I bid Tonomo good-bye and wept, not because of what he told me. I knew it wasn't true. Sakon was dead; I felt it.

In my twenty-sixth year, I retired and became the teacher destiny decreed. The work filled my days and eased my pain. My heart never stopped yearning for Sakon; my soul resonated with the memory of our love. Even in old age, my body burned for his touch. I never again in that life experienced the passion I shared with him.

On July 13 of each year, the feast of the Dead, I lit candles for my love. As they flickered, I felt him in the room with me, felt his touch. The memories warmed my heart and swaddled my old bones when the cold, north winds blew and brought the snow that lived in my heart since the day he died. I'd find him again someday. He waited for me. I was certain of it.

Chapter 5

> My Mars angles a complex pattern of Richard's natal Moon, affecting his emotions and 8th house of deep relationships, triggering major complexities for us, common in deep relationships. Venus square Neptune in his natal chart triggers fear of engulfment in a relationship and fear of abandonment, vacillating between needing and wanting me and fearing the pain it can bring him. The Universe challenges us to deal with, overcome and outgrow our outmoded ways of relating and coping, to heal our hearts and grow from our experience together.

Richard and I frustrate, confound and infuriate each other. Our mutually strong emotional defense systems guarantee a difficult relationship. We need each other. We love each other. We punch each other's emotional buttons, engaging in Plutonian conflict and power struggles, igniting deeper issues around intimacy and commitment in our relationship. It's what we've come to do. It's important for us psychologically and karmically.

He dredges up my daddy issues like demons from hell. I project on him all the impossible neediness of my little girl. I will him the task of healing my pain and filling the emotional void left by my father. I rage at him when he fails me, as he unfailingly does. The problem is: I expect a man with no legs to carry me to safety.

He didn't want to fall in love with me, but he had little choice. I have what he needs to connect him to his emotional expression and heal it. It's the major factor in our relationship. My energy deeply attracts him, stirs his emotions to a fervor that terrifies and repels him. He can't sort it out. He holds me tightly with one hand and pushes me back with the other, creating an emotional impasse. I'm the irresistible force to his immovable object.

In Richard's case, his Virgo Moon is like a little nun sitting on his shoulder, injecting doubt into every positive thought, ruining pleasure with guilt, reminding him duty and responsibility come first. This morning after our first night of passion, the nun incites his thoughts to run furious laps around his heart until they collapse from indecision. Fear and confusion ride through his thoughts like twins joined at the hip. His ultra-responsible Saturn energy joins his Virgo Moon, scurrying between responsibility and worry, chewing at the ragged edges of his self confidence like a rat with a piece of cheese.

His Gemini Sun fears loving me means being held back, forfeiting his dreams to an unfettered life—committing to me an emotional trap to be avoided at all costs. Even more frightening, our passion connects us in a way that touches a special place deep in each other, triggering a kind of yearning that burns a hole in the heart that only the other one can fill. This kind of intense emotion doesn't make sense to the logical side of his Virgo Moon. His Gemini Sun seesaws the possibilities back and forth; his Virgo Moon analyzes his feelings into paralysis.

I have my own problems. Confused, emotionally fragile and wary, I don't trust my feelings. I still reel from the humiliation of surrendering my virginity at nineteen to a handsome but emotionally damaged soul with the IQ of a tree frog. And the sex was much ado about nothing, making me question why everybody but my mother thought sex was so great. I couldn't believe she could be right about something so important. After several futile attempts to see if the sex would improve, I decided to become celibate.

Too late, I was pregnant. We never used protection because he told me an old football injury left him sterile. Impossibly naïve and inexperienced, I believed him. I had to get married, just like my mother had done, and having to walk in her moccasins devastated me. I held strong judgments about the life choices my mother had made. The Universe gave me a needed lesson in humility.

The baby, born three months early, died shortly after birth. Losing the baby emotionally devastated me. I took the pain and horror of that experience and buried it as quickly and deeply as I could. But I knew subconsciously I'd been given a reprieve. The Universe had better plans for me than a dead end life with an uneducated, abusive, pathological liar. Divorcing the handsome tree frog was easy. Caring for laboring women and attending their births helps me heal the loss of my first baby and offers reassurance that there's a happy ending for me someday. It will take years for me to stop tearing up during each birth I attend.

If I'd stuck to my intention to never have premarital sex again, last night with Richard would never have happened. Now, I find myself in a situation where the old rules don't apply. I question the limits and restrictions I've put on myself. My values are changing in ways I haven't anticipated, leaving me unsettled.

I decide it all boils down to stockpiling memories that warm your heart and body when you're in the rest home, rocking on the porch. I want those memories. From now on, my decision to have sex hinges on whether I will kick myself later for missing some experience because of someone else's rules. Without a doubt, last night gave me a major memory for my golden years.

Peace comes as I make the very Aquarian decision to make my own rules regarding sex. As long as I'm true to my own code, it doesn't matter what anyone else thinks. When Shakespeare wrote, "To thine own self be true," all the free spirit Aquarians in the Universe must have been singing the Aquarian theme song in his ear—"I Gotta Be Me."

His Virgo nun convinces Richard to stick to his game plan and concentrate on his career in law enforcement, with no time or place for emotional commitment. He longs to be a Secret Service agent. He doesn't think it would be fair to a wife and kids with the long hours and absences that the job would require. He doesn't want to end up like his older brother who's been married twice and headed for number three.

I know something's wrong when I see him briefly that afternoon. I still glow from our night together; he looks distracted, pensive and remote. When I ask him what's wrong, he tells me not to get *hung up* on him because he doesn't want me to get hurt. I play it cool and tell him it isn't a problem. I'd see him around. I'm hurt and bewildered at how he can so easily dismiss what we shared last night. I'm humiliated and furious at his rejection.

Last night, I'd experienced the tender, passionate side of him, the upside of his Venus square Neptune and the sweetness of his Virgo Moon. Now, I get my first taste of the negative side of his Virgo emotions and the ambivalence of his Gemini Sun. The darker side of his Gemini-Virgo combination throws me a painful curve. I vow to avoid him, but he sits securely in my 7th house of relationships, my 5th house of romance and my 8th house of mystical sex. Our yearning for each other keeps us on a short leash.

College Fair Apartments
March, 1964

Jennie and I partied until midnight. Loaded to the gills and looking for trouble, we head for apartment 105. I tell myself I don't care if Richard is there or not, but I do.

Faces of Love, Death and Transformation:

Jennie knocks once and opens the door. Richard sits at the table studying; his roommate Greg rifles through the *Sacramento Bee*. Bobby isn't there. Jennie and Greg have major hot pants for each other. They go to the refrigerator to find something to eat. Greg leans over, and Jennie caresses his backside. They forget about food and head for the bedroom.

To my surprise, Richard looks happy to see me. "Have a seat and stay awhile." He reaches out and pulls me onto his lap. "I missed you, Constance."

The use of my formal name makes me smile. It presumes a certain intimacy. My determination to protect my heart vanishes like a politician's promise. The dormant spark in my belly bursts into flame; instant desire leaves me breathless. Our cheeks touch lightly; I feel his breath on my ear as his teeth graze my ear lobe. His fingers run through my hair, creating warm sparks of energy in their wake, leaving me dizzy. "I think we should go upstairs." I stroke his neck, tracing a line down his chest into his shirt. I love the feel of his smooth skin on my fingers.

We bolt for the door, bounding up the stairs at a full run. Richard rips his clothes off and jumps into bed. I pull at the pins holding my hair. He watches me with impatience. My hair cascades into my face; my usually nimble fingers fumble and flail with the buttons on my dress. It falls to the floor, and I catch it on my toe, kicking it with a triumphant flourish into the air. My bra unhooks easily, and I cast it over my shoulder. Taking deliberate aim, I throw my naked body on top of Richard and impale myself on his waiting, erect organ.

Instead of the tender magic of before, we roil in glorious, animal passion, coupling furiously like felines in heat. The bed creaks and bangs in response to the thrashing of our bodies as we move in fluid synchronicity. The sound of ecstatic moans and grunts of exertion mix with the musky smell of sex in the air.

My brain whirls from exhaustion. Sleep quickly moves to suck me down into its warm depths. Then I hear him saying something about his parents sending him away at age thirteen. This has to be important. I fight my way back to an alert state.

He tells me the story. With no high school in Garberville, the remote logging town in northern California where his family lives, his parents sent him and his brother away to school. They worked on a dairy farm for their room and board in Ferndale, hours away. His childhood ended abruptly.

I cannot begin to fathom the emotional pain of being abandoned like that. I flood with feelings of protectiveness and compassion for him, connecting to the lonely heart he briefly lets me feel. The emotional hook sinks even deeper.

He tries to be matter-of-fact about it, but I hear the hurt and anger in his voice. He didn't mean to pick the scab of that unhealed wound. He realizes he's revealed too much of himself and quickly changes the subject.

In the morning, we agree to be lovers and take care of each other's sexual needs with no strings. I'm not being honest; I love him, and I have other plans.

Sacramento, California
February 20 1965

> The planets plot a surprise for Richard and me. Expansive Jupiter returns to my 5th house of romance and new experiences. Richard's ultra responsible Saturn energy quakes in anticipation of being dog piled by an intense Mars, Neptune and Venus angle, creating a highly charged emotional and sexual energy capable of triggering his *fight or flight* response.
>
> A configuration of aggressive Mars, loving Venus and soul-to-soul connecting Neptune entice me to throw caution to the winds and do something I've refused to do until now.

Our relationship follows a set pattern. Richard resists until the yearning reaches critical mass and he has no choice but to come for me. The absences, coupled with our chemistry, make each encounter seem more intense. Each time, he renews his vow to stay away from me until he succumbs yet again.

Jennie plans to culminate her month long siege on Dr. Williams tonight; she sits on our couch with the hospital lothario, readied to sate her desire.

Pulled from a deep sleep, I hear banging on the door, the doorbell ringing furiously, and loud voices. Karen, our roommate, is in a state of panic.

"He's trying to climb in my bedroom window! You've got to stop him."

I sit up in bed. "Who?"

"Richard. Stop him!" She's hysterical now.

Jennie opens the apartment door; Greg bursts into the room, Eddie and Bobby in tow. They bolt for Karen's bedroom where Richard hangs precariously from the second story sill. I know he has to be really drunk to do something this stupid. Greg pulls him through the window to safety.

Jennie's heartthrob cowers on the couch, looking like a poacher caught in the headlights of a pickup with a redneck's shotgun aimed at his crotch. Furious, she sees victory being wrenched from her grasp.

"You better do something about those stupid friends of yours!" She plays the lady of the manor beset by the unwashed masses.

"Constance, they wouldn't let us in." Richard sways like a drunken cowboy. He spies Jennie seated on the couch with her friend. "Genevieve, what are you doing with a wimpy son-of-a-bitch like that?" He stands menacingly in front of them. "I ought to kick his ass. Constance, don't you think he's a wimpy little son-of-a-bitch?"

Jennie throws herself in front of her quaking date. "Don't you touch him, you dick head," she hisses. "He's a surgeon; he has to be careful of his hands." She puts one foot forward, menacingly, "Lay one hand on him and I'll drop kick your balls."

Richard bursts into uproarious laughter; the others join him. Jennie grabs the wimpy son-of-a-bitch's hand and dashes out the door to safety. "Get them all out of here," she shouts at me. "They better not be here when I get back!"

"Okay, guys. What do you say we blow this place and get a drink?" I know what motivates them. "I'll drive."

Richard's eyes narrow, glaring at me. "Give me the keys."

"I'm driving my car."

"Give me the goddamn keys, Constance," He moves toward me. I give him the goddamn keys.

Richard gets behind the wheel. Greg sits in the front seat and pulls me onto his lap. We take off down Howe Avenue, heading toward Fair Oaks Boulevard. The Mustang hits the Fair Oaks/Howe Avenue intersection at 90 mph. The light flashes green. I close my eyes and clutch Greg's leg. I know we aren't going to make the sharp turn. The big trees that line the road bear old wounds in silent testimony to the curve's dangers. I silently make my peace with death and wait for the crash. The car sways and throws me against the door. I open my eyes and blessed relief replaces my terror. We made it.

Richard hoots with glee, speeding down Fair Oaks Boulevard. "Goddamn, Constance," he says pounding the steering wheel. "This car has guts! I owe that wimpy Mustang salesman an apology."

Greg laughs. "Richard got into an argument at a party and told this Mustang salesman that all Mustang's were wimpy cars and anybody who sold them was a wimp too. He was going to kick his ass. The guy looked like he was going to pee his pants."

Richard pulls the car into the parking lot at the side entrance to The Fireside. It's now 1 A.M. The others wait at the curb. Bobby bends over the gutter.

"Wait a minute; Hansen has to puke," Eddie reports.

Bobby heaves three or four times, wipes his mouth with the back of his hand, grins and says, "Okay, I'm ready to drink some more."

Richard strides to the bar and plunks down fifty cents. "Drinks for the house, Neal."

Neal, our favorite junkie bartender, smiles and stumbles off. Drunk or stoned he pours a reliable drink. Neal forgets to pick up the fifty cents; Richard puts it back in his pocket and caresses my thigh. An old woman, plastered with garish makeup and wearing a moth eaten fur coat, casts a look of disdain.

"So, where you going to live now, Richard," Greg asks.

"Aren't you living with Gary?" I ask.

Greg laughs, "Not after tonight, he isn't."

Richard smiles weakly, "We had a little fight."

"Richard ran Gary's head through the wall."

I'm mildly shocked. I've never seen a violent side to Richard, but I've heard tales of brawls at the Blue Moon bar in Garberville. Gary must have punched some major emotional buttons for Richard to do that.

At 2 A.M., Neal insists we all leave. Greg drives back to my apartment. Richard sleeps with his head on my shoulder.

I want them to go home. I'm not in the mood to face Jennie's wrath, and I have four hours left to sleep before I have to be at work. "I have to work, guys. I'll see you later, okay?"

"One more drink, Constance," Richard pleads. "Then we'll go."

As I pour the wine, Richard disappears. We find him passed out on my bed. Bobby and Greg pull vainly at Richard's limp body. "Oh, just leave him," I say in resignation. After they leave, I study Richard sprawled motionless on his back, eyes closed. I sigh and take his shoes off, unbutton his pants.

"Why do you put up with me, Constance?" He sounds quite sober.

"Let me get your clothes off, and I'll tell you."

Naked, I slide into bed and put my arms around him, cradling his head to me. "I do it because—I love you." I can't believe I finally said it. Euphoria explodes in my brain and terror grips my heart in anguished delight.

My words unleash a torrent of emotion in Richard. The intense energy he feels crashes over the wall around his heart like a tsunami. The nun runs for cover.

Richard's arms tighten around me. "What do you think we should do?" He sounds tortured.

My long held feelings tumble out in a torrent, "I think we should be together. We belong together, Richard. There's so much we could do." I know I'm saying too much, too fast, but the force of my emotions override my deep fear of rejection.

"We're so good together." He holds me even tighter, burying his face in my neck. He kisses me with a yearning tenderness I've never felt from him before. I've never felt so close to anyone as I do him right now. I intuitively understand how deeply he feels and how terrifying it is for him. We stop talking. Our lovemaking binds us in a way it hadn't ever before. Euphoria fills me; if God struck me dead, I'd go with no regrets. We sleep entangled in each other's arms.

At work, I think about how much I love him. Even though he didn't come out and say it, I know he loves me, too. He let me feel it. For the first time, I have hope we'll be together.

The nun can't budge Richard out of my bed; he's waiting for me when I get home—a good sign. I tear off my uniform and fling myself into his warm arms. I study his face, run my fingers through his short, cropped hair. We smile at each other; his fingers move down the middle of my back. He reaches for my hips and pulls me to him. I feel the familiar sharp, hot sensation of him inside me; the shock runs through my body. I've thought about this all day.

At 5 o'clock, I drive him to Eddie and Patrick's apartment—his new home. Richard says nothing about my declaration of love. I know he'll do what he always does after we have an intense encounter—disappear for a while to analyze what happened between us and do his Gemini indecision waiting game. He kisses me tenderly, smiles at me with unmistakable love in his eyes and says, "You're an angel."

I'll see that look many times over the years.

March 1965

The nun wins again. Back to square one. I haven't seen or heard from Richard in two weeks. I go to a party by myself. Eddie lurches around the room in a glassy-eyed stupor. He moves resolutely toward me, drops to his knees and sticks his hand up my dress. I react instinctively, clamping my hand over his to halt the invasion. I'm in no mood for his bad little boy antics. As he clings to my upper thigh like a leech on a piece of fresh liver, I prepare to strike a violent blow for liberty. A strong hand reaches out and frees me. Richard puts his arm around me, and we move to the dance floor.

"I was ready to hurt him." I'm pissed.

He doesn't acknowledge my comment. His mouth moves close to my ear. "I don't know what it is. I can't explain it, but I desire you, Constance."

The word "desire" takes me by surprise, romantically archaic and peculiarly out of place coming from Richard. When he drinks, he reveals parts of himself not otherwise accessible.

"I try to stay away from you and I can't. You know how I feel about relationships. I don't know what to do."

I feel his anguish. "I guess we need to talk."

The stinging cold hits our faces, the stars bright in the crisp March night. Our warm breath and the cold air collide, exploding in white wisps of steam. We kiss deeply for a long time, clinging to each other, not wanting it to end, not knowing what to say. The yearning becomes unbearable.

I turn at a familiar sound: Eddie pees loudly in the bushes, solidly on my shit list now.

"Come home with me, Richard."

He holds me close, "I can't, Constance. I can't. It's too hard. I have to stay away from you. I have to find a way."

"Please, just tonight. You can give me up tomorrow."

He holds me at arms length. "I have to go."

I go home, demoralized, sick of the uncertainty in our relationship.

It isn't as if I don't try. I date other people, even tried sex with a few of them, but I'm always disappointed. I keep my occasional lapses of grace to myself. As far as anyone knows, I only have sex with Richard. The chemistry, that alchemical fusion with Richard, holds me as seductively as any addiction. And casual sex doesn't work for me. I need the emotional connection, and I truly love Richard. I spend most of my time with Eddie, Bobby and Patrick, passing my time in platonic pursuits, waiting. I apply to the Peace Corps.

April 1965
Coyote Lake, California

Bobby and I are on our way to Coyote Lake for spring break. Eddie and Richard plan to meet us there. At this time of year, cows graze in pastures under oak trees and drink from man-made ponds. Vineyards dot the countryside around Lodi, and the peach orchards of Ripon ready to bloom.

Bobby drives my Mustang to the San Luis Reservoir, picks up 152 and cuts across Pacheco Pass, bypassing Gilroy, the garlic capital of the world. We head up Canada Road to Coyote Lake in the timber ridge area in the Santa Clara County mountains.

We arrive at the cabin, rustic and comfortable. Tall trees and dense brush surround the small house, giving it a secluded, safe look. I can see why Bobby calls this his Walden Pond. The air smells of wildflowers in bloom.

Holly and Jack enjoy martinis in the kitchen with some neighbors. Holly gives me the same look as she had the first time we met. I decline the offer of a drink to wait for Eddie and Richard's arrival.

Four little kids sit on the floor in the living room playing Chutes and Ladders. I love kids, and within ten minutes they have me laughing uproariously to gross and disgusting bodily function jokes only eight year olds can love or tell—except maybe Eddie.

The hours melt away with the ice in the martinis. Holly tends a stew for dinner, but it seems to be in a holding pattern. The contents of the pot hold enough food to feed maybe three people, not the ten or so who will be dining. Every so often, she throws in more water and another potato, but the only thing getting stewed is the cook.

Fierce hunger gnaws at me by the time Richard and Eddie arrive. Eddie celebrates his new appointment. "You won't believe this, but I got an internship with Alcoholic Beverage Control. I'm going to get paid to drink!"

"Geezus, Ed. How can you live with yourself? Arresting people for drinking; that's chicken shit," Richard grumbles with mock seriousness and obvious envy.

"You're jealous, Richard. Admit it: I'm a lucky sonofabitch. Right?"

The cocktail hour continues until 9 P.M. when Holly gives everyone a plate with one piece of meat, a quarter of a potato, one small carrot, and some thin, watery gravy slopped over the top. Toothpicks would taste good by now.

Richard and Eddie want to go into town to get a drink and decent food. We land in a dark little tavern. A lone sailor sits at the bar drinking solemnly and with obvious purpose

Richard strikes up a conversation with the sailor, and they begin a spirited political discussion. I stand by the jukebox, listening to snatches of the conversation.

Bobby loses himself in the passion of a solo flamenco dance. He clenches several straws in his teeth in absence of the traditional rose and stomps on the floor loudly, clapping his hands. The bartender remains steadfastly unamused.

Eddie's tired of Richard's preoccupation with the sailor and the conversation in general. He sits next to Richard, puts his arm around him in a possessive gesture, kisses him on the cheek and informs the sailor that he's brought Richard for himself. He doesn't want to share him with anyone else. Richard studiously ignores Eddie, who lisps and flutters his hands.

"You're just doing this to make me jealous, you big tease," Eddie says as he rubs Richard's back affectionately.

The sailor flees. The bartender blames us; the sailor sucked up suds and shooters like a water vac. He's not happy. We're asked to leave.

Back at the cabin everyone settles down somewhere to sleep. Holly assigns me the second bedroom with Bobby's eight-year-old half brother Joey. Holly and Jack have the other bedroom. The guys bunk in the living room: Richard on the couch, Eddie on the floor in a sleeping bag, Bobby on a day bed against the wall. Flames dance brightly in the rock fireplace.

It takes about five minutes for Eddie, in a drunken coma, to start moaning like a mountain lion in heat. No one moves or makes a sound until Holly calls from the bedroom with great exasperation, "Well, let's either help him or kill him."

I hear Richard. "Ed, No! No! Not there. Oh Geezus!"

The fire hisses as Eddie's urine meets flame.

I dash into the living room. Steam rises from the fireplace. Richard stands next to Eddie.

"Goddamn. Ed." Richard mumbles.

We lead him back to his sleeping bag and tuck him in. He never wakes up, but the moaning mercifully stops.

"What's going on out there?" Holly inquires.

"Nothing, Holly. Ed's just sleepwalking, Richard calls. "He's back in bed now. No problem."

Bobby sleeps soundly through it all. Richard pulls me quietly over to the couch. I sit on the edge and he draws me down and enfolds me in his arms and nuzzles my neck.

"Let's go outside," I whisper into his ear, my tongue teasing him, my right hand exploring familiar territory. I unzip his pants to reduce the strain.

"We can't. We'll wake someone up."

"Please."

Richard stops further negotiations by kissing me. We try to crawl silently into each other's skin. He pulls my pants down; our bodies move into each other with irresistible force. My teeth dig into his shoulder to keep from making any noise. We know it's crazy, but we don't care. It doesn't take long maybe a minute. We hold each other quietly.

"I still can't stay away from you." Richard strokes my hair. " That's bad." He kisses my eyes. "Don't let me be selfish and talk you out of going in the Peace Corps just so I can keep you here with me. I'll miss you, but I know you have to go. It's your chance to do something really worthwhile."

What can I say? I don't really want to go. I just don't know what else to do. I say nothing. I kiss him tenderly and go back to my bed.

Joey, Bobby's little brother, in his sleepy voice says, "I'm in big trouble. Whatever happens, they always blame me."

"No you're not, Joey. I'm the one in trouble."

The next morning Holly fixes breakfast. Forget bacon and eggs. She serves ice cream gin fizzes—her specialty of the house. The icy cold, smooth texture of ice cream comforts our hung over bodies. We succumb to the crisp bite of soda, the soothing warmth of gin.

Eddie raises his glass in a toast, "Nothing like a liquid breakfast to set a man straight. Another glass of your finest, innkeeper." He crosses his eyes for effect.

We drink fizzes until noon then switch to martinis. I sit on the floor with a gin fizz in one hand and a martini in the other, caught in the change of shift. The group considers it impolite to waste booze; it won't be tolerated. I continue to drink.

Faces of Love, Death and Transformation:

Eddie and Richard want to water ski. Eddie feels macho after the morning's quota of libations. Bobby brings the boat around, and we set out for the middle of the lake. Eddie doesn't really want to water ski, he just wants to wear a wet suit and swagger around with a beer in his hand. Bobby drives the boat back, aims for the dock but he's going too fast. Richard yells for Bobby to slow down, but he spazzes out and hits the dock with a resounding crash. Bobby fumes and waves his arms around in impotent rage, stuttering obscenities.

"Hansen, you dumb shit!" Eddie yells. "What the hell were you thinking!"

Richard thinks Bobby has been embarrassed enough. "This calls for a drink." He puts a comforting arm around Bobby and my heart warms at his sensitivity to Bobby's humiliation.

Bobby grins and exclaims, "The shit house mouse rides again." It's very drunk out again that night.

In the morning, Bobby gets up on the roof to remove some tiles that need replacing per Holly's request. Eddie and Richard catch the tiles and stack them.

Inside, I help Holly with the breakfast dishes. She looks at me and abruptly asks, "Just who are you with?"

"All of them. I'm one of the boys." I dry a plate and avoid her gaze.

"You don't look like any boy I've ever seen," Holly replies looking at my breasts.

I don't blame her. It does look pretty strange for one girl to be running loose with three guys. I'm more than one of the boys; I'm like their den mother. I nurture and fret over them. "Mother Constance and her boys," as Richard often describes us.

A cry of dismay rings through the air as a familiar figure hurtles past the kitchen window. We know from the blond hair it's Bobby. We hear the thud, then, "Shit!"

Holly slams down a pot and heads for the door.

"Hansen, you dumb shit!" Eddie yells.

Holly stands over Bobby with hands on her hips and that same tight smile on her face I remember from Bobby's birthday. "Can't you do anything without screwing up, for Chrissakes! Just leave it. I'll do it myself later," she fumes. "Why do you always have to be so goddamned clumsy?" She strides back into the house and slams the door.

Bobby lays on the ground with his arm over his eyes, not moving.

"Hansen, you okay?" Richard asks. He's pissed at Holly for embarrassing Bobby in front of his friends.

Time to go home. Bobby wants to go to San Francisco for a few days and asks to borrow my car.

"Are you out of your mind, Constance!" Eddie warns me. "The dumb son of a bitch will wreck it." Bobby is infamously accident prone.

"Shut up, Eddie," I reply. "Nothing's going to happen."

Eddie and Richard give me a ride back to Sacramento. Eddie has his Dad's pickup with a camper shell covering the back. Eddie borrowed it to go hunting. Richard and I paw each other all the way home with increasing fervor. Eddie watches us with envious glee. "Why don't you two get in the back and have at it," he suggests. "Nobody can see you."

For one brief moment, I actually consider the possibility. God, help me, I think, I'm truly out of control.

Richard smiles widely at the thought but rejects Eddie's suggestion. At least one of us has some sense.

When we get back to the guys' apartment, Richard quickly disappears into his bedroom without a word. I hang around for a few minutes, hoping to assuage my passion properly before going home. It never occurs to me Richard waits for me in the bedroom. I need a formal invitation. I leave disappointed. We have a definite communication problem.

June 1965

> Structure loving Saturn in my 4th house brings completion to what has been and germinates new beginnings, encouraging me to set boundaries and bring some security and stability to my life. I can't live with the uncertainty anymore.

> **Energetic Mars in my 9th house of travel and social activities whips my restlessness to try something new. Adventuresome Jupiter in my 7th house of relationships sparks an optimistic desire to expand my horizons and meet new people. When one door closes, Jupiter opens the next.**
>
> **Time to move on.**

Jennie joins the Air Force. Richard, Gary and Filben graduate from Sac State. Bobby flunks Life Science for the third time, delaying his graduation. Since he'd rented the cap and gown and sent out invitations, he shows up and hopes no one will notice. We all agree: no one but Hansen has the balls to do what he did. He confesses to Holly later, takes the predictable emotional flogging like a man, and signs up for summer school.

Richard's dream of being a Secret Service agent died a year ago when he flunked their eyesight requirements. He went on a lone bender, drowning his sorrow in martinis at the Fireside. He had sense enough to know he couldn't drive and he called me to come get him. He was trapped in a phone booth in the parking lot and couldn't figure how to get out. He hung up before he could tell me where he was, but I figured it out and went to his rescue—the angel once again.

I don't know Richard has a pathological aversion to good-byes ever since he left home at thirteen. He moves to San Jose and starts his new job as a Special Agent for Alcoholic Beverage Control without a word to me. I don't understand; we aren't fighting. He calls when he hears I plan to move to Miami with my new friend Ann Marie, as a heart murmur precludes my joining the Peace Corp. He doesn't want me to leave without our seeing each other one more time. A faint spark of hope flames again.

The young Highway Patrolman clocks me at 100 mph on Interstate 80 at Davis on my way to San Jose. I tell him he can't give me a ticket for how fast I was going because I can't afford it. I need money to move to Miami. We negotiate, and he writes me up for 70 mph with a warning to slow down. My car radio plays, "*Do You Know the Way to San Jose?*" I do, and I can't get there fast enough.

Richard waits for me in the bedroom. I smile at him from the end of the bed; he puts his hand out to me. "Where've you been, Constance? I expected you hours ago."

"I'm glad you called me; I missed you."

Richard pulls me closer. I lean over and he kisses me softly on the lips.

"I thought we could drive to Santa Cruz for the day and have dinner."

"Let's talk about that later." I undress and he reaches for me, kissing my eyes, lips, neck, and nipples. He continues downward, parting my legs. Knowing this is our last time adds force to our passion. The sweat rolls down our bodies, making erotic, sucking sounds as we move in and out of each other. I breathe in the intoxicating smell of sex, the musky fragrance heightening my excitement. The cadence and rhythm of our bodies increase the frenzy of pent up energy.

We lay beside each other drenched in juices and sweat. I love these times of total exhaustion, when my body feels so light it floats above me. Richard holds me tightly; we stroke each other absently, lost in our own thoughts.

"Think we should take a shower?" Richard asks.

"We are a sweaty mess." I leap out of bed and dart toward the large shower across the hall. "Come on."

We turn the water to a cool temperature; Richard lathers my body with his long fingers. He strokes me with a tender sweetness that makes me dizzy with wanting him again. Water beats down, spraying cool droplets onto our tongues.

I stand on tiptoes in a silent invitation. He pulls me up and settles into me; my arms cling to his neck. We're just the right height for each other to make it work. Richard leans against the wall for support. I move my hips in a clockwise rotation as he thrusts inside me. I hope to God we don't slip and kill ourselves but I don't care anymore.

"Well, it's four o'clock, you horny woman." Richard laughs, looking at the clock. We've been in bed since noon. "It's too late to go to Santa Cruz."

"I've seen Santa Cruz."

"*What's New Pussycat*" plays downtown. After the movie, we go for cocktails and dinner. We sit at the bar. Richard talks again about his dream of having his own boat and sailing the South Seas someday.

"I could help you get your boat. We could save all our money. Probably take a couple of years, but we could do it." I search his face, hoping.

Faces of Love, Death and Transformation:

He smiles and shakes his head. "I'm going to have to join the National Guard to keep from getting drafted. I need to get that out of the way. Six months is better than two years and getting my butt shot off in Vietnam."

"Do you want me to write to you, send you cookies?"

"Sure." He laughs and gives me that look.

The menu covers Richard's face; he reads the options for dinner and surveys the prices. "Don't order the lobster." He peers at me over the top of the menu.

Back at his apartment, we make love one more time. He kisses me good-bye and tells me to enjoy myself.

I weep copious tears on the three-hour drive home.

I have to get far away from him. I pray Florida is far enough. I can't keep doing this to myself.

Chapter 6

Somewhere in Florida
August 1965

An ominous darkness on a lonely stretch of Florida freeway surrounds my Mustang. The headlights cut weakly through the dense blackness, revealing nothing in the moonless night. Rain falls, not a soft California rain lightly pelting the windshield, tapping comforting counterpoint to the slap of the wipers, but rain in brutal, blinding sheets like a living thing determined to crash through all barriers.

I lift my foot off the accelerator, hesitantly, trying to decide what to do. The car slows; I turn the wheel slightly to hug the shoulder of the road I hope remains rather than some swamp teeming with alligators.

Ann Marie's voice betrays the panic we both feel. "Don't stop! Someone behind us can run into us. Keep going, kid."

It doesn't occur to me at the time, but the situation is an apt metaphor for where I am in my life. What do I fear more: what lies behind me or ahead of me? Either way, I can get creamed. I keep going.

So far, this adventure hasn't been a lot of fun. I've been thrown off a horse in Idaho and kicked in the head, luckily with an unshod hoof or I'd be pushing up daisies. In Queens, New York, some Mafia types approached me in the bar of the hotel where we stayed. After they determined I was indeed a nurse, not a hooker trying to muscle in on their territory, they offered me a job doing abortions in the basement. I politely declined their kind offer, telling them I only knew about birthing babies.

In Chicago, a cop stopped us on some phony pretext, proposing a ticket or a date. I talked him out of both. In Fargo, North Dakota, Ann Marie struck up a conversation with the friendly farmer sitting next to her in a bar. He told her it was harvest season and he needed help to drive a combine. I reminded her we didn't know anything about combines. Ann Marie displays a tenuous grip on reality at times, but I appreciate her amiable, cheerful disposition.

Miami, sprawling and sleazy, gives me nothing to like. I hate the flat top houses, the sultry weather, the gaudy, seedy hotels that smell of sweat and cigars. I neglected to temper Jupiter's boundless enthusiasm with some Saturn based reality testing before we left California. Our Jupiterian adventure leads us not to a beautiful utopia but to a tropical neon paradise of pink plastic flamingos. This isn't what we had in mind.

Eleuthra the Bahamas
September, 1965

After a brief sojourn, we flee Miami for an out-island, staying with a friend of Ann Marie's from Idaho, a peach of a guy who gladly takes us in as house guests. He's lonesome, and we're at loose ends.

French Leave, the only resort on the island, has miles of white sand and water as warm as a baby's bath. The resort closed for off-season, we share the empty beach with a bad tempered macaw left behind for obvious reasons. He resists all Ann Marie's efforts to befriend him.

Sunday Simpson's Boarding House and Bar is the island's social gathering place. Sunday, a retired madam from the UK, had moved to Eleuthra ten years before. Mike adds us to his account at Sunday's; we drink free. Ann Marie's hollow leg rejoices.

Mike's sparsely furnished one-bedroom place comes without air-conditioning. The three of us jockey for space in the double bed. The nights, hot and muggy, make sleeping impossible. An industrial size fan blows irritating blasts of warm air across the room all night. The sheets remain perpetually damp. Mike snores. Various blood-sucking bugs torment us. We drink prodigious amounts of liquor each evening. The heat, booze, isolation and boredom make me a little crazy. This isn't what Saturn has in mind for me. Then it comes—a curve ball from the gods of change: Neptune, Pluto, and Uranus.

September 9, 1965

> **Neptune, also the god of the deep, ruler of water, weather, conjurer of storms, hurricanes and other natural disasters invite**

> some pals for a party: Pluto adds his intensity to the mix; Mars whips the energy higher; Uranus, the master of the unexpected, poises to wreak havoc. A near full moon fuels the volatile energy.

Mike gets the word over the teletype: Hurricane Betsy rages two hours away. The wind already blows at 60 mph. We hang onto each other, pushing our way through the howling winds from the store back to the apartment with our emergency supplies: gin, vodka, and mix.

Mike arranges a hurricane poker party with Gary, a sometime bartender at Sunday Simpson's, and Elijah, the owner of the only used car lot on the island.

Workmen come and board us into the second story apartment. Fear stabs at me like a dull knife as I hear nails pound into the boards covering the door and windows, sealing us in as tightly as a coffin.

Pouring a tumbler of warm gin, I settle into an easy chair in the corner of the living room and listlessly watch the poker party in progress. Totally oblivious to the increasingly howling winds, Ann Marie intently focuses on her cards. Elijah's lilting Bahamian accent fills the room.

I have come here to die, I think with fearsome self-pity, all this way to die in a ratty apartment on some God forsaken, obscure island. I wonder what the guys at home are doing. I wonder if they'll miss me when they find out I'm dead.

In a fury, the planets unleash their wrath. The sound rises from a loud, mournful moaning to a deafening roar, like a freight train in a tunnel. The wind reaches a crescendo at 126 mph. The ocean storms the beach and claws at the doorway of the second story. Cars float by and bang ominously into the building, which shudders in response.

I wonder how it will happen: Will the apartment building collapse? Will the wind or the water carry us away?

By six in the morning, the worst of the wind mellows into loud sighing as the storm moves away. I'm numb from fear. Ann Marie is ecstatic at winning sixty dollars.

The hurricane knocks out all the power on the island—no electricity, no fresh water, nothing but heat, bugs and booze. The hurricane destroyed the airstrip, stranding us.

Faces of Love, Death and Transformation:

Sunday Simpson sheltered a number of tourists during the storm, including a horse she tethered in the parlor afraid the creature wouldn't survive the hurricane. However grateful the animal may have been, he crapped all over the floor. The alcohol sodden guests survived quite nicely. A little horseshit in the parlor did nothing to dim their good humor.

Three weeks have past since we first came to the island, and a week since Hurricane Betsy moved on. I've hit bottom. Emotional limbo and constant ennui dog me. I move through the days in a fog. I walk miles on the beach every day, ruminating on what to do with my life and how to purge Richard from my heart.

Soul searching is 12th house work, deep and intense. It's the house of karma and the realm of the unconscious. It's a period at the end of a cycle before beginning the new. Mars in my 12th house accelerates the forcefulness of the messages from my unconscious. I wrestle with my demons around deep relationships—the limitations, the things holding me back—like my passion for Richard.

I don't need to ask the big question. I have the answer: I have to let him go. Time has run out on our relationship. I have no choice except to move on or start the cycle all over again when Mars moves into my 1st house of new beginnings. I know even at a conscious level how destructive that would be.

The long drive back to California gives me more time to ponder my future. I alternate between silent depression and loud crying jags, finishing the 12th house work of grieving and letting go.

Sacramento, California
September 30, 1965

> **Mars crosses my ascendant, signaling new beginnings, a fresh start. Pluto and Uranus the change agents deliver new possibilities and a new career.**

Ann Marie and I move into a rundown one-bedroom apartment on P Street with my old roommate, and high school friend Karen. We take turns sleeping on the saggy couch in the tiny living room while the other two share the double bed. I want my old life back, but it isn't there anymore. I need to see Bobby.

The garage, a grey stucco building in a nice neighborhood near the college, has steep stairs at the side leading to an upstairs room. Bobby answers my knock, standing there in wilted, paisley Bermuda shorts, shirtless and barefoot, surprised to see me.

"You're back." He looks confused. "I thought you were going to be gone at least six months."

"It's a long story."

Bobby's lost weight. His eyes betray a discernible sadness lodged in the core of his being like shards of splintered bone. He looks lost. Bobby looks like I feel.

A new stereo stands on the wall facing the bed in the cavernous, dimly lit room, a stark contrast to the other old, scarred furnishings. A dark blue, velvet picture of a deeply lined Mexican peasant in a sombrero hangs over the stereo. A double bed sits forlornly under the lone, cobweb-filled window. Clean and obviously soiled clothing pile together in a heap on the bare floor. His flag drapes across the bed.

"This is a very depressing room, Bobby."

"I know, but it's cheap. You're skinny, Constance, but your boobs are holding up."

"I've lost 15 pounds; it's what happens when you're too poor to eat. You look like you could use some food; how about buying me dinner?"

The enchiladas at *La Casita* on Fair Oaks Boulevard taste even better than I remembered. Two martinis apiece bestow a glow to our cheeks and lift our drooping spirits. It feels good to be together again. I think if he could just pass Life Science this time and I could end my angst over Richard, we'd be set. As if reading my mind, Bobby raises his glass in a silent salute.

After dinner, we go back to the garage. Bobby flops on the bed and stares at the ceiling. "Thanks, Constance. It's good to have you back. I spend too much time in this room."

"I don't start work until day after tomorrow, want me to spend the night?"
Bobby lifts his arm from his eyes and smiles at me, "Would you?"

"Move over." I fold the flag down and settle us under the covers. Sex isn't on the agenda. Bobby already knows that from previous experience. One lonely night last year, he asked to sleep with me. We kept our clothes on and assumed the spoon position, my back to him. After a few moments, I felt his erection throbbing against my back, posing the silent question. I answered wordlessly by feigning sleep. After a minute or so, he rolled over and I curled into his back. We fell asleep holding hands. I love that he loves me no matter what.

I pull Bobby to me and wrap my arms around him. His body melts into mine. He buries his nose in my neck. I hold him tightly like a mother with her child, wishing with all my might I could make his sadness go away—and mine.

My feelings for Bobby go beyond protective and motherly. Our hearts have a common bond through our mother's abuse and neglect. We've shared the same pain. And right now we're both adrift in the same boat of uncertainty about our futures—kindred spirits.

I start my new job on Monday, reluctantly taking a position in the emergency room at the Sacramento County Hospital where I trained. I don't have a choice. Although there is a position available in labor and delivery, the Director of Nurse's new policy of not assigning attractive nurses to that department precludes my working there. The interns have a bad habit of marrying the nurses in that department, and she meant to put an end to it. I need a job badly and I'm too depressed to protest her unfair policy. I take some consolation in being considered attractive.

The first month I immerse myself in the language, culture and practices of the ER. It hasn't changed since I was a student, still the same long, gray tiled, dark hall with narrow, dingy rooms off to the sides. Gurneys, and wheelchairs line the hallway. Assorted equipment jam into small spaces adding to the clutter. The sickening sweet odor of paraldehyde and bitter, antiseptic smell of cuprex mingle noxiously. The sounds of crying kids, adult groans of pain, and the voices of harried staff, meld into a ragged dissonance.

Growing up with my mother gave me great battlefield training for the ER. I instinctively know how to live and deal with unexpected violence and crisis. That hyper alert state is second nature to me. I easily shift into that mode where everything in my mind becomes bright and clear; I focus on the task at hand with a steely calmness. I have a sixth sense when a fist is about to fly my way from a combative drunk, deftly moving out of harm's way.

My fear of the unknown fades after a couple of weeks, but the patients and their circumstances remain relentlessly depressing. As a labor and delivery nurse, I'd experienced the joyful possibilities of new life. Now I witness the diseased distress at the end, along with all the horrible things we do to each other and to ourselves along the way. I sink into a dark hole that I don't know how to pull myself out of.

I have no money for food, but I would rather starve than ask my mother for a loan. She calls me weekly, demanding I repay her the $300 she'd had to fork over for my car insurance when I was stranded on Eleuthra. She knows I don't have it right now, but that doesn't stop her hounding me. Joan comes to my rescue, loaning me the money to get Mom off my back.

Joan and I fought fiercely as children. But in bed at night as sleep reached for us, we put aside the rage and frustration we heaped on each other during the day, all those helpless feelings we didn't dare direct at our mother. Our small bodies clung to each other. Throughout the night, we slept in the spoon position, comforting each other silently with our bodies.

As adults, my sister and I have aligned ourselves against our common enemy: our mother. Joan is two years younger than I, but she's functioned as my big sister ever since I had rheumatic fever at age fifteen and she grew to be taller than me. She's an imposing presence at 5 feet 9 and a half inches. I wisely acceded sibling dominance on the day she picked me up and turned me upside down, my head dangling inches from the floor. Since that time when she talks, I listen. She always tells me the truth, even when I don't want to hear it. I am grateful she took pity on me. I have enough to handle right now without our mother.

My gnawing hunger fades, replaced by a hollow emptiness. I don't think about food unless I smell it. I drink coffee and more coffee. I ignore the irregular, polka-like beats my heart makes at intervals from all the caffeine. I survive by pilfering chicken broth and jello from the hospital food cart. After a while, I cease cringing when I have to scrape the mold off the jello.

Richard hasn't called me. I know that he knows I'm back in town. I won't call him. I vow to let him go, but the Universe tests that resolve.

At the end of October just when I think things can't get any worse, I realize I haven't had a period since I left in August after seeing Richard for the last time. I'd stopped taking birth control pills in June, thinking I didn't need them.

I schedule an appointment with my doctor. I need time to think. What if I am pregnant? What am I going to do? Having the baby isn't the issue; it's the *how* that troubles me. I tell myself I can't count on Richard. Marriage and kids are not part of his game plan. Unwed pregnancy and illegitimacy still carry a major stigma. It won't be easy.

Faces of Love, Death and Transformation:

Sacramento, California
October 23, 1965

> An intense configuration involving Venus, Mars, Uranus and Pluto put immense pressure on me to resolve the issues around my love life. Saturn insists on limits and aggressive Mars fuels the intention regarding male energy in my life. Richard's energy reaches nuclear intensity. We face a romantic High Noon.

My weekend off Eddie calls. "Constance, I've got Richard here and he wants to go to Tahoe and gamble. He wants you to give him a ride cause I have to work tonight."

My stomach straddles my kneecaps. I have to face him sooner or later. "Okay, I guess I can do that." The Universe readies my test. I vow not to end up in bed with Richard, but I can't resist seeing him.

My feet feel like lead as I climb the stairs to Eddie's apartment. Richard opens the door and steps out before I knock. "Let's go, my dear." He sounds happy with anticipation, like a kid whose ride to the circus just arrived.

His warm smile kindles the old tenderness I feel toward him. This isn't going to be easy. We make strained small talk as my Mustang heads down Folsom Boulevard.

"Stop at that bar over there, and let's have a drink."

I didn't think he really wanted to go to Tahoe. The dark bar sits empty, except for two solitary drinkers. The jukebox plays Bobby Vinton's *"There I've Said It Again."* Our drinks come and we sip them in silence, each waiting for the other to make the first move.

"Let's dance." Richard stands and leads me to the dance floor.

I move into his arms; he holds me close. I feel his breath on my ear. The spark ignites and catches fire. My heart sinks as our bodies melt together and Bobby sings, "*I love you; what more can I say? I need you; there's no other way...*" The song says it all. My body clings to his. I feel like a heroin addict out of rehab about to plunge the needle into my arm.

"Let's go." Richard's husky voice demands. We leave our full drinks on the table. I follow him like a zombie back to the car. We start for Tahoe once again.

Richard has other ideas. "Let's find a rack somewhere." The longing in his voice sends chills through me. His eyes bright with fire, he caresses my arm through my thick sweater and he's got that look in his eyes.

I've never wanted him so much as I do at this moment. A fierce war rages between my heart and my resolve. My body physically aches for him. I'm teetering on an emotional tightrope and I could fall either way.

My mind snaps and my resolve kicks in. I stop the car, turn it around and drive back down Folsom Boulevard. "I'll take you back to Eddie's."

Richard grabs my wrist, "Just a damn minute, what's going on? Stop the goddamn car!"

I guide the Mustang to the shoulder. "I can't do this anymore, Richard. I just can't. I left to get away from you and try to make some sense out of our relationship. I have to face the fact things will never be any different between us."

He doesn't offer any rebuttal. We make the trip in icy silence. I wait for him to get out as we sit in the parking lot of Eddie's apartment building.

I don't want him to go.

"Why are you so bitter?" He stares at me intently.

I look away. "I thought I was pregnant. I hadn't had a period since we were together in August." I turn back to him.

"Are you pregnant?" His eyes soft and shiny look into mine.

His tender reaction shocks me. I realize I might have underestimated him. "No, I'm not." I meet his gaze. "It occurred to me that if I was pregnant, I couldn't count on you. I'd have to have the baby by myself. I want more than that."

"What *do* you want, Constance?" He hurls the question as a fiery challenge.

I look into his eyes. "Do you love me? Forget about commitment or marriage, or whatever; do you at least love me?" I'm desperate for some sign of emotion from him, a fragment I can cling to. Anything.

He stares at his hands stretched across his knees. "I don't know what that is. What is love? Do you know?" He glares at me.

I say to him, "I have to go." I know it's hopeless.

He slams the car door and bounds up the stairs to Eddie's apartment, leaving me with tears streaming down my face.

The timing is all wrong, I tell myself. Richard might never need a relationship, but I need him now. He's spent two years bouncing my heart around like a rowboat in a hurricane and it just shattered on the rocky shore of his unyielding ambivalence.

Confrontations are anathema to both his Gemini Sun and Virgo Moon. Gemini doesn't like being scolded and Virgo wounds easily. His inability to communicate his feelings doom any effort to resolve the issues between us. He wounds me with his challenge that I don't know what love is. Fact is: I don't. I won't for quite a while.

Chapter 7

San Diego, California
September 15, 1974

We comfort each other by being together. We talk quietly and laugh loudly at our bursts of black humor, trying to keep tears at bay. We remember the good times, reciting them like a rosary, over and over.

Eddie joins us. I resent his presence. He never really liked Bobby that much. He never loved him the way the rest of us did. I don't feel like he belongs here.

Richard, Filben and I go with Liz to make funeral arrangements. We tell her the story of the Buick, the legendary, green, corduroy sport coat of Richard's that held magical powers: Wear the Buick and you got laid. Bobby nailed Ruth in that jacket, Richard reminds us. We think he should be buried in the Buick, even though it's as long gone as our early years together.

We wonder whatever happened to George, Bobby's battered Volkswagen. We agree he should have kept it instead of trading it in for a flashy convertible when he finally passed Life Science after the fifth attempt and graduated. Instead of a casket, we think he should be buried in George with a jug of Red Mountain cradled under his arm, wearing the Buick, tie optional.

The funeral director listens to us, his face betraying unconcealed horror as we banter the possibilities back and forth. Liz, tired of our walk down memory lane, signs on for the traditional casket and ceremony.

We bury Bobby on a pleasant-looking hill at a cemetery that I forget the name or the location of. It doesn't matter. I don't visit cemeteries; I never go back.

Bobby kept us together; he was the glue for our group. With the exception of Eddie, he's the one everyone felt closest to. The structure of the group and our relationships to each other begin shifting into a new form. We have to grow up. Our innocence died with Bobby. We face our mortality and pray our close bond remains strong over time.

Faces of Love, Death and Transformation:

The long hours in the ICU reveal to me what I avoided until now. I can't fool myself any longer. I'm not happy and I deserve to be. I don't remember ever being truly happy; I experienced brief moments of intense joy that Richard and I shared making love, but I need more.

For the first time, I sense there is more.

Bobby kept the band-aid on my battered heart. His death ripped it off and I'm in need of major surgery. As painful as it is, only a major trauma like this could shake me loose. His dying plunges me head long into the deep psyche explorations that the 8th house demands, evaluating the deeper realities in my relationships. Bobby and his love will always be with me. Eddie is another story.

Sacramento, California
November 1965

> **Saturn nestles in my 4th house of new beginnings, home, family and stability. Optimistic Jupiter occupies my house of relationships. Sexy Pluto and Mars angle Venus in my 5th house of romance, play, and amusements—all perfect energies for courting.**

Eddie has hunted all his life; he knows a wounded bird when he sees one. I behave like an injured dove: dazed, unable to comprehend what has happened or what to do next, an easy target.

He senses my emotionally vulnerable state. A huge void opened when I closed the door on Richard. The immutable laws of the Universe dictate that something has to fill it. Eddie's been waiting for this.

My emotional pain brings out only the best in his usually self-involved, juvenile personality. He treats me with the same loving tenderness as he had when he courted me in a past life in Kentucky. We go for long drives, eat quiet dinners. He buys me ice cream sundaes after I pledge never to tell anyone he actually set foot in an ice cream parlor, protecting his bad boy reputation.

I'm laughing again. He's wormed his way into my heart with his little boy charm and devotion. He wants to marry me, telling me he'll always love me and never do anything to hurt me. More than anything, those words strike a powerful emotional chord in me. He makes all the right moves, says all the right things. He offers me a lifeline. I don't realize it's made of silly putty.

I'm not physically attracted to Eddie. He doesn't have the kind of looks that women generally find appealing. He isn't tall at 5'9" with a slight build and Irish white skin dotted with freckles like a spotted pony. His face is broad and long. His eyebrows form a thick, unbroken line over his round brown eyes; he's self-conscious about them. He once asked me if I thought girls would like him better if he plucked them. His nose is strong, his lips full; he has good teeth. His thick, dark lashes hide behind black, horn-rimmed glasses.

What I do find appealing is his playful, funny, self-deprecating, outrageous personality. He has one of those chameleon-like personalities where he can be whatever he thinks you want him to be at the time. Whatever demons he may have, he doesn't let me see them—yet.

The more I think about marriage to Eddie, the more sense it makes. I'd experienced consuming passion and I can't do it again. I feel that I wouldn't survive. Being safe, secure and happy becomes my priority. I want the pain to end and my overwhelming desire to nest convinces me that the implausible is possible, the unthinkable desirable.

Eddie loves me as much as his emotionally stunted little boy-self will let him, and I love him as much as my broken heart allows. True, I don't love him the way I love Richard or the way I love Bobby, but there are many kinds of love. Love is love: one type needn't be better than the other, I keep telling myself. And Eddie needs me to save him from himself. He's a child who needs boundaries that he can't provide for himself. He instinctively senses I can give him what he needs and keep him safe from the consequences of his irresponsible behavior—the way his mother has done up to now.

Our sexual union conjures no burning, erotic passion. Eddie loves whorehouse sex. He considers himself an *aficionado*, having spent most of his time and money at the brothels in Nevada every summer. It's what happens when you have Mars, Scorpio, and Uranus in bed together in the 8th house, and the Moon, Venus, and Neptune in a ménage a trois writing Forum fantasies for *Penthouse*. His Mars/Venus connection makes sex a little twisted. For Eddie, sexy is dirty and dirty is sexy. His strict Catholic upbringing doesn't help. He once told me he couldn't be alone without amusing himself by abusing himself. His mother's God decreed it a sin and that made it all the more fun.

Eddie doesn't see sex as a way to emotionally connect. Accustomed to limited fondling and foreplay with the meter always running, he focuses on the fast finish. He teaches me proper brothel etiquette. I learn the difference between a *half and half* and an *around the world*. He expands my sexual perspective. The act usually entails an enthusiastic romp done in and on unlikely places like the kitchen table or the toilet. Eddie loves sexual adventures. I've never laughed during sex before, but I deeply miss the kind of emotional connection Richard and I had when we made love. I'm hoping in time Eddie and I can develop that.

We bring no secrets to our relationship; Eddie as Richard's best friend knows how much I loved him. He watched our romance play out from a front row seat just as he did in the Japanese life. Most comforting of all is my belief Eddie will never ask me to give him the one thing he can never have—my whole heart. He doesn't want it anyway. We make a Faustian pact that brings a high price in tears and heartache. I plunge head long into that abyss which I hoped to avoid by marrying Eddie.

I'm comforted in the knowledge Richard remains in my life as my husband's best friend. We're destined to continue the eternal triangle we started in the Japanese life. Over the years, Eddie keeps Richard and me connected, yet apart.

In January, Eddie drives to San Jose to break the news to Richard that we're getting married. Eddie expects that Richard will beat the crap out of him, but it has to be done.

Eddie returns with no visible wounds. I ask how it went.

"When I told Richard we were getting married, he asked me why I would want to marry someone who's been around as much as you have."

I'm stunned. I can't imagine Richard saying anything like that, especially about me. I've never heard him say an unkind word about anyone.

Eddie puts his arms around me. "I told him that didn't matter to me, that I loved you." He wounds me and then comforts me. I don't perceive Eddie's motivation at the time.

Eddie lied to me just like he did in the Japanese life. Richard never said that, but I won't know it for certain for many years. Eddie wants to make sure I don't have any second thoughts about reconciling with Richard. He made sure that door slammed shut with his deliberate, hurtful lie.

By February, I sense a change in Eddie's attitude. He shows all the signs of someone having second thoughts about a permanent commitment, alternating between being emotionally needy and committing acts of casual cruelty. I tolerate the behavior because I understand his ambivalence. Like a child he needs me, and he doesn't always like that. I don't realize at the time he's testing my limits and boundaries to see how far he can push me. It's what emotional abusers do. Disenchanted with the relationship, I have second thoughts, too.

The phone rings insistently. Eddie. He can screw himself and the horse he rode in on. He infuriated me last night, calling me a bitch in front of his partner Russ at Alcoholic Beverage Control. Usually when he drinks, he's charming and flattering. Last night he'd ditched the charm and turned into a mean drunk.

"Hi! He chirps, sounding like the blue bird of happiness. "I'm ready for you to apologize for last night."

I slam the phone on the hook, pick it up and slam it down again, just in case he didn't get it the first time. That little boy shit isn't working anymore.

An hour later the phone rings again. I hear a whimper. "Constance, please don't hang up! Something terrible happened." The whimper rises to a plaintive whine. "Please, come over, now."

"What happened?" Eddie frequently employs a flair for the dramatic.

"Please, please, just come over." He sounds tearful.

I open the door to his bedroom; the smell of dirty clothes and stale cigarettes fill the air. Pulled shades darken the room. Eddie's body curls into a fetal position, the covers over his head.

"Well, what's the big emergency?"

His eyes, alive with panic, stare up at me. Oily hair plasters his scalp. A stubble of whiskers dot his pale skin, milky white with fright. "I've been drafted! Drafted! Can you believe that shit?"

"So?"

"I can't go in the Army. I'm not cut out for that shit." He babbles. "I've got to find a way out of this. Help me. Holy Geezus! They'll send me to Vietnam and I'll get my ass shot off. Oh, fuck!"

Faces of Love, Death and Transformation:

I stand silently.

"I know; you can shoot me in the foot. They can't take a cripple. I'll get my gun. You can do it right now." He sits up on the edge of the bed, looking toward the closet; his gun dangles in the holster.

I smile. "I'm not going to shoot you in the foot, Eddie." I'm enjoying his dilemma. Talk about the ultimate irony: Eddie who hates authority of any kind being forced to do what he's told 24 hours a day for two years. Maybe there is a God after all. Now I know that actually, there is a Saturn after all.

"Oh, God! I'm screwed—screwed, blued, and tattooed!" The wailing reaches fever pitch. I've never seen him like this.

Then it strikes him. There are things worse than getting killed. Who will take care of him? No sending his laundry to Stockton to his mother. No Patrick to make tequila meatloaf and remind him to do things. He'll have to live with a bunch of guys and keep things neat.

For the first time in his life he will really be on his own. Before despair swallows him, the epiphany comes like a shining light. He focuses on me, salvation at hand. "Constance, marry me, please. Don't leave me. I'm sorry for calling you a bitch. You know I didn't mean it." He claws at my hand like a drowning man. "I can just see us married, can't you? I think we should have four kids. It would be so great. Let's do it now. We can go to Reno and get married this afternoon. What do you say? Constance!"

"I don't know Eddie. Let's see how it goes."

The Army set the induction date for April 6, 1966. Eddie spends the next two months courting me like a presidential candidate needing one last vote for victory. The trick is convincing me I will live happily ever after if I elect him to be my husband. He wages a hell of a campaign.

Fair Oaks, California
June 15, 1966

Astrologically, disaster waits to happen. Enough planets converge in high tension angles in the heavens to cause a cosmic

blackout: A Venus and Moon conjunction, dealing with love and emotional issues, opposes a deceptive Neptune in intense Scorpio, masking blind spots, hidden doors, and unseen consequences to come. We fool ourselves and each other in thinking we can make this work, but fate decrees we take this path. The combination of all the planets involved set the dynamics that will play out in our marriage.

The music starts. Panic threatens my outer composure. I breathe deeply and take the first step. Eddie's work partner, Russ, sits in the back row. He catches my eye, "It's not too late," he whispers. "I have the motor running."

I shake my head no. I think about Richard. He finally needs me and I can't help him. What timing: as I walk down the aisle, Richard's at his father's funeral, wearing the suit he bought for my wedding. His mother is in the hospital in critical condition from the small plane crash that killed his father. My heart aches for Richard. I know how he feels losing his father, but I'm minutes away from being married. I can only do what I'm about to do.

The minister drones on and on about the ring and sacred commitment, ignoring my look of obvious displeasure at his rambling discourse. Eddie stands rigid, frozen in place. I want the ceremony over quickly.

The big, white Lincoln Continental cruises down Interstate 80 on the way to West Sac for the reception at my mother's house. I breathe a sigh of relief and smile at my new husband. He looks at me quizzically for a moment. "You in a white dress, that's a laugh."

My cheeks flame. A sick feeling rips through me, a deep anger settles inside me. I'll never forget what he said.

I drink several glasses of champagne to calm my jangled nerves at the reception. Bobby and I come face-to-face; we stare into each other's eyes. He reaches for me and we embrace, holding each other, no words necessary.

Eddie and I change clothes in my mother's bedroom. He stops me in front of the full-length mirror and puts his arms around me. He gazes at the two of us in the mirror. "We make a great looking couple, don't you think?"

I stare into the mirror and say nothing. I think about burning the white dress, preferably with him wearing it.

The twenty mile trip to the hotel is a nightmare. My little brother switched the spark plugs as a wedding prank and the car refuses to go over forty miles and hour, coughing and sputtering. Eddie screams obscenities. When I tell him it's just a tradition, he tells me he doesn't give a flying fuck about tradition and he's going to kill the little bastard. Any residual feelings of post wedding euphoria I have desert me.

We spend our wedding night at a hotel off Highway 160. The room overlooks a small man-made lake. Ducks swim listlessly in the murky water; a giant fountain spews water twenty feet in the air.

"Damn, I wish I had my gun; I could rip off a few and get me some ducks." Since he doesn't have his gun, he orders drinks sent to the room. I change into a pale blue nightgown with delicate pink flowers on a fitted bodice. The low cut shows my breasts to great advantage. I feel glamorous.

The drinks sweat on the nightstand, leaving rivulets of water on the dark wood. Eddie jumps up and down on the bed like a chimpanzee on a trampoline.

"What are you doing?"

"I won! I won! Richard wanted you. Bobby wanted you. But I got you." He jumps up and down, rhythmically.

I'm a trophy. It never occurred to me before. He doesn't seem to realize he didn't win me; he got me by default.

We don't have sex; he doesn't feel like it.

The second night we spend at a remote cabin courtesy of a friend. It's forty minutes from Lake Tahoe and Eddie wants to gamble. I hate gambling; I want to stay in and have a romantic dinner and get my feelings back on track.

Eddie begs and wheedles, promising to be back in two hours. He leaves at 8 P.M. and arrives back at 4 A.M. sloppy drunk. I'm thinking marrying him was not such a hot idea, but I console myself with the hope that he will grow up in time. Our next stop is Disneyland—his choice, not mine.

Sacramento, California
October 5, 1966

> Saturn sharply angles Richard's Venus, hurling the hammer of reality of love in his face with my marrying Eddie. Uranus hurls more major changes at him with my leaving for Germany.

The apartment brims with people for my going away party. I join Eddie in Germany on Monday. Richard walks in. My heart lurches. He looks thinner. Lines of fatigue rim his eyes. His mother survived, but his father's death has obviously taken a toll.

"Hey, look who's here! Richard, you asshole, how you doing?" Filben roars with drunken good humor.

Richard accepts a beer and greets me with a subdued, "Hello, Constance."

His eyes look tired and sad, bloodshot from drinking. I wish I could find the right words to say about his father's death, but I know he doesn't want to talk about it. I study his face. "I didn't know you were coming."

"How's Mr. Ed doing? I hear he's already adding to the annals by peeing on a sergeant." He's referring to the night Eddie drank too much German beer, sleepwalked to a stairwell balcony looking for the latrine, and let loose on a hapless sergeant standing watch below. "He needs you to keep him out of trouble, Constance." He studies my face intently, his eyes dark and bitter. "Why did you do it? Why did you marry him when you knew I loved you? How could you do it?"

I stand frozen, trying to comprehend what he's just said, my brain on pause mode. I try to form a response, but nothing comes. I've waited a long time to hear those words: "…I loved you." Improbably, I smile, turn around and leave him standing there. He came too late, too goddamned late. I am so angry at him and terribly sad for both of us.

Richard had two years and a six-month engagement to make his feelings known. He's paying the price for his unwillingness to make a decision on his own. Change came, but not the one he wanted. Without wanting to, we've broken each other's hearts—a necessary step at the time. A broken heart trumps a closed heart in the game of love.

We've done our little *pas de deux* over several lifetimes. The only time we've actually been together was during an Indian life in Arizona right after Japan. The complicated scenario sounds like a soap opera: I loved Richard's best friend, but he wanted me, so he killed my betrothed, made it look like an accident and married me after I finished my grieving—bad karma, great sex.

We met up again in London in the 1700s where I flowered as a promising ballerina named Leah Strom and Richard assisted the dance master. We fell madly in love again, and there were no societal or cultural barriers as in the Japanese life, no other man as in the previous life. We promised to marry. Then he got some fever and died on me. Foiled again. Maybe stealing me in the Indian life meant he couldn't have me in that one.

When Richard died in the dancer life, we gave each other a piece of our souls. We wanted to keep our soul connection alive until we could find each other again. We wouldn't return those soul pieces to each other for 400 years.

On a soul level, this passion between us has to move to a level worthy of the deep intimacy of the 8th house. We have to finish our karma with each other. There's a reason we have the connection we do. In my heart, I know we aren't really done with each other, but right now I have to attend to my karma with Eddie.

Chapter 8

> Eddie's strong personality comes from a potent Scorpio/Mars combination. He stubbornly embraces the negative side of Scorpio: power and control. Mars adds the fiery, forceful aspect to his personality and opposes both his Saturn, the disciplinarian, and the unpredictable, explosive Uranus. In layman's terms—he was born with a major bug up his butt.

I'd experienced isolated snatches of Eddie's unpredictable anger before we married. I attributed it to his impatience and immaturity, things I thought he would eventually outgrow. I wasn't aware of how full and deep his anger ran. I'm puzzled as to what feeds it.

His mother differs from the ones the rest of us have, a sweet, devout woman with endless patience, a nurse who spoils and dotes on her oldest son. But with her passive, martyr personality, she didn't have the courage to give him what he really needed: boundaries and the opportunity to experience consequences. He grew up thinking the rules of polite society didn't apply to him and she never dared tell him otherwise. He repays her misguided love and loyalty with arrogant contempt. I have married my mother.

Eddie's father is an ex-cop, a tenderhearted, tough old bird who calls Eddie "Honey." I find that endearing. He's a life-long binge drinker whose own father drowned in Lake Michigan after shooting a hole in the boat while duck hunting drunk. The times his father fell off the wagon and got trampled by the hooch horses from hell, as Eddie describes it to me, his mother sent him to search the flophouse hotels on skid row looking for him. He watched his mother pound on his father's chest in angry frustration, desolate her prayers couldn't keep her husband from the bottle. I see where Eddie could be angry, but not the way he is. The rest of us had more traumatic childhoods.

Eddie's anger presents a formidable obstacle to intimacy in our relationship, stirring up all the ego issues love should never be about—power, struggle, control and mean-spirited competition: the dark side of love.

My inflexible, stubborn will collides with his rebellious nature, creating a struggle for dominance. Instead of equal partners in marriage, we fall into a parent-child relationship. I play the mother demanding he grow up. He adopts the role of the little boy running through life screaming, "You can't make me." I'm betting I can.

Baumholder, Germany
October, 1966

We live in base housing, where Rommel's troops bivouacked during WWII. Our apartment is a cavernous hole inhabited by gray, worn furniture, moth-eaten damask drapes and an aged, wood counter in the kitchen in advanced stages of black rot. My gossamer winged fantasy of a quaint German apartment adorned with geranium filled window boxes dies a quick death.

It didn't have to be this way. The Army offered Eddie a commission and a slot in their prized Criminal Investigation Department, requiring an extra year of service. He flatly turned it down, unmoved by the professional experience he would get and the nice addition to his résumé. He wasn't giving the Army one more minute than the required two years, preferring to spend his time typing with one finger in the personnel unit, while frequently "misplacing" the files of those who displease him—a covert use of his limited power.

We drive around in an ancient battered VW Eddie bought for $100. Old Blue, as he names her, has no muffler and a large hole in the floor on the passenger side. We have to keep the windows down even in winter to keep from being overcome by the fumes. The broken driver's seat necessitates a sewer pipe in the back to hold it upright. Eddie loves this car.

Our year in Germany sets the tone for the marriage, and our first battle wages over garbage. I want him to be responsible for dumping it. He informs me he can't do that because he's too busy protecting me from the Red Communist menace, fighting on the frontiers of freedom.

The rotting bags of garbage sit in the entry hall for two weeks like a compost pile; I add a new bag everyday. The smells of the growing ferment greet him as he comes through the door each afternoon. I close myself off in the bedroom with the window open to the chilly autumn air, bundled in my winter coat, reading *War and Peace* for the third time. I feel a kinship with Tolstoy's tortured Russians. I have nothing else to do. Eddie won't allow me outdoors alone. He lectures me on the evil lurking in the hearts of the lonely, horny troops on the base.

When the stench reaches critical mass, he capitulates and dumps the garbage; I enjoy hearing him gag with each trip to the dumpster. Victory is mine, but I lose the next two rounds.

I want him to stop leaving his clothes all over the apartment. He demonstrates his disdain for my request by hanging his underwear on the light fixture in the living room. The next morning, I pick up all his clothes and throw them out the bedroom window into the snow. He comes home for lunch, surveys my handiwork, picks them up, marches into the bedroom and dumps them on the floor. "So, ridin' the cotton pony are we?"

In March, the Christmas tree stands in the living room, dry and dangerous. Pine needles litter the floor, a funeral pyre waiting to happen. My need for safety compels me to give in and drag it to the dumpster.

We have different expectations for marriage. He wants a caretaker/mother, not a wife. In his heart, he's a bachelor, not a husband. He wants to do what he wants to do when he wants to do it and fiercely defends what he believes is his inalienable right to be free. He's a teenager.

Our battles follow a pattern. I expect a traditional marriage where he does man things and I do woman things. We skirmish; we fight, sometimes openly and loudly, sometimes silently and covertly. After we unofficially declare a victor, we hold a brief truce, retreat to regroup, then march to the battlefield again.

When he gets bored or senses I'm too content, he pouts, telling me he can't stop thinking about my having sex with Richard. It bothers him. I see it for what it is—deliberate emotional manipulation to make me feel guilty and unworthy, another way to try and control me.

My Aquarian rebels against his Scorpio fueled power play. The unfairness infuriates me and feeds resentment that grows strong over the years. Two things keep me going: his uncanny ability to make me laugh and my stubborn will. I'm determined to make this relationship work—my dogged Venus in Capricorn insists the toad will become the prince.

Faces of Love, Death and Transformation:

St. Helena, California
February 1968

I'm back in Sacramento apartment and job hunting. Eddie won't be out of the Army and returning home until next month. I'm overjoyed to be home after suffering long bouts of homesickness and isolation. I feel like I've been let out of prison.

Gary and his longtime girlfriend June are getting married. Richard is best man. Filben, Karen and I drive from Sacramento together to the house Gary and June rent in St. Helena, a quaint little place in a secluded area with a stream running through the property.

The rest of the gang arrived earlier. They're drinking and watching Richard and Gary frolicking in the stream, wrestling in the frigid, shallow water like two bear cubs. I study Richard as he sits on a rock drying off. He's changed: his college brush-cut now a mass of dark curls falling around his ears in appealing disarray. A Zapata-like moustache straggles over his lip. The look suits his new job as an undercover narcotic agent—dangerous and seductive. Richard meets my hesitant gaze. "Hello, Constance." He greets me in a neutral tone, but stares intently at me.

I look at my watch and announce the ceremony starts in thirty minutes. Pandemonium ensues. Gary cuts himself shaving and Richard yells for me to come stop the bleeding while he fixes Gary's cummerbund. Once dressed, they speed off in Richard's Porsche with the rest of us following.

We arrive in the church parking lot, but no sign of the Porsche. I see a familiar figure standing and waiting for us. It's Bobby in his Army uniform. I didn't know he would be here. I run and throw myself into his arms. He holds me tight and we giggle like a couple of teenagers. I can't stop kissing his cheeks. He looks almost handsome.

The groom and best man arrive thirty minutes late for the ceremony. Gary, already more than a little drunk, insisted on one last cocktail at his favorite pub. Richard reluctantly obliged.

The infuriated priest agrees to perform the ceremony only after Filben, Irishman to Irishman, convinces him the groom isn't on drugs; he's merely drunk.

I hold my breath and Bobby's hand during the ceremony. Gary is out of control, weaving and waving drunkenly to everyone. The ceremony starts. The priest asks the couple to kneel during the prayer. Gary pitches forward and June deftly grabs the back of his collar to halt his face forward trajectory. I pray for June's sake he makes it through the ceremony before passing out. I'm angry for her. I think Gary needs to be horse whipped.

The deed is done and I join the raucous circle at the reception telling war stories and reminiscing about old times. I'd heard through the gang grapevine while we were in Germany how Bobby dropped out of Officer Candidate School because he couldn't learn to read maps, Life Science all over again. He refused to repeat that pain, became a sergeant and volunteered for Vietnam.

I think Bobby went to Vietnam to shut Holly up and to do penance for his father's sins, to do what his father refused: fight for his country and be a man.

Somewhere in those jungles, Bobby buried the sins and the ghost of his father by proving to himself he wasn't the hapless loser Holly decreed him to be. He wasn't his father, after all.

His war experience helped him to see the strength and courage he had all along and it gave him new confidence. He found purpose and meaning to his life in the emotional connection he made with the men in his platoon. It's ironic that the experience that gave him new life would also take it. Agent Orange comes home with Bobby and mutates into the Hodgkin's that will kill him.

Bobby tells us the story of the firefight in Vietnam that caught him by surprise when he was on the latrine. The shooting started and he had to jump into the latrine for cover. We all laughed at the thought of him standing knee deep in shit and firing away madly with his pants down around his knees. He said he was determined he wasn't going to get killed in a shit hole. It would have been too humiliating.

When he mentions going to Singapore on leave I tease him. "Tell us you met someone you knew."

Bobby grins. "I ran into the Canadian nurses I lived with for a while on Ruth Court."

We all groan. His legend lives.

The guys excitedly share their work experiences. Richard, Filben and Gary are

Special Agents for the Bureau of Narcotic Enforcement. Gary won't last long: his first buy as an undercover agent will go sour when he unintentionally blows the doper's head off in the scuffle for his gun, killing him. He'll resign and become a junior college teacher.

Patrick couldn't be here. He and Nancy currently live in Los Angeles where Patrick works for the CIA. No one knows exactly what he's doing. The clandestine is right up Patrick's Scorpio alley.

Richard puts his arm around my waist and draws me in close. I relax against his shoulder. It feels comfortable and natural. The innate intimacy we share draws us. No matter how much time goes by, it's always there.

The party continues back at Gary and June's house after Gary incites his mother's old world Italian wrath by inviting everyone to get drunk, get naked and fall in a pile. Her bridge club bubbled with embarrassment.

We all drink too much. I fall asleep on the couch and waken slightly in the wee hours. I turn, shifting to a more comfortable position. The quiet tells me everyone finally sleeps. I feel the presence of someone else on the couch with me. A hand reaches out and pulls me forcefully. In a flash, Richard's mouth finds mine. Reacting instinctively, I kiss him back with a passion I thought was, if not dead, under control.

"Constance. I love you. I've missed you so much."

Intense feelings sweep over me, then reality hits; I'm married. It's hopeless. "I love you," I whisper, "But I can't do this." I start crying.

Richard buries my face in his neck and strokes my hair. "Shhh, shhh, it's all right."

My tears soak his shirt. Nothing has changed. I still love him; I'm still married to his best friend. We kiss feverishly for a long time, feeling each other's bodies, aching to have each other, but going no further.

"What are we going to do?"

I tell him I don't know. What can we do? I made a commitment when I married Eddie and I can't betray that. "We'll just have to pretend to be friends so no one will guess how we really feel. We don't have any other choice."

Richard falls silent. It doesn't occur to me that's not what he has in mind. I have to be rational. Just because he says he loves me doesn't mean he'll do anything about it. I can't throw everything away in the off chance he will finally commit to me. I still have hope Eddie and I can make things work. Richard has already broken my heart once; I can't let him do it again.

In the morning we say our good-byes. Richard and I turn to each other awkwardly. He gazes into my eyes, looking for what to do. I move gently into his arms and hug him. "Good-bye, Richard," I whisper softly.

"Good-bye, Constance."

I can barely hear his voice. I see the longing and confusion in his eyes. We hold hands briefly and part.

Bobby waits in the car; he's riding back to Sacramento with us. He looks at me with anger and I hear the hurt in his voice. "You bitch."

I realize he wasn't asleep last night. He heard Richard and I, and I can tell he thinks we had sex. I'm too emotionally exhausted to set him straight. He'll get over it; he always does.

April 1968

> Somewhere between ages 28 and 30, Saturn returns to where he starts in a natal chart. Back in my 5th house, he brings important changes to my life, demanding I look at my life and get real about what's working and what isn't, time to grow up. Relationships make major changes that affect my life from now on. I have the chance to alter the blue print of this life, the opportunity to redesign the little house of horrors I was born into and turn it into my own Taj Mahal.
>
> The main theme of Saturn in my 5th house this year has to do with emotional needs, children, parenting and building something tangible for the future.

The yearning comes and won't go away. It's appeared at various times over the last few years, but this time it won't be ignored. I want a baby. My strong maternal instinct decrees it's time. Eddie doesn't favor the idea at all. He's been my only child for three years and he likes it that way. Having a baby conjures up the kind of change he isn't ready for, like maturing into an adult. I tell him if he doesn't want a baby, he can give up sex. I know he can no more give up sex than a dog can keep from licking himself. By October, my maternal instinct prevails, but my joy short lived.

The noise from the living room angers me. Eddie holds court for several of his friends. They've been drinking for hours. In bed, consumed with worry and fighting a feeling of impending doom, I feel abandoned. I started spotting three days before. My doctor tells me to stay in bed, keep quiet and hope for the best. I know I'm losing the baby.

Eddie appears at the door of the bedroom. "Hey, you think you could fix us something to eat?"

Furious, I shake my head no. Self-pity consumes me. The depth of his insensitivity astounds me. His disregard for my emotional pain reminds me, once again, that I can't count on him when I need him most.

Instead of looking at the blatant realities of my relationship with Eddie and running for my life as I should do, I get pregnant again. But there's a reason that I don't leave the marriage yet. I owe Eddie.

**Frankfort, Kentucky
1860**

This life came to me in bits and pieces over many years until I could see a clear enough picture to put it together. I know my name was Mary Suellen Atcheson, born sometime in 1842. The names of my parents and husband never came to me.

My most vivid memories center around the strong emotional connections I made in that life and the circumstances of my death. The rest I can only surmise by the times in which I lived and the events of the Civil War that influenced my destiny.

I strongly sensed my ego came first in that life. I expressed arrogance, conceit and self-pity when thwarted. I displayed immense charm and kindness when things were going my way; I could also be stubborn and hard hearted. I offered immunity to no one from my sharp tongue and formidable temper. I exhibited an unfounded self-confidence.

A vivid scene shows me determined and angry, as I stomped my way down the street berating my mother struggling to keep up. Petite and quite pretty, dark curls swirled around my face. I wanted a special dress for a coming ball. Exasperation and capitulation reflected in my mother's eyes. I am not an easy child. I read my mother like a beloved, worn, old book whose pages I'd long since memorized. I found constancy her most endearing quality—and the most useful.

I may have been preparing for the annual masked ball to honor the legislators at the Capitol Hotel, probably marking my unofficial entry into Kentucky society since I'm about 18 at the time. Important politicians from all over the state would be there. The kind of man I envisioned marrying would surely be at that ball.

My passion for self-expression drove me to find a husband who could provide the means to fulfill my desires. In the times in which I lived, it was the only avenue open to me as a woman. A politician would be a perfect husband to bring the power, position and wealth I coveted.

Marriage itself held no interest for me, but what it could give me did: attention, privilege, travel, security, comfort and excitement. Wealth topped the list of prerequisites for anyone who might ask for my hand. The right position in society and profession were next. I had specific plans for this life.

My strongest memory and attachment is to my childhood house, a splendid blending of architecture in the Greek Revival style. Six impressive white columns supported the second story. The back of the house bore a balcony on each floor that ran the entire length of the house, overlooking a large, peaceful pond. A separate building, housing the kitchen, sat in back of the main house along with the stables and carriage house. The grounds boasted well-tended walkways through the thick forest of pine, cedar, hickory and maple trees. Azaleas in full, fiery bloom nestled at the foot of the budding tulip trees flanking the narrow road to the house. The landscape blazed in mind-dazzling, life-affirming color. I loved that house more than anything.

My father in that life thought me a handful. He admired my determination and persistence. He loved me beyond reason.

It would have been easy to categorize me as a junior grade Scarlett O'Hara, but that would have been a mistake. There would be no Ashley Wilkes, or Rhett Butler in that life to ignite my passion; I didn't want one.

I wasn't consciously aware of what drove me. I'd come from a previous life where I'd spent years training to be a ballerina. When my beloved, the assistant to the dance master, died before we could marry, I spiraled into a destructive depression. I ended my life by deliberately by walking in front of a coach. My inner joy left with my lover. I vowed never to give that much of myself away again. No passion could ever be worth that kind of pain.

In this life, I hungered for comfort, security and the adulation that would have been mine had I lived up to my promise and become a ballet star in the previous life. Those memories lived in me at a cellular level. I experienced the hunger for adulation and acceptance and held a deep fear of losing myself.

Another strong connection to a house imbedded itself into my memory. At some point before the Civil War, I had to have been a guest at Federal Hill in Bardstown, the home of young John Rowan who'd come home from Europe to Federal Hill to live with his beautiful wife Rebecca and their ten children after his father died. I experienced this house as resounding with the laughter of happy children and glamorous guests enlivening the energy. I would have wanted a house like Federal Hill and a husband like John Rowan.

Although my fertile imagination worked out most of the details for my future, I hadn't seriously contemplated the more practical aspects of the marriage contract. I didn't want children but hadn't any idea how I would prevent that. The mysteries of birth, sex and death interested and repelled me. The thought of my tiny, prized waistline blown to cruel proportion made me nauseous. I'd think of something when the time came.

In March 1860, Kentucky prepared for inevitable war. The legislature gave Major General Simon B. Buckner the power to organize the Louisville Citizens Guard into the Second Regiment of the Kentucky State Guard. This war was about to destroy my dreams and my future.

It would take something as life changing as the chaos of war to make somebody like me look beyond myself. My deeper qualities of compassion and empathy might have blossomed with a prolonged period of strife and hardship, bringing opportunity for growth. I would have none of it.

I don't know all the details of what happened to my family and me during the war, but I know we lost our house and I was separated from my parents somehow. My father developed a dementia and I felt abandoned by him with no desire to take care of him or comfort my mother.

My life fast-forwards to a wagon train headed west. I'm married to Eddie who res-

cued me from a life of poverty. I didn't love him and he certainly didn't fit my dream of a wealthy, well-positioned husband, but I had no choice. I sensed Eddie was a good man who loved me. He wanted children.

I was pregnant and in labor. The contractions started midway through the journey west. Early into the labor, I hovered tentatively above the figure in the narrow bed, thrashing and screaming in pain. I had a choice: I could stay or go. I chose the latter. My dreams died and I didn't want to live. Blood gushed in a torrent and drenched the small bed as the afterbirth detached prematurely from the womb. The blood loss killed my unborn baby and me. I left the still figure in the bed and soared away, lessons unlearned, opportunities lost, a pot load of karma I couldn't escape, only postpone.

What goes round does come around. In this current life, Eddie's personality eerily mimics mine in the Kentucky life: spoiled, willful, self-involved and bad tempered. It's like we've switched roles. Back then he wanted children; I didn't. Paybacks are a bitch, and there's more than a touch of irony that I'm here to give him the children he wanted in that life and now he doesn't want them.

I consider what would have happened if I'd chosen to live: I could very well have turned out to be the kind of mother I had in this life.

If I'd left Eddie last December when I had the miscarriage, I would have moved to San Diego with my old roommates and probably had another go-round with Richard. That would have thwarted fate's plan for me to go back to Sacramento, where my destiny waits.

San Diego, California
April 1969

> A Venus retrograde loop pushes me to reevaluate my relationship with Eddie, and deep emotional adjustments come in response. A Venus loop can result in positive outcomes, but in this case, an unraveling begins.

By the third month of pregnancy, I bask in the pregnancy hormones that make my skin luminous and my emotions labile. Ecstatic one minute and crying over the homeless doggie of the week in the newspaper the next, I ride the roller coaster of emotions typical in early pregnancy. The critical period when miscarriage might occur has passed. I'm going to be a mom this time. I love, and I want to be loved.

Eddie indulges in one lone outburst when I give him the news I'm pregnant again. He throws one of his temper tantrums and tells me I'd better not get any ideas about cravings and all that pregnant bullshit. I'd better carry on as usual with my duties, and don't even think of quitting work. He blusters and flails haplessly, like a kite in an updraft, before falling silent. The reality hits home for him. I can tell how frightened he is, but my unshakable optimism tells me he'll get over it and get with the program.

We drive to San Diego to spend a long weekend with the gang. I look forward to reveling in my impending motherhood. My old friends, Karen and Ann Marie, live in a charming but tattered around the edges 1930's house on Mission Bay, the sandy beach right outside their door. The water shimmers like a giant prism in the sunlight. I have fleeting thoughts of how I could be here instead of married to Eddie.

We settle into the joyfully raucous energy that emerges whenever we're all together. Richard comes and so does Donna, an old girl friend of his who'd bonded to the gang during her brief affair with him. We met her at a gathering for Bobby. Richard supplied Donna as Bobby's welcome home gift from Vietnam last year. She happily serviced him, even though she'd never met him before. Richard has always been generous with his castoffs.

Donna, obsessed with her sexuality, makes frequent, crude references to her sexual preferences, which are pretty out there. When she complains to me that Richard is selfish in bed. I suggest maybe she doesn't inspire him. It's the most fun I have all weekend. She reminds me of the long line of Okie broads Eddie used to plank in the Lodi vineyards in the backseat of his Corvair. She makes me cringe.

Nothing could have prepared me for Eddie's reaction to Donna. He publicly secedes from our union and declares his independence. Our three years of skirmishes escalate into all out civil war. He fires the first shot when he grabs Donna in front of everyone, sticks his hand down her low cut blouse, his other hand up her mini-skirt and his tongue down her throat in a full frontal assault. She squeals, weakly trying to deflect his advances, but she clearly enjoys the attention.

Dead silence settles over the gathering. They're all waiting for me to react. This is off the charts, even for Eddie. The nervous tension in the room stays as taut as a drawn bowstring. I zoom past pissed and rocket right into murderous rage at mock speed. I hide my anger and humiliation behind a tightly controlled façade of indifference. I do nothing; I say nothing. The tension lifts as everyone assumes I've chalked this up as nothing more than one of Eddie's immature escapades.

I hold that façade through the weekend as he continues his amorous attack on Donna; it reaches a crescendo at poolside when he pours wine into her navel and laps it up with his tongue like a dehydrated dog. They disappear somewhere. Too despondent to care, I won't let myself speculate about what they're doing.

Eddie's joy comes from ruining mine, and he's done a stellar job. He's made a very public declaration he isn't sailing away on the S.S. Parenthood with me. He's on the dock, giving me the middle finger salute. I'm on my own.

On the drive home, I rage and cry, wallowing in betrayal. I tell him, "You keep this shit up and the day will come when I'll divorce you." I add in frustration, "You're a socially insensitive slob and an asshole."

Eddie tells me he doesn't believe I'll ever divorce him. He laughs and tells me to write down the insensitive slob and asshole part so he can remember to tell Richard. I have to accept he'll never be any different. A toad is a toad is a toad.

We emotionally divorce each other that weekend. He deeply resents my forcing him into being a father, after making it abundantly clear it isn't what he wants. I have to pay the price. The Kentucky life is kicking the crap out of me.

San Francisco, California
July 1969

Eddie and I have different schedules. I work the 3-11 P.M. shift and he works 9-5. Once in a while we have a weekend off at the same time, like now. I propose we go to a romantic place up the coast and have a quiet weekend to talk about our baby in progress. He has other plans. He's going to Lake Tahoe to gamble with a buddy.

I go where I usually go when I need love and comfort. I call Bobby in San Francisco and tell him I'm coming to see him. He tells me he's scheduled to go to a party that evening but no problem.

We go to the party with my pregnant belly preceding me. Bobby introduces me to everyone as his girlfriend. His friends look at my stomach with shock and stammer that they hope everything works out for us. Bobby excuses us and we go giggle in a corner like a couple of naughty kids.

I've come to the right place. Bobby and I cuddle in his bed. I put his hand on my stomach; he grins and his face lights up when my baby kicks. We talk and laugh. He holds me, his hand on my belly as I fall asleep. He is such a gift to me. What Bobby gives me is what I want and need from Eddie. He knows that; it's why he won't give it to me.

I arrive home an hour after Eddie. He wants to know where I've been. I tell him I was with Bobby.

He pauses for a moment and asks, "Where did you sleep?"

"With Bobby."

"Oh."

Stockton, California
October 5, 1969

At 7 A.M. my water breaks and the contractions start. Eddie slept on the couch, over trained on champagne while celebrating the impending birth once again—any excuse to drink. He passed out before making it to bed.

"Eddie, wake up! My water broke. We have to go to the hospital."

"Oh, my God!" He rolls off the couch and dashes for the shower, leaving me standing there with amniotic fluid running down my legs. I hear the shower running.

"Eddie, what are you doing?"

"I'm getting ready. Do you think the nurses will like me? Where in the hell is the hair spray?"

The nurse checks me and tells Eddie it will be sometime late that afternoon before I have the baby. My contractions come without a break. A half an hour later, I reach for the call light.

A Spiritual Memoir

"What are you doing?"

"Get the nurse. I'm having this baby—now!"

"Stop that! You're embarrassing me. The nurse said you wouldn't be ready until this afternoon."

"You'll be a lot more embarrassed if I have this baby in bed, you idiot!" I don't have to be a labor nurse to know when I have a head about to explode between my legs.

My daughter, Melissa Lynn, arrives at 9:04 A.M., two hours after the contractions started. Melissa has a fuzz of pale blonde hair, blue eyes and beautiful, almost translucent skin. I can't stop looking at her perfect little face and body. I plunge into motherhood with a boundless joy even Eddie can't ruin. I've experienced the receiving end of unconditional love from my Gramma and Bobby, but now I understand what it feels like to give it in return. I vow to be the kind of mother I never had.

Eddie doesn't care that he's a new father. The parenthood thing is all mine. He wants excitement. He's become bored busting teenyboppers for buying beer. He wants to be a narcotic agent like his buddies who've moved on from ABC.

Two weeks after Melissa's birth, we move to L.A. from Stockton where we've lived for the past 15 months wrapped in the warm bosom of friends and family. Joan has just given birth to her first daughter and I looked forward to our sharing our babies and motherhood with each other. I grieve over being yanked from my comfortable cocoon. I hold Melissa tightly in my arms and cry silently on the six-hour drive to L.A. Eddie doesn't acknowledge my tears.

I hate L.A., the endless warm weather, the shaggy palm trees, the sprawling suburbs connecting endless freeways and the blue-collar neighborhood where we live on the edge of Compton.

Once again, Bobby saves me. He works out of the L.A. office with Eddie. Bobby's stakeouts are often in our neighborhood. He comes by our apartment frequently, has dinner and plays with Melissa. She sees more of him than she does Eddie. Bobby stares at my daughter in wonder. She looks like him with her blond hair, blue eyes and fair skin. I imagine he thinks a lot about what if we'd gotten married. I see it in his eyes and it makes me sad.

Bobby's become a minor legend in the Bureau of Narcotic Enforcement with his unique approach to his work. Like the afternoon he was driving through Manhattan Beach with the top down on his convertible, wearing Bermuda shorts, shirtless and barefoot. At a stoplight, he glances at the car next to him and recognizes the driver as a wanted murder suspect. Bobby gets out of his car gun in hand, strolls casually over to the bad guy and puts the gun to his head and arrests him. Afterward, the guy says he was caught totally off guard because he'd never seen a half naked cop before.

My favorite story: Bobby's been tailing a doper out of Detroit for a week, waiting for him to make his buy. The guy's been carrying a black suitcase around with him all week. The plane taxis down the runway headed back to Detroit. Bobby drives onto the runway and stops the plane, boards and hauls the doper off. He opens the black suitcase. It's empty. Bobby screams at him, "What kind of a doper are you! It's empty, you stupid sonofabitch. Where's the dope? What've you been doing all week? Shit!"

"I'm sorry. I'm sorry. I couldn't make my connection. I'll do better next time."

Eddie, enthralled with his new job, swaggers like a cowboy, talks like a doper, lets his hair grow into a Prince Valiant do, held in place with copious amounts of Aqua Net hair spray, and sports a thick moustache. He's a dead ringer for Sonny Bono. It all fits his flair for the dramatic. When he isn't working, which is almost all the time, he sleeps. He's found heaven. I wallow in hell.

This job isn't a good choice for someone like Eddie. It feeds his dark side. He thrills at kicking down doors, screaming with impunity at "pukes" and punks, intimidating and threatening them. The power that comes with this job is his aphrodisiac, his high, and he can't get enough. You can't live in the underbelly of society and not be affected. He embraces a dark world that will eventually erode his humanity and dim the light in his soul. He doesn't see that he isn't that much different than the dopers he arrests. Instead of heroin or speed, power is his addiction and drug of choice.

In May, fate intervenes and frees me. The bureau transfers Eddie to Sacramento. I've been working at the Kaiser in Bellflower twenty hours a week; Sacramento Kaiser has an opening in labor and delivery. A critical part of my destiny waits there.

Sacramento, California
May 3, 1972

> Uranus fans my flames of discontent with my marriage. A Venus-Mars conjunction in hard angle to transformative Pluto prompts me to question my values, beliefs and the realities of my relationship with Eddie. This energy is similar to the one that ended my relationship with Richard. Good relationships survive this kind of angle, but the unstable ones often don't.

I've just had my second daughter after another short, tumultuous labor. I'm made to have babies.

I'd considered the wisdom of having another child with Eddie. I'd forced him to see a marriage counselor with me two years ago; he told Eddie if he didn't shape up, I was going to divorce him. He charged us $300—wasted time and money. I'm disillusioned with the relationship in every respect, but not with the marriage in general. I love my house; I like the friends we have, my part time job at Kaiser and I've developed a close relationship with Eddie's parents. I'm not ready to rock my boat in life at this point, but I figure if I eventually divorce Eddie, I'll just have one less kid to care for. I view my motherhood as separate from my marriage. Eddie is nothing more to me now than a reluctant sperm donor.

I hold Stacie Ann in my arms. Doris, my labor nurse, escorts Eddie into the delivery room. "Geezus! That's the ugliest kid I've ever seen. No one's ever going to marry her. She's going to be living with us the rest of her life."

I ignore Eddie's assessment of my new daughter. Her shock of black hair stands on end. Her little soul probably contemplates life with Eddie as her father. Dark, impossibly thick lashes frame her large, dark eyes. Eddie's prediction proves false. She grows to be a beauty with a sweet personality and a genius IQ that she certainly didn't get from him, although his mother would disagree.

He makes it clear he's not interested in this baby, either. He visits me in the hospital the next day, stands several feet away from the bed, mumbles a few words about being busy, looks at his watch, turns and leaves. He lives for two things: his job and drinking.

My retreat from the marriage begins in earnest. I busy myself with work and being a mother. We're a self-contained unit; my girls and I get along fine by ourselves. Our house functions as kid central for the neighborhood. Engulfed in joy and laughter, I soak it in like a sponge. Being surrounded by little kids makes me happy, their energy healing balm for my heart. They remind me of my carefree days before Sister Mary Christopher.

I've stopped nagging Eddie to do anything since I asked him to change a light bulb and he told me he couldn't because he didn't have the right tools. He thinks I've finally gotten used to his job, the unpredictable hours and his being away frequently. I haven't. I just don't care anymore.

May 12, 1974

Richard visits us frequently. Our house is his refuge when he's broken up with his latest girlfriend or needs recharging from the stress of his job.

It was only a few months ago when he found himself on the floor face down with a doper's shotgun at his head, seconds away from having his brains blown out. His wire wasn't working. One of the other agent's instincts told him something wasn't right and he stormed through the door in the nick of time. Richard sat in shock as his buddy beat the doper senseless. He took a week off and made a beeline for our house.

It's Mother's Day and I'm working. I've left the girls with Eddie and Richard. At 9 P.M. the phone rings. Charlie, the nurse who works with me, says, "You might as well get it; you know it's Eddie." He calls me precisely at 9 P.M. when I'm working to scream at me to come home because one or both kids are crying. My response is always the same: I hang up on him. He hates watching the girls; it's only two evenings a week and it's the only thing I insist he do, and he's going to do it.

It's Eddie, but he's not screaming. He's whimpering. "You've got to come home; I think I've killed Richard."

I think this is one of Eddie's pranks; I hang up and go back to work. The phone rings again. "Please, don't hang up. Something terrible has happened; I ran over Richard with the car."

He has my attention. "What happened? Did you call an ambulance?"

"No. Just come home!" He's crying.

I pull in the driveway. The garage door is up and I can see the back wall has been pushed back several feet. I study the imprint of Richard's knees in the sheetrock. This can't be good. My heart pounds so furiously I can hear it in my ears like a drum. Eddie and both girls rush to me. Melissa and Stacie hug my knees and cry. I put my arms around them. Richard reclines on the couch. He looks in great pain, but feigns nonchalance.

Eddie tells me the story: they drove into the garage and something was in the way of the car. Richard got out to move it; Eddie's foot slipped off the brake and the car lurched forward pinning Richard against the wall.

"How much have you two been drinking?" I'm furious they've been out drinking and driving with my girls in the car.

"Just a few beers—I swear." I don't believe Eddie. He can't stop at a few beers. This is a man who fixes a fresh bourbon and seven at bedtime and puts it on the nightstand just in case he wakes up in the middle of the night.

We get Richard into my car and I head back to Kaiser.

"Constance? Please don't be mad at Eddie; he didn't mean to wreck the garage."

"You two deserve each other." I sound furious, but I'm terrified.

The doctor tells us Richard has to be on total bedrest for two weeks until the swelling in his knees go down; they're the size of cantaloupes by now. He could look forward to traumatic arthritis of his knees as he gets older. He's lucky he wasn't killed. I'm still terrified he'll throw a clot and die, but I don't tell him that.

I settle Richard in our bedroom so he can have the TV to pass the hours. I bring him three meals a day and empty his urinal. The neighbor kids come every day to check out the strange man in Connie's bed.

Eddie suffers post traumatic stress syndrome. "I almost killed my best friend." He repeats it over and over. I haven't seen him this distraught since he got drafted. "I know you two are getting after it while I'm at work, but that's okay. The least you can do is give him a blowjob. I owe him."

Eddie's quite serious. It's clear I have chattel status in his mind. I'm appalled, but nothing he says or does shocks me anymore.

Faces of Love, Death and Transformation:

Richard and I have never spent concentrated time together without Eddie. We both feel a little awkward, so much unsaid between us, our emotional connection the six hundred pound gorilla in the room. I'm bringing some clean underwear to him.

"Constance, sit down." He pats the bed. "I want to play a game one of my girlfriends taught me."

I sit, curious and a little anxious.

"You walk down a path and you come upon various objects. As you encounter each object, tell me what it looks like and what you do with it. The first thing you encounter is a trunk. Tell me what you see."

I see the trunk in my mind's eye: "It's like a treasure chest with a key in it. I open it and see it's filled with books. I sit down and read them."

"Move on down the path. The next thing you see is a mirror. Describe it."

"It's long and slim, has a plain frame around it. It's functional like the kind you see hanging on the back of a door. Nothing special."

"The next object is a house. What does it look like?"

I see the house, but I'm confused. It isn't anything I've seen before. "It's a big, two-story, white house with lots of windows. It's filled with sunlight and happy children. Birch trees surround the house; it looks like it's from another time."

"Continue down the path. Now you come to a lake."

"The lake is blue, not really big, but pretty. I go to the water's edge and put my toe in. Then I take my clothes off and plunge in."

Richard laughs delightedly and squeezes my hand. "I knew you'd do that; I knew it!"

"Okay. So what does it all mean?"

"The trunk is how you view knowledge. The mirror is how you see yourself; the house is who you are and the lake is your sexuality."

"Tell me what you saw on your path."

"I took the key from the trunk, put it in my pocket to save for later. My mirror was a piece of broken glass nailed to a tree. My house was deep in the forest, small with a large porch. I let people visit me on the porch, but I didn't allow anyone inside. In the back of the house was a beautiful, deep canyon of trees. My lake was about the size of yours with a sign that said "Forbidden." I approached the water anyway, tested it, took my clothes off and eventually went for a swim."

I wonder if he knows how much of himself he's revealed. He sees himself as broken, unwilling to let anyone inside his heart or explore the deepest parts of himself in that dense forest behind his house. I instinctively know the lake isn't just sex; it's also about intimacy and his sign says it's forbidden. It all fits.

As for me, I'm disturbed I perceive myself as nothing special. I'll be changing that perception in the next few years.

We gave the test to Eddie that night: He ignores the chest and throws the key away. His mirror is the same as Richard's—exactly. His house is small and remote. A cranky old man lives there and won't let anyone near. He runs them off with his shotgun. His lake is big and full of fish. He stands on the shore with his long fishing pole, casting. He never gets near the water. No surprises there.

The end of the second week is near. The phone has been ringing off the hook ever since the accident with calls from fellow agents across the state. They all ask me if the story is true: Did Eddie catch Richard and I in the garage enflagrante delicto and did I really have tire tracks on my head. Cop humor.

I'm exhausted. There's been a steady stream of visitors come to pay homage to the fallen warrior. They always come for cocktails and stay for dinner. I'm sitting on the couch with Richard taking a breather.

Eddie bursts through the garage door. "Get your ass off the couch and get this place cleaned up; it's a pig sty and I got guys coming for drinks." I know this performance is for Richard's benefit.

I remain outwardly calm, but my blood pressure is shooting through the top of my head. I sense Richard holding his breath. He doesn't like unpleasantness. I pick Stacie up and head to her bedroom to change her diaper; Eddie follows me.

"Did you hear what I just said?"

My rage unleashes itself. "You can clean this pig sty up yourself you sonofabitch—I hate you!" And I do.

Stacie flinches and throws her arms around my neck, squirming her little body to get closer to me.

The fury in my eyes tells Eddie I mean every word. He stands there momentarily bewildered. "It bothers me when you say things like that." He turns and walks away.

The unraveling continues.

Chapter 9

Sacramento, California
September 19, 1974

> Some years are just a killer. The kind that put you through the fires of hell and you either come out tempered steel, dead, or wishing you were. Pluto can be the epitome of Nietzsche's maxim, "What doesn't kill me makes me stronger."
>
> Saturn continues his work in my 8th house of sex and the psyche, evaluating relationships and monitoring the transformation in progress. Uranus takes his sweet time bringing change. Neptune and Mars slow the process to a snail's crawl.

I stand in front of Dr. Marshall's desk. Tears glisten in my eyes. I don't know what to do. I've missed my period. He examines me and tells me I have an enlarged, soft uterus consistent with early pregnancy.

I'm still in grief and shock over Bobby's death five days ago. I've moved to the other extreme of having no water in my chart. I'm in major emotional meltdown. Dr. Marshall quietly watches me. He's never seen this side of me before. We've worked together for four years. He knows the always together, cool-in-crisis Connie, not the emotional wreck I am right now.

I have my own judgments. He's impossibly handsome in a Greek god kind of way: black, curly hair, tall at 6'4", broad shoulders, a slim waist and a classic Roman nose, straight and strong. His golden brown, Scorpio eyes peer out from under dark eyebrows. He's perfect—too perfect.

He's my gynecologist. His fingers have traced circles around my nipples, explored the contours of my breasts and probed deep inside me. He knows my body intimately, but not who I really am—neither do I at this point.

I tell him I've been at a dying friend's bedside for the last week. I don't know why, except I can't think about anything else. I move to the office window and look out at the parking lot so he can't see the tears flowing relentlessly down my cheeks. I'm embarrassed. My life is like the Tower card in the Tarot, tumbling down around my feet; my demons rage through the rubble, and I have no defenses left to protect me.

I don't want another baby. The timing is awful. I'm back in school, and this would derail my plans to finish my bachelor's degree. Stacie isn't even two years old. Eddie and I, in the eighth year of marriage, barely exist together. We fight fiercely and continually. We bring out the worst in each other. I struggle continually to stay positive, but his constant anger, arrogance and negativity pitch me into such dark, deep places I'm emotionally drained.

Eddie seems to savor his frequent outbursts like fine wine; they pleasure and relax him, give him a sense of power and control.

The unending conflict takes its toll on the girls. Melissa wets the bed every night, and Stacie clings to me almost constantly for comfort. I fear the damage we're inflicting with our dysfunction. I want better for them—and me.

"I'll run a pregnancy test. When I get the results, I'll call you. Are you okay?" His concern surprises me. He tends to be reserved and private, like me.

I can't talk; I just shake my head and walk out of the office before I break down completely. For one insane moment, I want to throw myself into his arms and sob until there's nothing left. Poor Dr. Marshall, he'd probably have a heart attack. I wonder if he ever comes down from that ivory tower of his.

Kaiser Hospital
November 5, 1974

The pre-op meds make me giddy. Dr. Marshall's intense eyes stare at me over his surgical mask. He's tying my tubes after the big pregnancy scare. I'm immensely grateful that I won't be repeating that experience. The uncertainty went on for too long. Eddie and Richard hounded me not to go through another pregnancy. Eddie includes Richard in every aspect of our marriage; we're still the eternal triangle.

"How are you doing, Connie?"

I look up at him and think he has the most hypnotic eyes I've ever seen. Must be the drugs. "We have to stop meeting this way; my husband's getting suspicious." I see him recoil in shock. I hear snickering in the background. Just as I thought: no sense of humor. I smile and surrender gratefully to the drugs, drifting off to the blissful oblivion I need.

Sacramento State College
November 1974

The Death and Dying class should be renamed *Cry Me A River*, because that's all I do. Every class reduces me and everyone else to a blubbering mess; Kleenex boxes ubiquitously dot the room. I dutifully trudge to class three times a week, enduring the gauntlet of emotions literally overwhelming me as I listen to the stories and poems about death, rubbing salt into my open wounds. I surrender to it, the key to the 8th house energy; I don't have the strength to do anything else. Of course, I think about Bobby. The grieving pulls me out of the numb state that clenches my heart like a vice. It's intensely painful, but cathartic—very Plutonian. Transformations are a bitch.

Human Sexuality is a different story. It's the first class, and we're going to see what the instructor refers to as normal heterosexual intercourse. The enthralling film stars an anonymous medical student and his wife, a passionate couple with great sexual chemistry; it's obvious they love each other. Memories of my first night with Richard flash through my heart like volts of electricity, igniting the old yearning.

I watch the couple with growing dismay. It's as though Venus whispers to me, "See, this is how it's supposed to be." My yearning now has a face, and I can't turn away. When the film ends, the instructor asks if anyone has any questions. I say what every woman in the class is thinking. "Do you have his phone number?" Laughter breaks the tension we're all feeling.

Psych 105 drives it all home. Annabelle Gross, a psychologist in private practice, teaches this class. She's a middle-aged, rotund, chain-smoking woman with blonde hair, bright blue eyes and a warm heart the size of Texas. This time, teacher Saturn manifests in a nicer form than Sister Mary Christopher.

"All right," Annabelle tells the class, "I want you to write down who you are." It's a perfect 8th house, deep psyche question.

I write quickly: mother, friend, nurse, wife. Annabelle asks me to read my list. She contemplates my answers for a moment. "That's not who you are. Try it again."

Her words shake me at a profound level. The false foundation of my current reality cracks like an earthquake fault line under stress. At age thirty-three, I realize I don't know who I am. Questions fly around me like bats out of a cave at sunset, fluttering and chattering in my mind. Saturn smiles smugly from my 8th house like a teacher whose backward student finally gets it.

At home, I sit on my bed and sift through my thoughts. I've spent my whole life being what I thought other people wanted me to be, a pattern of behavior that's now second nature. I've tied my entire self-worth to my relationships with the people in my life. If I perform my life roles well, I'm validated. The realization renders me senseless.

Human Sexuality this week deals with the dynamics of orgasm. The physical description of orgasm and the accompanying sensations are new information to me, so much for the sex and nurse mystique. I've never given any thought to female orgasms. For me, sex ends when my partner climaxes.

I have a strong sex drive. I truly enjoy it and never had any feelings of missing anything. The fondling, kissing and physical connection allows me to reach high states of arousal, perching on the edge of the orgasmic platform but never plunging over the edge. It's a fifties kind of conditioning, I think. Good girls only go so far and, obviously, I've learned to stop short. Pluto in my natal 8th house destines me to plunge deeper into the mystical aspects of sex. It's another hurdle I have to navigate.

In class, we see a film of a baby in a crib, lying on her stomach masturbating by rocking back and forth. I have absolutely no recollection of ever doing anything like that as a child. I'm sure if I did someone put a screeching halt to it. Until this class, I didn't know women even did that. Guys, yes, but babies?

My curiosity compels me to try the vibrator I'd bought for Eddie's dad when he'd broken his legs and had muscle cramps. I plug it in and place it between my legs. The powerful sensation makes me jerk the vibrator away. I pause for a few moments, take a deep breath, close my eyes and try again. I have an orgasm within seconds. All those years, it waited there. I feel it: the tingling, the unbearable itch, the uncontrollable urge for release, the waves of vaginal contractions and the euphoria. The sensations trigger memories.

West Sacramento, California
August 1956

At fifteen, I had my first steady boyfriend, a blond, brown-eyed, hot-blooded Italian. We made out in the front seat of my parent's car, parked in the garage. I'd never been kissed the way he kissed me. It seemed to go on for hours. I reached the state of arousal where I lost any sense of myself, totally enveloped in the passion. Involuntarily, I thrust my pelvis forcefully against him. On contact, I ignited into a full-blown orgasm. "La petite mort," as the French call it—the little death.

We were both confused as to what happened. Dazed and embarrassed, I thought, somehow, I'd done something terribly wrong. I thought about those sensations in bed that night. I decided I couldn't let that happen again.

It did happen again, but not until I was in labor with Melissa. When her head descended into the birth canal, the pelvic engorgement triggered an orgasm. Not an unusual physiological occurrence. It happened again with Stacie's birth. The sensations seemed vaguely familiar at the time, but I didn't connect them with anything. I sit with the realization of all I've denied myself. My Saturn 8th house connection taps into the hidden parts of my self and the needs that wait there for recognition. I'm not sure what to do with it. I've come to a difficult emotional crossroads.

The crying starts every time I get in the car to go to work. I'm longing for the kind of love I've never had. I want a deep connection with someone who knows how to love. I think about Richard; I sift through the crumbs of those memories; I know he isn't able to give me what I want and need. The forbidden sign on his lake of intimacy decrees it impossible, at least for now.

The headaches come around 5 P.M. whenever I know Eddie's going to be home. Insomnia denies me the oblivion of sleep, forcing me to lie there for hours, my mind marching through the wasteland of my marriage. My raw emotions roast slowly over the fires of transformation.

We're driving home from a friend's party. A persistent melancholy comes over me; I start crying. I hate it when this happens but I can't control it. Ever since Bobby died, I'm totally at the mercy of my emotions.

Eddie looks at me with disgust. "If you're so damned unhappy, why don't you do what your mother did and just kill yourself?"

Faces of Love, Death and Transformation:

The words hit me like a neutron bomb. I breathe in sharply with the impact. Everything becomes deathly still and motionless inside me. With those words, he drove a wooden stake through whatever was left of our relationship. He irrevocably killed the last vestige of feeling I ever had for him. I cannot let my girls grow up in the same house with this man.

May 21, 1975

> *The polar energies of Neptune hover near my natal Mars in my 1st house. Neptune can fog and confuse, bringing indecision and long waiting periods before things ripen into action. Action oriented Mars wants things done yesterday. The opposing energies of the two planets create an impasse. Meanwhile, Mars' current movement in the heavens has him popping in and out of my 7th house of relationships at various points during 1975. Things brew and stew.*

The next evening when Eddie gets home from work, the determined look on my face tells him he's in deep trouble. I've been crying again. "I can't do this anymore, Eddie. I've tried everything and nothing has ever worked. I have to divorce you before this relationship kills me."

It's Eddie's turn to sob. "You can't do this! You can't! I have to call Richard; he'll talk you out of this. Don't do this, please! Why didn't you tell me things were this serious?" He's wailing pitifully.

Richard tries to reason with me. He's as devastated as Eddie over the possibility of a divorce. "You can't divorce Mr. Ed, Constance. Who'll take care of him? You know he can't survive on his own."

"I'm tired of taking care of him. I'm tired of the whole thing. You know what he's like to live with."

"I know, but If you two can't make it, who can?"

Richard has that Venus square Neptune idealized vision of me as always doing the right thing, being strong enough to handle anything, even marriage to Eddie. My pain falls on deaf ears.

I have a dream that night:

I walked in a garden with Richard. He smiled at me and took my hand. We walked down a path and encountered a yawning pit. Richard jumped across it effortlessly and motioned for me to do the same. I looked down and saw a mass of writhing snakes. Terror seized me, but Richard beckoned again. I jumped, reaching for his outstretched hand. I missed and fell into the pit. I screamed but no sound came out. I silently begged Richard to help me; I put my arms out to him. He looked down at me, not moving. He didn't seem to understand what was happening. The snakes slithered and twisted over my body, attacking me.

I'm pretty skilled at interpreting my dreams. The pit symbolizes the deep psyche. The snakes represent transformation and the pain that comes with it. Richard wants me to avoid the changes I need to make. He can't comprehend the pain I'm in, and I can't count on him for help.

It isn't a level playing field. My tough Capricorn and abundance of masculine Mars energy can't compete with Eddie's swings from blustery warrior to poor me victim at will. I have to accept that Richard sits squarely in Eddie's corner as the identified underdog. Richard never considers I might need him. I do, desperately; I just can't tell him.

We start counseling with Annabelle, but I'm going through the motions. I know it's too late. It's going to be a long year. Eddie treads carefully through the fractured landscape of our marriage, the jagged rents and gaping fissures he created and stubbornly ignored ready to give way with one misstep.

The yelling and fighting stop, but the silence is worse. We're like two shipwreck victims clinging to the same piece of debris, floating on a sea of despair, waiting for one or the other to let go and quietly float away.

Dreams come to me every night. My powerful Neptune transit during this time helps me tap into the deep psyche and subconscious through my dreams. I remember them and think about the possible meaning of each one. In dreams, my subconscious and higher conscious meet and speak to each other, offering direction and answers to my questions through the symbols. This dream comes in Technicolor, the details vivid and sharp.

I walked into a hospital lobby on a sunny, spring day. People stood in groups, talking and laughing. I wondered why I was there. A nurse walked up to me, put a tightly swaddled baby in my arms and walked off. I moved the blanket away from the face and recoiled. A pitifully deformed baby stared up at me. Overwhelming panic seized me. I couldn't take care of that baby. It wasn't my responsibility; I didn't want it.

I approached a group of nurses and doctors; I told them the baby wasn't mine, but no one listened. They ignored me. I tried several other people with no response; my frustration grew. In desperation, I took the elevator up to the nursery floor. A nurse stood at the desk; I walked forcefully through the door, placed the baby securely in her surprised arms, and walked out the door. I didn't look back. Triumph and euphoria surged through me like a powerful wave carrying me to safety on a distant shore.

On the main floor, I strode purposefully past the groups of people who'd refused to help me, my head high. I pushed the door open; warm sunlight hit my face; birds sang. I smiled with a joy I'd felt only at the birth of my girls, that incredible lightness of being, the end of pain and the beginning of love.

The song in Cinderella says, "A dream is a wish the heart makes." It doesn't take any great soul searching or insightful interpretation to know what the dream means. It takes me by the throat like a pit bull and shakes me to my core. The deformed baby is Eddie. I don't want the responsibility anymore. No one will listen to me, but I have to do what's right for me and my girls.

Kaiser Hospital
May 20, 1976

I knock on Dr. Marshall's office door and enter; he's putting his lab coat on and smiles warmly at me. I've been spending time with him in the clinic for a school requirement.

"Good morning." He's unusually cheerful. "Ready to see patients?"

"Thanks for letting me spend time with you."

"I'm happy to do it. It's a nice break for me. I like teaching." He looks at the chart he's carrying. "This patient had a cervical biopsy last week. She's here for a follow-up visit."

He opens the door to the exam room and walks in. I follow until he stops so abruptly I careen into his back.

"Ah, we won't be examining you today. You can put your clothes on. I'll see you in my office—when you're dressed."

I check out the woman on the exam table. She's young, very attractive and very naked. The exam sheet lies on the floor in a heap. One leg rests casually in a stirrup, one arm behind her head; her other hand rests on her abdomen in a Playboy-like pose. She looks disappointed he won't be examining her.

"That's a perfect example of a seductive patient," he tells me as we walk back to his office.

"She wasn't exactly subtle. Does that happen very often?"

"Often enough."

He seems genuinely perplexed by such inappropriate behavior. He's obviously unaware of how attractive he is; I'm surprised.

May 25, 1976

> **The planets spend nearly a year lining up to form a perfect celestial symmetry for my life to move on. Warrior Mars has finished his stay in my 7th house and moved into my 8th house evaluating deep relationships. High energy Mars connects with revolutionary Uranus to bring sweeping change, the kind that occurred during the French Revolution, only this time, it's Eddie's head on the chopping block.**

Eddie wants sex. I lie on my back and close my eyes. He gets on top. I grit my teeth and squeeze my eyes tight. When he touches me, I stiffen and involuntarily recoil. I swear I can hear screaming in my head. He rolls off.

"We need to get some sexual counseling."

I stare at the ceiling, "It won't do any good."

He stands by the bed and bursts into sobs. "I can't take this anymore. It's over isn't it?"

"Yes."

Faces of Love, Death and Transformation:

He dresses. I hear him on the phone talking to Richard who's in town for a meeting. Good. He can spend the night with him. I smile; there's always somebody to catch Eddie when he falls. In a way, I envy him.

It's exactly one year to the month after I first told Eddie I had to divorce him. It's finally over. Freedom nestles against me like a warm body on a cold night. I lie in bed and luxuriate in the quietness, the peace and liberation that Uranus birthed for me.

Eddie's leaving ended the karma of the Kentucky life with him. He provided the opportunity for me to experience what it's like to be married to someone who is selfish, volatile, emotionally unavailable and terminally immature—just like I was in that life. Ten years is enough. I get it.

I still have my broken heart, courtesy of Richard. I've let Eddie spend the last 10 years tap dancing on the debris. It's time to pick up the pieces and move on to the next phase of my experience. Jupiter in my 5th house of love and romance opens a new door, the one I've been waiting for all my life. I leap into the void.

Chapter 10

I'm ready for the simple life, but Saturn has different plans for me as he moves into my 9th house of travel, broader horizons, urging me on to the new experiences and the opportunities coming. The 9th house reveals the bigger picture of life. The lighter energy brings a welcome change from the intensity of the 8th house and the heavy emotional and psychological work it demands. In the last two years, I've plumbed the depths, hit bottom, kicked my way to the surface, and now I'm enjoying that first burst of air into my depleted lungs. I'm feeling the sun on my face, just as I did in my divorce dream. In the 9th house, I float on my back, gaze at the sky, contemplate my navel, the meaning of life and my connection to the Universe. I'm in the fertile void.

Earlier in the month, a Venus and Jupiter conjunction passed near my natal Jupiter in my 5th house of romance, inspiring me to live my life fully and with true love. Jupiter isn't buying my limited vision of the future. He's whipping up a sweet potion of love, romance and adventure. He intends to turn my black and white Polaroid life into a vivid Technicolor movie.

Now that I've made the changes Uranus and my Higher Self demanded, the Furies come to call, showing up in external events and in the people who find the changes threatening.

The immense relief I feel at Eddie's leaving alternates with mild panic over being the sole provider. I've always been the sole parent, so that hasn't changed. The financial reality of what I've done hits home. I take a hammer to Bruce, Melissa's blue dog bank, and count a hundred dollars. It'll tide us over until my first full-time check from Kaiser. I take a deep breath; I know I can make it.

I'm ready to live my life without a man. Two bad marriages and my relationship with Richard convince me: I'm staying single, finishing my bachelor's degree, raising my girls and concentrating on giving them the tranquility and stability they deserve and couldn't have with Eddie around.

Stacie is sad at the breakup, but relieved. She needs peace, and that's my gift to her. Melissa has mixed feelings: she's glad the fighting has ended, but she's unsure of the future and her anxiety levels are high. Frequent stomachaches keep her home from school. She's highly intuitive, and I sense she's picking up on my fears. The three of us cuddle together in my bed every night when I get home from work. We sleep entangled in each other's limbs and our love.

I want my life simple. I'm like a concentration camp survivor. I celebrate the small things and simple joys. I have my girls, my house, my vibrator.

Eddie's not doing well. He stops by the house frequently, following me around and cataloging all the reasons why I can't divorce him, like a lawyer giving an impassioned closing speech to the jury. "You have to stay married to me because of God, the flag and apple pie. Divorce destroys the fabric of American society." He's whining.

I sense he's grieving not so much for the marriage, but for the loss of his caretaker trophy wife. For Eddie, there are only two kinds of women: snakes and sweat hogs—his words. A large part of his self-esteem has centered on being married to me, being able to show off his snake at social functions. He's lost a large chunk of his identity and he doesn't know how to fill that space. He can't replace me; I was his one shot at a trophy wife and he won't get another.

He's fought fiercely the last ten years to live like a bachelor, and now he's got the real deal. I'm frustrated and disgusted with him. More importantly, I'm done with him.

"You want to screw?" He looks at me plaintively, already knowing the answer. "You never loved me. You deprived me of love and affection for this whole last year."

I have no desire to even try to reason with him. I maintain a determined silence. He turns to leave. "Don't get any ideas about Richard, cause I'll see to it he never comes near you again."

"I want your key to the house."

He stares at me in stunned silence then rips the key from its chain. The door slams. I lock it and I hold Stacie tightly, breathing deeply. In a fury, Eddie kicks the door in a rage several times before leaving. Stacie clings tightly to me in terror.

I know he's in a lot of pain, but he's experiencing the consequences of his actions, something that's never happened to him before. Eddie's dodged a lot of bullets in his life, but this one nailed him right between the eyes. He counted on me being like his mother and hanging in there forever no matter what. I'm not playing by the old rules. He's in shock, but I'm not responsible for him anymore. I feel the same way about Eddie as I felt when my mother died—blessed relief. But the constant badgering wears me down. I lean against the wall and start to cry in frustration. I have the fear he'll never leave me alone.

Melissa comes and hugs my legs. "It's okay, Mommy. I always feel better after I cry. It really is better just the three of us. No more screaming and fighting."

I hug her gratefully. My seven-year-old daughter shows wisdom beyond her years.

Eddie's mother sympathizes when I announce I'm divorcing her son. She tells me she doesn't know how I managed as long as I have—that lasts a week. After further reflection, she decides I have to stick it out. She repeats the spirit killing, Catholic aphorism: "You'll get your reward in heaven, dear."

I'm not buying that martyr bull crap. I've set myself free and there's no going back.

When Eddie isn't lobbying me for a reprieve, he goes on the road with his personal *Passion Play,* beseeching one and all to behold his wounds, his pain and suffering. His act plays to good reviews.

Eddie doesn't spare the girls; he lacks the moral compass and conscience. He parades his pain for them in a manipulative ploy to enlist their support. When his efforts at reconciliation fail, he calls for retribution. Stacie ignores his histrionics, but Melissa takes up the banner and becomes his avenging angel. She also inherits the emotional abuse he can no longer heap on me.

The friends we made as a couple melt away like soft butter on a hot August day. I don't care about the people Eddie works with but, ever the optimist, I was certain his parents would still love me. They don't. Eddie's mother calls me with a list of things she's given us over the years and she wants them all back so she can make sure her son gets them. And Richard's anger wounds me deeply. The only one who doesn't abandon me is Filben who remains neutral, flatly refusing Eddie's ultimatum to choose between us. I pull away from everyone in a defensive posture.

I've taken on a punishing load: working full time, going to school, taking care of the house and being a mother to my girls. I've lost 10 pounds; I'm skinny the way

I was when I got back from the hurricane in the Bahamas. Stress kills my appetite. Work saves me and takes me out of myself. I use the eight hours like a moving meditation. I barely hear the screams and moans of the laboring women.

My friends at work cheer me. Charlie just separated from her husband. We share our trials and stresses, supporting each other emotionally.

Dr. Dickie Poo, the junior resident, wants to talk to me. He acquired that name when he whined about the nurses not referring to him as doctor and showing him the proper respect.

"The other residents and I have a proposition for you. Dr. Marshall's been on the rampage lately; he's making our lives miserable."

"What's that got to do with me?"

"We were thinking: now that you're single, maybe you'd be willing to take care of him and calm him down. We've talked about taking up a collection. We're desperate."

"You want to pay me to have sex with Dr. Marshall so he'll get off your backs?"

"We don't think he's getting any at home. Will you do it?"

The male solution for all problems: sex. My smile betrays my cynical amusement. "Sorry, Dickie, I can't help you."

It's quiet in labor and delivery. I'm alone at the nursing station. Dr. Marshall stands looking down at me. "I've been thinking: I should take you out to lunch as a way of thanking you for all the help you gave me in the clinic. Of course, I'd have to ask Eddie's permission."

"You don't have to ask his permission for anything; I'm divorcing him." I surprise myself with the vehemence in my voice.

I see the look in his eyes, like a kid seeing Disneyland for the first time. There's no mistaking the meaning. *Oh, Oh. Here it comes.* He follows me to the coffee room, a dazed look and an unmistakably dreamy grin on his face. I can see the possibilities running through his brain.

"I had no idea. I thought you were happily married."

"Now you know."

Fun loving, risk-taking Jupiter sits in his 5th house of romance urging him on. Over the next month, he repeats the invitation to lunch. I make excuses; the last thing I'm going to do is get involved with a married man. It's against my values and my vow to keep my life simple. But time wears me down. I haven't done anything for myself and I need some diversion from my daily struggle for survival.

I've heard all the rumors about Byrne Marshall's reputation with women—how he and his wife live separate lives and the swarm of nurses from the Med Center who compete for his attention when he makes rounds there once a month. I have a difficult time reconciling that image with the one I've experienced. He seems to me peculiarly passionless and too restrained emotionally to be a dedicated womanizer. Over the last six years, he's been unwaveringly reserved with the nursing staff and even his peers. If he has a sense of humor, he keeps it to himself. Unfailingly polite, he calls us by our last names with the appropriate appellation of Miss or Missus. He's aloof, but not unfriendly, and occasionally displays an intellectual and social arrogance we attribute to his supposedly aristocratic, wealthy background. For all of the rumors, no one seems to really know him. I think it might be entertaining to experience him in action, see how he operates before politely declining to join the reported harem. No harm in a free lunch.

Red Lion Inn
July 7, 1976

He's waiting for me in the lobby. He strides purposefully towards me, dressed in one of his elegant, custom made suits. He looks like a doctor. And he is handsome; I have to give him that. He greets me with a wide, friendly smile.

I'm wearing my hair in a chignon. My yellow linen slacks fit loosely on my too slim frame, and my striped cotton shirt hugs my breasts. I'm tottering dangerously on Famolares, the fashion statement of the moment: high platform sandals with thick, clunky 3-inch heels. I look pretty and I know it.

We sit at a small table in the center of the room. He seems nervous, making polite small talk. He orders a Perfect Manhattan. I smile. Leave it to Dr. Marshall to order something perfect. I order a martini.

The drinks come. His hand shakes slightly as he takes a sip. I'm relaxed and friendly. I let him ramble, patiently waiting for the pitch. After a bumbling, circuitous route, he gets there.

"The problem is my wife and I aren't sexually compatible. I couldn't possibly get a divorce. The perfect solution would be a sexual surrogate situation."

He's trying to sound casual, but his face blanches white with fright.

"Why can't you get a divorce?"

"Because," he intones dramatically, "there'd be a death in the family."

"Who'd die?"

"My father-in-law."

"How old is he?"

"Ninety."

I burst into uproarious laughter, not missing the puzzled look on his face. He's quite serious.

"So, when you talk about a sexual surrogate, you have me in mind." I'm looking directly and unflinchingly into his eyes. I wait.

He pauses, looking like a treed raccoon. "Ah—you'd be quite acceptable."

This is entirely different than I imagined it. This man is no polished seducer. He's petrified. How did he ever find the courage to ask me to lunch, let alone to have an affair? There's something about him that touches my heart, an innocent vulnerability I'd never seen before or suspected. "Instead of having an affair, why don't you go to counseling with your wife? An affair just complicates matters."

"She'd never do that; she doesn't like anyone knowing her business."

We walk out to his car together and stand there. He looks at me expectantly, like a puppy waiting to have his head scratched.

"It really wouldn't be a good idea to have an affair when we work together. There are a lot of things to think about, like when it's over could we still be friends and work together without it being horribly awkward?" I shake my head, "I don't know; I'll have to think about this." I can't believe I'm saying I'll even consider having an affair with him. It's like someone else took over my brain. I'm outside myself thinking: *What in the hell are you doing?*

Relief floods his face. I hadn't said no. I hadn't embarrassed or humiliated him. I actually considered it. A quiet joy flushes his face.

I step closer to him, look up into his face and kiss his lips softly. I feel him quiver. He doesn't move, doesn't touch me. "Could you do that one more time?"

I kiss his full lips again. It's sweet. "I'll think it over and let you know."

I do think about it a lot for the next week, almost constantly. I need some fun, some diversion. Eddie has the girls every other weekend. Byrne has Wednesday afternoons off. Logistically, it's workable. We could have a short-term affair, until he talks his wife into counseling. He could be my stopover before I start dating. I begin to see it as a mutually beneficial situation. God knows, I could use the sex. The last years with Eddie were a sexual wasteland: brief, obligatory couplings with no love or feelings between us. My vibrator gets the job done, but it can't kiss me and hold me.

Charlie, not as cautious as I with her new found freedom, plunges happily into a sexual liaison, bedding the handsome young carpenter she's hired to do some work around the house. Along with her cabinets, he refurbishes her sex life.

She's been out sick for a week and calls me at work, crying with pain. "I've had a temperature of 103 degrees for days, and my bottom hurts so bad I can't walk. I'm scared. I've never been this sick before."

"Come in and let Scotty check you out. We're quiet right now."

Charlie walks into labor and delivery bent over with the pain. I take her to the triage room and help her on the table. Dr. Scott puts the speculum in her vagina. "You've got a pretty bad primary herpes infection there."

"Oh, no. The carpenter. It has to be that damned carpenter!"

I peek over Scotty's shoulder and recoil. Her vagina oozes crater-like, green sores. It's like a bomb-scarred battlefield in there. Sores cluster around her anus.

Oh! Shit! I've never seen anything like that before. Dr. Marshall looks better and better. It's either that or become a nun. It's too dangerous out there.

Byrne finds me in the coffee room. He stands in the doorway and looks at me smiling, a questioning look in his eyes. We're alone.

"I've thought it over. We could do it as long as you can guarantee me we could still be friends when it's over. It would be short term until you get into counseling and I start dating again. I want you to be absolutely sure this is what you really want. Think about it for a while and let me know."

"Okay." His grin is full with intoxicating promise. I hear him whistling down the hall. I already know the answer.

A few days later, he appears at the door of the coffee room again. He has a faraway look in his eyes, a kind of Wind Song perfume ad look. "Let's just do it!"

I smile at the unpolished innocence of him.

We meet at the Buggy Whip for a drink to discuss the ground rules and the implementation of our affair.

"This is the kind of place my mother would describe as clandestine, the kind of place men take their mistresses to."

"Kiss me, Dr. Marshall," I tease, pulling him to me. I'm warming to the adventure of a forbidden affair. I'm becoming a whore of Babylon.

We kiss briefly. His eyes stay closed when the kiss ends. He sighs. I feel his longing. It's obvious he needs a lot more than sex. I kiss his cheek and hand him his drink. We decide to do it in his office on Saturday. I have no idea what I'm getting myself into.

Chapter 11

Byrne's Higher Self planted seeds of discontent in 1974, and Uranus began whipping up a major mid-life crisis. His Self demands major changes to realize his unfulfilled longings, to live a more authentic life in tune to his life's purpose. Uranus is all about being true to yourself.

A powerful confluence of long running planetary energies come together, devoted to transforming his world. The next five years will bring him the kind of deep psyche exploration and soul searching that happens once in a lifetime.

Mars and Neptune in Byrne's 8th house of sex and the deep psyche create an intense desire to experience transcendent, mystical sex with someone that will lure him through a powerful vortex of transformation, the kind a Scorpio yearns for from deep within his subconscious. I'm to be the catalyst.

Kaiser Hospital
July 31, 1976

I walk hurriedly across the deserted clinic parking lot. I'm dressed for the occasion: a halter-top, no bra, slacks that slip off easily, no underwear. I'm ready to jump Dr. Marshall's bones and give him the ride of his life. Mars positively angling my Venus in the heavens make ideal energies for romance and sex. I'm revved and giddy with anticipation.

Byrne peeks around the door from his office. He reaches out, pulls me into the room and locks the door quickly. A bottle of newly opened Blue Nun sits on his desk. He kisses my cheek, his hands ice cold; he looks like he might faint. My plan to rip his clothes off and have at him fizzles; I realize this isn't going to be the fevered coupling I envisioned.

We drink a little wine. He wistfully tells me how beautiful I look. I take his hand

and put it inside my blouse. He feels bare skin and looks panicked. My desire is dead on arrival; my heart melts at the sweetness of him.

We sit on the floor; I kiss him gently and caress his face. His eyes close and he relaxes. I pull his shorts off slowly, stroking his thighs, dancing near his erection, but not touching it. I kiss his neck, run my hands languidly down his body.

"Touch me. Touch me." A dreamy smile plays on his lips. His eyes close.

I stroke him; my fingers skim the base and briefly touch the head. He moans. I straddle him and gently make love to him. He surrenders to my touch and the soft rhythm of my movements. This is so different than anything I'd ever experienced before. Instead of the passionate tango with Richard, or the raucous polka with Eddie, Byrne is a sensual waltz.

We sip more wine. He's saving the cork as a memento. On top of everything else, he's a romantic. He looks at me with utter adoration. There's no doubt in my mind he's never done this before.

Driving home, I'm disoriented. This is so unlike what I'd expected. I'm both disappointed at not experiencing my fantasy of wild sex and immensely intrigued by what did happen.

Galt, California
August 12, 1976

> It's a great night for romance. Passionate Venus harmonizes
> with powerful Uranus in the heavens, delivering erotic, electric
> sex to the mix.

Byrne takes me to the Golden Acorn for dinner. It's far enough out of town to make it safe; no one will see us. Throughout dinner, he looks at me with the yearning of a teenager in the throes of first love.

"I'd give anything to kiss you right now."

I'm totally disarmed.

After dinner, we go to a motel in West Sacramento.

"I have to warn you, I'll probably say I love you during sex. I have a hard time not saying it. Don't take it personally."

I smile. He's really something.

As predicted, he utters, "I love you," in the middle of sex. I'm on top; I take his face in my hands, and look into his eyes. "Just fuck me." I only use that word during sex. I kiss him passionately, do a double shunt and it's over.

I coax him into the shower, lather his body, put my arms around his neck and smile up at him. "So, how does it feel to fall out of your ivory tower right onto your butt?"

He looks down at me pensively. "I really have, haven't I?"

I can tell by the look on his face, he's feeling considerable guilt and acute discomfort at having adulterous sex in a motel. I'm not crazy about motels either, but I don't want our affair intruding on my regular life. I want it separate. I won't confuse my girls with temporary relationships. They've been through enough.

I dress. Byrne's in the bathroom; I hear the water running. He's at the sink washing small bloodstains off the bottom sheet. My period is a few days away and I've leaked a few drops during sex.

"What are you doing?"

"I'm washing the sheet. We can't leave it this way. Someone might call the police."

I shake my head. He's wound way too tight. He needs to learn how to relax and have fun.

I reconsider my decision. The neighbors might get suspicious, but I don't care anymore. The motel thing isn't going to work. We can see each other when the girls are with Eddie or at school. No one has to know.

It's our first Wednesday afternoon at my house. I have a split of champagne waiting in the bedroom. Byrne knocks tentatively on the door. He asks if we could sit on the couch for a few minutes; he just wants to look at me, hold my hand and talk first.

The sex gets better and better as Byrne relaxes and we explore new ways to please each other. The sensual, tender way he touches and strokes me incites a new found passion in me. We don't hear the doorbell.

I wave good-bye as Byrne's car turns the corner. Eddie pulls into the driveway. He seems in shock. "I was here earlier. You didn't answer the door. I ran the license plate on the car. He's married." There's genuine anguish in his voice.

"Yes. He is." I refuse to be intimidated. "This is a short term deal. It's just sex."

Eddie looks hard at me. "If you want him, you'll get him." The vehemence in his voice startles me.

We sit on the couch in Byrne's office that same afternoon. "I think it's only fair I tell you Eddie saw your car today. He ran your license plate. He knows who you are and that you're married. I don't think he'll do anything, but you never know."

He's appropriately panicked. "You don't think he'd shoot me, do you?"

I laugh. "No. He would have done that this afternoon."

"Maybe we shouldn't see each other for a while."

"It's your call." I say it, but I don't want to stop seeing him. Our time together has become important to me. The realization makes me uneasy. Uranus triggered an unexplored space in my psyche I need for my growth on a soul level. Byrne's energy can take me there. The sabbatical lasts three days. It's Sunday morning as usual.

Eddie flies to San Diego to cry on Richard's shoulder. They spend the whole time gutter crawling drunk with Eddie sobbing and tearing at Richard's heartstrings with his story of my adulterous infidelity. Now Eddie can tell everyone I cheated on him and left him for a rich doctor. The divorce really isn't his fault. Accepting responsibility isn't part of his warped reality.

Byrne and I settle into a routine of Wednesday afternoons, when the girls are at school, and Sunday mornings on the weekends Eddie has them. They know nothing. I intend to keep it that way.

Our Sunday mornings begin at 7 A.M. I'm not a morning person, but Byrne can't wait, having been awake since 3 A.M. fantasizing about me.

We make unhurried love. I straddle Byrne, put my middle finger inside me and then put it to his lips. He moans and licks my finger. I move my hips over his face.

"What are you doing?

I smile down at him, "I'm going to sit on your face."

"Oh. God." His eyes close, and he reaches to hold my hips. No one's ever done this to him before.

He has a special gesture: immediately after orgasm, his right hand goes behind my neck, his other arm around my waist. He pulls me on top of him, burying my face in his neck. He holds me there in that protective embrace for long, silent moments, savoring our connection. It's an exquisite gesture of intimacy that leaves me breathless with joy. I've never felt so safe as when he holds me like that. His quiet strength comforts and intoxicates me.

I've experienced other kinds of sex, now I'm learning about the deep sensuality of a Scorpio—a Sun and Moon double Scorpio. That kind of intensity powerfully attracts me. I want to plunge to the core of his being.

After sex is just as wonderful. We lie in bed naked, holding each other, drinking champagne and talking. I love his slim, muscled body, even the dark, fine hair on his chest that makes a thin trail down to his hard stomach. I've learned to love the softness of it. But, it's his hands that captivate me. They're strong with long, exquisite fingers, sensual hands that feel like silk on my body.

We laugh at what people at work would think if they knew what we were up to in our spare time, thoroughly enjoying the covert aspects of our liaison.

"What attracted you to MJ?" I'm curious about his wife.

"I don't know. We met in college and just fell into a relationship. I can't say now I was ever really in love with her. It's funny: the day of our wedding, I knew I was making a mistake, but it was too late. Things were okay for the first ten years, before we adopted the boys. We had some pretty good times, but I never realized how bad the sex was until you."

"Don't you ever have oral sex?"

"No. We don't do much of anything. I get a hand job on Sundays if I beg."

"It's probably a good thing we didn't meet when you were in medical school. We'd have spent all our time having sex, and you'd have flunked out."

"It would have been worth it. I only had sex with two other women before MJ, quickies in the back seat of the car or hand jobs. I don't have a lot of experience. I worry I won't be able to please you."

"You do nothing but please me."

We've finished making love again. I look down at him. "Now, isn't this a lot more fun than teaching Sunday school?" I make a teasing reference to his short-lived, previous Sunday morning pastime.

"Oh, God. We'll be struck dead. But, yes, this is a lot nicer." His smile radiates contentment. "You have totally corrupted me."

Over the weeks, Byrne shares himself with me. He tells me about his mother going to the TB sanitarium for a year when he was six. He and his younger brother went to live with an aunt in Ann Arbor. The separation devastated his already sensitive psyche. He spent a year terrified his mother would die. Bob, his father, told him when his mother got home that he had to be a very good little boy or she might get sick and go away again. That defining moment changed him into a hyper-responsible, fearful, emotionally controlled little boy. He felt his mother's life depended on his being perfect. And he loved her deeply.

He shares his insecurities. He still thinks of himself as the same shy, gawky sixteen-year old who asked someone for a date by saying, "You wouldn't want to go to the dance with me, would you?"

He knows something about everything. His innate curiosity and memory astound me. He knows art, opera, sports, literature, classical music. I'm in love with his mind. And I love that we never run out of things to talk about.

I cook him breakfast on our Sunday mornings: Mexican omelets or Eggs Benedict. This is a man who lives to eat, and I love to feed him. He thinks he's found Paradise. As he tells me, a bite of omelet poised on his fork, a boyish smile on his lips, "Nobody's been this nice to me since my mother."

Our stolen times together become an oasis from the stress and frustration of our everyday lives. We develop an intense need to share everything with each other.

Byrne brings me little gifts like a silver and turquoise stone bracelet. He tells me he had to buy it because it reminds him of me: slim, elegant and lovely. His gestures of affection leave me in awe. No one has been this nice to me—ever.

He calls me everyday right before noon when he's seen his last patient before lunch. The tender, intimate way he talks to me makes my spirit soar to dizzying heights.

We have fun at work, touching each other surreptitiously when no one can see. He tells me: "You touch me, and my thoughts scatter in a million directions." He says it with utter wonder at how that could be. It's agonizingly romantic.

Faces of Love, Death and Transformation:

Chapter 12

October 13, 1976

> The planets prime Byrne for major change. The seeds of discontent sprout. Neptune, another god of change, adds a powerful energy to the mix, summoning deep examination of his inner and outer life, bringing confusion, dissolving things built on false foundations and values. Uranus fans the flames of his growing inner tension between the life he has and the one his Self will insist on.
>
> Saturn in his 8th house of deep relationships prepares to do a thorough house cleaning, just as he did for me. This kind of major transformation runs right up a Scorpio's cosmic alley.
>
> A Mars and Uranus conjunction throws him the major curve ball.

Byrne's quiet and distracted. We're having lunch at the East Indian place near my house. We order; he looks at me thoughtfully, "There's something I have to tell you."

I'm not sure I want to hear whatever is coming. I stop breathing.

"I'm in love with you."

The words stun me. Anger wells uncontrollably. My eyes blaze brightly. "I don't want you to love me! It doesn't change anything. You're married. This relationship isn't going to last. Don't tell me you love me!"

"I'm sorry; I didn't mean to upset you. I just had to tell you." He looks stricken.

"I'm going to San Diego this weekend to see my friend Karen. We'll talk about this when I get back."

I'm in the fight or flight mode, aware of the danger. I lecture myself on how stupid it would be to surrender to this. No good ever comes from loving a married man. I've read the statistics: even if a man leaves his wife, only one in five ever stay with the mistress. I'm big on statistics. I've come too far to throw myself away on another hopeless situation. Byrne loving me breaks the rules we'd set for the relationship, breaching our safe status quo. We're like two dark stars on a collision course, whirling in a cold Universe. The inevitable explosion will create the heat and energy of a bright new world for us. But right now, all I can see is disaster.

I have to see Richard. I feel like I'm on the edge of a precipice and I need something to hang onto. I need to know if there's any future for us before I let go.

San Diego, California
October 15, 1976

> **Neptune opposes Richard's Sun, dissolving any illusion of control he has over me. He refuses to accept the reality and surrender gracefully.**

Karen and I have been friends since our sophomore year of high school. I think more clearly when I'm around her. Her common sense Virgo grounds me. We go to Ann Marie's pool party. Patrick and his wife Nancy greet me warmly. Richard's with them.

"Hello, Constance." The tone of his voice tells me he's still angry.

Patrick puts his arm around me protectively. "Constance is all right, Richard."

The air taut and tense, we stare at each other unflinchingly. "Richard, you're pissed off at me now, and you probably will be again, but you'll get over this." I turn and walk away so he won't see the tears. I'm right; he knows it, too, but it will take a year. And it'll be too late again.

I hadn't really expected Richard to do anything other than what he did. But I had to know for sure. I tuck him back into that special place in my heart reserved for him. I'm ready to move on emotionally.

I stare out the window of the plane going home and think about Byrne loving me. All my life I've wanted to be loved the way this man loves me. What if I never feel like this again? An involuntary sigh brings me out of my contemplation. Screw it; I'll do it, go with my feelings and just see what happens, jump into the void. I'll settle for whatever time we have together and treasure it. I know I'll regret it if I don't.

Sacramento, California
October 20, 1976

We're sitting on my couch. Byrne asks how my trip went.

"It was okay. I have something I have to tell you."

He looks frightened, waiting for me to go on.

"I tried not to—I didn't want to, but—I love you, too. I can't help it. You're the most wonderful thing that's ever happened to me."

Tears rush to Byrne's eyes. He pulls me into his arms and holds me tightly, kissing my hair. "I love you so much. I was so afraid I'd lose you, but I had to tell you. God, I am so happy."

His tears of joy melt any resistance I have left. I surrender and know I've made the right decision.

Sacramento, California
December 3, 1976

> **Venus and Jupiter, the most fun, pleasure, life loving planets in the zodiac, link happily for us, dispensing sweetness and pleasure for his birthday celebration. A mystical Sun, Mars, Neptune conjunction gives him a special gift, plucking the deeper chords of his soul and affirming the magic of our connection.**

Byrne turned forty several weeks ago. He'd been in LA at an OB conference with MJ the weekend of his birthday. He told her he needed to get home early for the kids' soccer games. He took a midnight flight Sunday morning back to Sacramento and drove straight to my house so he'd be with me on his birthday. He brought me a thin leather and gold chain belt. He tells me when he saw it he had to get it for me. I'm making plans to cook his belated birthday dinner Friday, and I have a special gift for him.

Byrne tells me he thinks about me constantly. He's drawn to me on levels he never knew existed within him. Our love brings him an anxious joy. He doesn't tell me that for the last two weeks, in quiet moments between patients or driving home, the same scenario intrudes into his thoughts. First, he sees my face, then the song starts: *The Windmills of Your Mind...a circle in a spiral, a wheel within a wheel, never ending or beginning on an ever spinning reel...* the image of the circle in a spiral floats through his thoughts, haunting him.

The circle symbolizes unending love and the spiral reincarnation, the perfect metaphor for our relationship. That consciousness stirs from deep within him, giving a glimpse of what has been and what will be.

He stands in the doorway, his classical guitar in his hand. He plays all the greatest hits from the 15th century. "Are you going to serenade me, Dr. Marshall?"

"I had to bring it. I told MJ I was going to a recital for my guitar teacher."

I built a fire; the lights are low. A silky comforter waits in front of the fireplace. Romantic music plays. Dinner simmers on the stove. The rich smells permeate the house with seductive aromas. Champagne sits in a bucket of ice. I love orchestrating these romantic encounters. Venus and Jupiter join us again in our own version of Love Potion #9.

Jack Jones sings The Songs of Michel Legrand: songs of poetic beauty, speaking from the unconscious of love and loss. It's very 8th house music—perfect. We drink champagne in front of the fireplace, undress, and make love on the comforter. The firelight dances over our naked bodies. I'm on top; I like looking at Byrne's face while we make love. My eyes can't get enough of him; he takes my breath away, his black hair a mass of soft curls; his eyes glow with love. My heart aches at how perfect it all is.

"This is the most wonderful birthday I've ever had. I don't even mind turning forty."

We hold each other. I trace a line down his stomach with my finger, thinking. I take his hand, brush it against my cheek and kiss it, a spontaneous gesture that surprises me. I feel so safe with him. "I have something for your birthday. Here, open it." I smile expectantly.

Byrne opens the small package. He takes the silver medallion out of the box. When he sees the circle in a spiral, his conscious and subconscious mind melt into a brief moment of cosmic illumination. He's stunned by the connection—speechless.

In the background, Jack Jones sings: "*….like a tunnel that you follow to a tunnel of its own, down a hollow to a cavern where the sun has never shown.*"

I can't tell by the look on his face whether he likes it or not. All I see is shock and bewilderment—not what I expected. He couldn't tell me about his visions at the time; it was just too weird. Nothing like this ever happened to him before. Everything means something, and some things mean everything.

"I wanted to give you something to remember me by. I had a jeweler make it. Years from now, you can look at it and think of our time together."

"I could never forget you." His voice chokes with emotion. He holds the medallion tightly in his hand.

The song plays softly: "*Through all of my life, summer, winter, spring and fall of my life, all I ever will recall of my life is all of my life—with you.*"

I touch his hair. "I've been thinking about the timing of our situation. I know, someday, you're going to divorce MJ. It may take a few more years, but you really don't have a choice. You're too unhappy. It makes me sad to know that by the time you do, I'll be long gone." I sigh and kiss his forehead. "The timing is all wrong for us."

Byrne remains silent, caught up in the mystical, dreamy soul-to-soul connection between us. Tonight gave him the kind of poetic experience his Scorpio soul yearns for, offering a relationship that will take him on an adventure to the deepest parts of his soul and psyche. Tonight is a small sample of what is to come.

"Come on sweetheart, your lover is ready to feed you."

Byrne loves the rich fish stew; he's never had it before. The prawns, oysters and crab rest quietly in a sea of diced tomatoes, red wine, fish broth and garlic. He dunks the hot French bread into the juices. His face tells me he's one happy man.

"Isn't it nice I keep expanding your culinary horizons?" The way to this man's heart is definitely through his stomach. The sex got his attention but the food won his heart.

"Where did you learn to cook like this? You're amazing."

"It's one of my many talents, my love. So, tell me. What did MJ get you for your birthday?"

Byrne smiles wickedly. "Odor Eaters for my shoes and a bottle of wrinkle cream. Think she's trying to tell me something?"

We laugh, hold wine glasses high and toast the Odor Eaters.

"I've been thinking. What do you think about my starting a retirement plan at work? I've got to start planning my future."

Byrne stares into my eyes with a faraway look. He doesn't say anything, just shakes his head slowly and goes back to eating.

Kaiser Hospital
December 1976

Hospitals are a microcosm of the cultural and collective consciousness. Power struggles, gossip, jealousy, intrigue and sex run rampant through our cloistered Kaiser world. Divorce rules; sex reigns.

Rumors of assignations fly faster than the speed of light. A janitor caught a pediatrician who resembles Dr. Dickie Poo and a nursery nurse who looks like me having sex in a clinic office. Dickie thinks it's funny. I keep my mouth shut.

Four of the eight OB residents and the entire day shift nursing staff are bitterly divorced or in the process. Ex-spouse bashing is the favored sport.

The PM shift fares better. Even though Charlie and I are in the throes of divorce, we aren't bitter or celibate. We're careful to keep our private lives private. I feel like a spy in deep cover. I'm pleased at my success in managing my affair with Byrne. The girls seem content spending every other weekend with Eddie. It's enough for them.

Dr. Bouchard gets a cup of coffee and sits in the break room with me. He looks pensive. "I think Marshall is having an affair."

I steel myself. "What makes you think that?"

"Because, he goes around the clinic whistling all the time. He's too happy. It only means one thing."

I relax. "Who do you think it is?"

"I don't know, but I'm going to find out."

I sip my coffee in relief. "Let me know what you find out." I know his quest will be futile.

Dr. Graham strolls leisurely down the hall of L&D, a grin of expectant pleasure traversing his well-worn face. He's on call, but he has other plans. "I'm going out for a couple of hours. I'll be on the beeper. If my wife calls, tell her I'm seeing a consult in the ER then beep me." He grins. "I don't want her hunting me down; you know what I mean?"

I nod. Graham feels a certain kinship with me. We knew each other from San Joaquin General. He did his residency when I worked there. The battles between he and his wife were the stuff of legends—drunken, violent, furniture breaking, screaming matches ending in hot sex that would have made Virginia Woolf cringe with sinister delight.

Graham toddles off to a rendezvous with Diana, the cute ward clerk from the surgery floor. I wonder if he knows she's entertaining one of the other OB residents at her place right now. The girl needs a scheduling clerk.

Doris works the PM shift with Charlie and me this evening. We're sitting at the nurse's station, discussing the mysterious charms of Enright our chief resident, who cuts an impressive swath through the nursing staff and ancillary personnel, bedding any and all comers. We can't figure it out. He's skinny with wispy, unkempt hair, a straggly moustache and watery blue eyes. He looks more like a junkie than a doctor.

"What do you think he has?" I ask.

"Joyce tells me he recites poetry while he's doing it," Charlie says.

"All I can figure is he must have the fastest tongue in the West," Doris chimes.

I see him out the corner of my eye; my face flushes a bright red.

Dr. Enright walks slowly to the nursing station. "I heard every word."

"So, which is it? The fast tongue or the poetry?" Doris isn't backing down.

Enright shakes his head in disgust and walks away.

Charlie spends time with the newly divorced resident Stewart McGeachin, a strawberry blonde, blue-eyed Scotsman. Stewart is arrogant to a fault, exceptionally bright, rebelliously abrasive and frighteningly intimidating to most people, a true gray lizard Scorpio. Cross him, and he guarantees retribution delivered at a proper time of his choosing, but I like him immensely. We're friends; he admires my confidence and knowledge as a nurse. Stewart tells me I'm the least neurotic person he knows, a high compliment coming from him. He enjoys spending time with Charlie and me, visiting in the coffee room during breaks. The three of us meet frequently for drinks after work. He prides himself on knowing everything that's going on in the Kaiser world. His favorite expression is, "Spill! Tell all," delivered in an imperious manner. He's relentless until he gets whatever gossip or data he's after. He would have made a good KGB interrogator. I know I have to be exceptionally careful to keep my affair with Byrne secret from Stewart, but he's caught the scent.

"Constance, I think the Big M has his eye on you. He seems to be sniffing around labor and delivery a lot lately when you're here."

"Oh, really? I hadn't noticed." I try looking disinterested. "He's hardly my type, Stewart. Could you see me with the Big M?" I laugh. "He wouldn't know what to do with me—and he's married, remember?"

"Yes, the infamous Mean Mary Jean."

"That's cute. You make that up yourself?"

"It's what even her friends call her from what I'm told."

December 16, 1976

Fran, one of the day nurses, hosts the department Christmas party this year. I buy a striking red outfit: pants, matching blazer and red and white striped silk blouse. Byrne will be there with Mean Mary Jean. I'm curious to see her again. I'd met her briefly at a retirement party for one of the doctors a couple of years before. I don't remember much about her, except that she's short.

The party is in high gear when Byrne and the missus arrive. He has on a navy blue Christmas blazer with snowflakes and a white turtleneck sweater, festively dashing. He's wearing the silver medallion.

MJ's dressed provocatively in a low cut jump suit to show off the boob job she had the year before. She has a good body, but she's not a beauty. She and Byrne just don't compute as a couple. His tall, handsome elegance and deep intensity sharply contrast her short stature and exhibitionistic, superficial charm. They're a clear mismatch.

She's feeling the effects of the drinks she'd had at the previous party they'd attended. Byrne tells me she hates these department things. She doesn't like associating with what she deems as her social inferiors. But she's careful to seem friendly and show the flag. She wants Byrne in private practice because it has more status. And she wouldn't have to go to functions like this. I watch her ramp up her flirty, teenybopper charm and start working the room like a politician at a fundraiser. She's good.

Byrne mixes her a drink at the makeshift bar, a table shoved against the wall. I stand at his elbow and watch as he pours her a triple shot. "What are you trying to do, knock her out?" I'm whispering, trying to look casual.

"Yes, I am, so she won't notice us. Meet me outside in five minutes. I have to kiss you."

Byrne sneaks out the door to the backyard. I wait a minute or so and then follow him. We stand in the darkened yard and kiss passionately.

A Sun and Mars combination generates a hot, impulsive kind of energy in Byrne. The ecstasy of raging hormones, and the agony of having to control himself, make him reckless and willing to walk a little on the wild side—quite unlike him.

"This is crazy. What if someone sees us?"

"You're right." His hand brushes my cheek. "Go back in. I'll be there in a minute, as soon as this erection goes away."

I walk nonchalantly in the door to find Stewart waiting to pounce on me.

"Alright. Spill! What were you doing out there with the Big M?"

"Why, Stewart. Whatever do you mean?" I reply in my best Scarlett O'Hara voice, moving past him to the bar.

Stewart asks MJ to dance and then walks off. She doesn't notice he's gone, dancing on by herself in drunken abandon. Byrne takes her home before she passes out. On the way home he asks her, "So, was there anyone you thought was attractive at the party?"

"The tall blonde in red," she mutters before passing out. Byrne smiles; he's being quite wicked. He doesn't fathom the depth of his anger toward her.

Stewart and the entire day shift wait for me in the tiny coffee room when I come on duty the next afternoon. "Okay, Constance. Spill! Tell all about you and the Big M,"

The air tenses and crackles in anticipation. I feel like an accused heretic at an inquisition; I have to think fast. "Well, I asked him if he could kiss as good as he looked, and he invited me outside to find out."

The looks on their faces tell me they hadn't expected me to be so candid. They're also waiting for the answer to the question I posed to him. I shrug. "He kisses as good as he looks."

The room remains in confused silence. I turn and casually walk out. No one can see the huge grin on my face.

New Year's Eve 1976

I always work New Year's Eve. I don't like parties and the drunken, desperate way people behave in the name of fun. I tired years before of Eddie's drunk, cop friends deliberately spilling drinks on my chest and offering to clean it up for me.

Hepler's on call; he's having his dinner in the coffee room. I join him.

"I have here a fine bottle of Bordeaux. How about a little glass with me to bring in the New Year?"

We have no patients. "Okay, just a little." I silently toast Byrne who is at a party somewhere with MJ. He's coming over in the morning.

New Year's Day 1977

At 7 A.M., I answer the soft knock at the door. Byrne stands there looking shell-shocked. He steps inside without a word, pulls me tightly into his arms and collapses against the wall, holding me in a desperate embrace.

"What's the matter, sweetheart?" I've never seen him this way.

"It was terrible. The party. She got horribly drunk and threw herself at every man in the room, vomited and passed out. I had to carry her to the car. It was so embarrassing. Her drinking is totally out of control."

"I'm sorry,"

"All I could think about was you, being here. I love you so much." He holds me tighter.

"I know. I know. I thought about you, too. Come here." I take him to my bed, make comforting love to him and feed him. Neptune slowly dissolves his ties to the old. Uranus poises ready to throw a bomb into the status quo when the time is right.

A note to report to the Assistant Director's office waits for me at work. No one on the day shift will look at me. The Furies rage again.

Denny, the Assistant Director of Nurses looks severely at me across from her desk. "The day shift reported to me that you were drinking on duty with Dr. Hepler last night."

"I had some wine with him," I readily admit it. "I showed extremely poor judgment. it will never happen again."

Denny's mouth stands open, ready to counter any excuses I make. I have none; there isn't anything else to say.

"Is someone going to say something to Hepler about drinking on duty?"

"The Chief of Staff will deal with him,"

I know no one is going to say squat to Hepler about anything. I'm pissed. How did the day shift find out?

Hepler passes me in the hall; he's making rounds on his patients. I grab his arm and stop him. "How did the day shift know you and I had wine last night?"

He grinned, "I brought the bottle out at change of shift and made the comment that you and I had polished off the bottle last night. I threw it in the waste basket."

"Thanks a lot. The day shift reported me to the nursing office. I just finished doing a major mea culpa to Denny."

"Oops, Sorry." He really isn't. He's an arrogant clod, always has been and I will be forever grateful to him for that. He was my doctor before Byrne and his crass insensitivity made me switch—fate at work again.

Phoenix, Arizona
January 26, 1977

> **Jupiter links with Venus and Mars sits on my Venus guaranteeing hot sex, romance and all pleasures of the senses and flesh. The energies sizzle.**

Byrne and I are taking our first trip away to an OB conference in Phoenix. It's my birthday and we sit in the restaurant of the hotel and smile at each other, savoring the days to come. Our drinks arrive; Byrne's converted me to Perfect Manhattans. He looks at me with tears in his eyes.

"What's the matter?"

"You only have one coat."

"How many am I supposed to have? You make me sound like Cinderella."

"That's how I think of you."

"Well, if I'm Cinderella, you must be Prince Charming—I like that; you really are my Prince Charming, you know."

Byrne has a major sinus infection, but that doesn't curb his enthusiasm for making love to me every chance he has. I sleep in each morning and order breakfast from room service. During breaks and lunch, he lopes into our room and happily hurls himself on me.

I'm having orgasms, primal and deeply satisfying. Byrne treasures every erotic moan I make. He's freed me to express an inner joy I've never known before. He gives me the profound sense of safety I need to express my sexuality. The karmic connections between us are powerful enough to light up the motherboard at Cosmic Central.

We drive around Phoenix in a rented green Gremlin with a gas tank that sloshes ominously at every turn. We joke about being blown up. We have no sense of direction and keep getting lost. We don't care.

He takes me to the Camelback Inn for dancing. I wear an electric blue halter dress that clings to my breasts and highlights my eyes. I bind my long hair and wear it up. On the dance floor, all eyes are on us.

"Why is everyone staring at us?" He whispers nervously.

"Because we're Prince Charming and Cinderella; we're pretty together."

Byrne puts his arm around me and takes my hand. I automatically move my hips into his.

"What are you doing?

"I'm dancing."

"You can't dance that way. You're in my space."

"Who says?"

"Arthur Murray. I've taken thousands of dollars worth of dance lessons, and you can't do it that way. Let me show you."

I sigh as Byrne moves me into the proper dance position. The band begins a waltz, a dance I've never done. He has a strong, graceful lead and moves me easily around the floor. All those lessons paid off; he's an amazing dancer. I flash to the ball scene with Cinderella waltzing with Prince Charming for the first time. I have that same radiant look in my eyes. There's no end to this man's talents. He just keeps surprising me.

Faces of Love, Death and Transformation:

The best surprise is his dry sense of humor. It frequently jumps out of nowhere like a mischievous child to delight me. I love everything about him.

That night after making love, he looks thoughtfully at me. "Sex with you is so intense; it's like hearing the music louder than it is. And kissing you is better than having an orgasm."

He leaves me joyously speechless.

On the plane home, Byrne tells me he's been a little worried about our spending concentrated time together. He puts his arm around me, "Even after four days, I'm not looking forward to leaving you."

Byrne and MJ vacation in Bermuda for a week at a tax-deductible conference, the kind doctors love and the IRS hates. I warned him the trip wouldn't go well. Uranus made sure it didn't. Enforced togetherness can be lethal in a rocky relationship. I divorced Eddie after a seven day cruise to Mexico. I know how much pain they're both in. Byrne hangs onto the moribund relationship because he can't bear the thought of losing his boys. MJ isn't about to give up her lifestyle. He doesn't see any way out. He knows she'll punish him with the kids if he divorces her, and I'd never ask him to do that.

I go to Aldo's, the up scale eatery in Town and Country Village. It's Opera Night. You get drinks, dinner and opera singers. I'm meeting the single nurses from the day and PM shifts.

I'm the first one there. I go to the bar and order a drink. A man sitting next to me strikes up a conversation. As soon as I tell him I'm a nurse and more are joining me, the feeding frenzy began. The mystique lives on. The guy runs to a back room where his company is having a meeting and spreads the word. By the time the others arrive, I'm surrounded. The salesmen act like a bunch of fishermen eagerly waiting to dip their poles in a new watering hole.

Opera night is fun. We sit at communal tables. A nice looking guy and his friend sit next to me. The nice looking guy asks me out. I decide, why not? He lives in San Francisco; he's a banker. Seems like a nice guy.

Afterwards, the girls and I go to the Coral Reef to have a drink. The talk turns to work, of course. Fran dates one of the older, single doctors; she prides herself on having all the inside scoop on everyone.

At an opportune time, I casually ask Fran, "So, what's the story on Dr. Marshall and his wife?"

Fran's eyes light up. "Well, they lead totally separate lives. He has a lot of girl friends and does his own thing. He's discreet, quite rich and can't afford to get a divorce, so they stay married. It's a financial thing."

"Interesting." It's obvious Fran doesn't know squat about Dr. Marshall.

It's all over labor and delivery the next day—the story of the salesmen swarming me at the bar like worker bees around the queen. And don't forget the cute guy who asked me out. I'm unjustly becoming the scandal of the department, and they don't even know about Byrne.

I get two letters from Byrne: one before he left for Bermuda so I'd be sure to hear from him while he's gone, one while he's there. It's going as predicted. He asks me not to be smug. Please. He's miserable; he loves me.

Byrne takes MJ home and drives straight to my house after the long flight back from Bermuda. He's desperate to see me, hold me, talk to me, love me.

We lay in bed naked, stroking each other quietly, thinking.

"In Bermuda, I heard that Roberta Flack song, *First Time Ever I Saw Your Face.* I broke down in tears, thinking about how much I love you. MJ must think I'm nuts."

His life slips through his fingers like a greased pig at a picnic, impossible to hang onto.

Faces of Love, Death and Transformation:

Chapter 13

I have dinner with the banker a couple of times. It impresses me that he's willing to drive all the way from San Francisco to date me. He's four years younger, but it doesn't bother him. I like him. I'm not interested in him long term, but feel like I have to do something. I can't continue with Byrne forever, no matter how much I love him. I learned that lesson with Richard. Maybe, it's time to move on—or try to.

Sacramento, California
March 5, 1977

> Uranus whips the tension in Byrne's life to unbearable levels. Saturn forces him to look at the hard reality of freedom versus the inevitable consequences. Neptune squaring Saturn dismantles his defenses and demolishes the walls to his future. His mid-life crisis arrives. His Self declares it's time for major change.

It's Sunday, a Byrne morning. We sit on the couch drinking champagne after breakfast. He's in a buoyant mood.

"So, when do you think you'll start dating again?"

His cavalier attitude annoys me. It's not like him. It's time.

"As a matter of fact, I've been dating a banker from San Francisco. He wants me to come to see him for St Patrick's Day. I'm going." We both know what that means: sex.

Byrne's smile fades. His face turns the color of a hospital sheet, panic obvious in his eyes. He jumps to his feet. "I have to get out of here. I can't stay here. I'm sorry." He sounds like he's having trouble breathing and bolts for the door. I let him go.

A cold, empty feeling settles in my stomach. When the door slams shut, I swear I can hear the sound of my heart breaking.

An hour later, the phone rings. "I'm sorry. I had to call you. MJ and the kids are waiting in the car. I had to tell you I understand. I do. I understand. I love you. I have to go." He's crying.

The next day, I sit at the nursing station, alone with my thoughts. I feel Byrne's hand on my shoulder; he's standing behind me. My heart sinks. I resist the urge to take his hand and put it to my cheek. I turn and look up at him. His eyes have dark circles under them, his face haggard. He doesn't speak; the tears run down his face relentlessly like snow melting under a warm sun. He turns and leaves without saying a word. He didn't need to. I want to go to him and hold him, make the pain go away, but I sit there. It's done.

He comes to L&D again, looking at me with wrenching anguish. This time I take his hand. "You can't keep doing this. You've got to get some help. You're on the verge of a breakdown."

"I know. I know. I don't know what to do. I can't lose you. I can't. I love you. I love you. That's all I know. It's all I can think about. I had this dream. I wrote it down. Here."

He pushes a piece of paper into my hand. I put it in my pocket. "Call Annabelle Gross. She's a really good counselor. She'll help you." I press his hand to my cheek, closing my eyes for a moment. "I won't go to San Francisco. I can't do this to you right now. I love you, sweetheart. I can't stand to see you like this. Talk to Annabelle."

He takes a deep breath and swallows hard. "You'd do that for me?" Relief floods his face. "Thank you, thank you." He clutches my hand briefly, kisses it and strides through the door, hiding his face so no one will see the tears.

I'm frightened for him. He's so fragile. His whole world crumbles around him. Having just come out of the same kind of pain, I understand what he's going through. Now, it's his choice. I have no regrets. I haven't asked him to do anything; I haven't expected anything. I've only loved him.

At home that night, I read Byrne's dream:

"I was out in the very dark rainy night on a bike by myself. The bus left at 10 P.M. I

had to find you. The bus depot was crowded. I saw your beautiful face and held you. I don't care who sees me. You said, 'I'm glad you're here; I thought I was going to have to leave without you. Go buy your ticket. You'll have to climb the hill to get the bus.'"

I marvel at the power of the dream. It mirrors the depth of Byrne's pain, fear and loneliness. The ticket is his divorce; the hill represents the struggle he faces; and the bus is our new life together. The power of his dream rivals my divorce dream. The message and direction for Byrne is just as clear.

He calls me at home. I'm so relieved to hear his soft voice say my name.

"Con, sweetheart. I saw Annabelle. She told me I had to get away from MJ. I have to have some distance from her—and from you—so I can figure things out. I'm moving into an apartment as soon as I tell her."

"I'm glad. I've been so worried about you. I love you." I'm on the verge of crying.

"It'll be all right, sweetheart. Con? We'll work it out. Just remember how much I love you and want to be with you. The thought of losing you—I couldn't survive it."

A day later, he tells MJ he's having some problems and needs some distance for a while. He breaks down in tears. She coldly tells him he's going through male menopause; he can read all about it for fifty cents in the latest issue of Reader's Digest. He doesn't need to spend good money on counseling or an apartment. She might as well have gift wrapped him and left him on my doorstep.

March 12, 1977

> Byrne doesn't know the places in his heart, soul and emotions this journey will take him. His authentic life is just beginning. He needs this experience for his soul's growth and his happiness.
>
> Over the next two months, a Venus retrograde loop puts his relationships on pause so he can evaluate and make the necessary adjustments—one will go, one will remain.

> Pain can be very transformative. The heart of Scorpio energy is all about transformation and the insistent drive to merge deeply with another human being. We've done this before.

Oia, Greece
5th Century BC

I made my way down an incredibly steep path to the ocean below and the tiny, secluded cove where I met my lover.

I wore a long, white tunic, my dark blonde hair in a long braid down my back. I was sixteen years old, my lover 18. My heart filled with joyous expectation. We'd been meeting in secret for a year now, waiting for our parents to give us permission to marry.

He waited for me: tall, with black, curly hair, handsome as a god, looking exactly as he does in this life. He came toward me. I was so happy and in love. We embraced passionately, our lovemaking intense, our emotional connection so strong we knew we would die without each other.

We married, had two children and a wonderful life. I was an artist of some kind, Byrne, a renowned teacher, taught history and mathematics. Students came from all over to study with him. We filled our house with famous, interesting people, our life together rich in every way.

Byrne died at the age of 86. We had his funeral. The next day I died. My spirit left my body and soared upward. A brilliant, white light came to meet me— Byrne; our energies came together and burst into a dazzling white light. We became one again. The joy was indescribable. That's the happiest life we'd had together.

We've had countless lives together. Most of them haven't been idyllic, rather fraught with pain, suffering and the untimely death of one or both of us. This one brought a welcome respite.

Byrne moves to Selby Ranch, an apartment complex. No one at work knows. He's on call tonight and we spend my eight-hour shift touching when we can, passing longing glances when no one can see, just happy to be together. We're headed to room four to examine a patient.

"I love you," I whisper, briefly brushing his hand.

"I love you—hopelessly."

I walk to the nurse's lounge to change and go home. Byrne's hand reaches out of the dark conference room and pulls me inside. He shuts the door, silently gathers me into his arms and kisses me. It's the kind of kiss a woman dreams about her whole life: long, slow, deep, achingly tender. A kiss that means everything, says everything: I love you; you have my heart—a kiss of total surrender to the love between us. Without a word, he leads me to the door and quietly closes it behind me.

I float on the energy of that kiss all the way to my car, lost in the wonder of it, the promise of it. I think to myself: *no woman should ever die without being kissed like that at least once.*

Faces of Love, Death and Transformation:

Chapter 14

Selby Ranch nestles off American River Drive in a forest of mature trees and lush landscaping. Rich people in transition live here while putting their lives together after divorce. Single women of all ages come here to husband hunt.

Byrne's beige one bedroom unit begs for color, but he doesn't see the drabness. He sees liberation. He's like a college kid with his first apartment. He needs to learn to live with himself to prove he can do it. He buys a sleek, white Cordoba with Corinthian leather, a tangible symbol of his new independence. New directions beckon, and he isn't resisting.

Byrne looks at me, his eyes dancing with light. "I told MJ about you. You know what she told me? She already suspected I was having an affair. She said she's been having them for years, and it's no big deal. Her last fling was the mechanic at the Porsche dealership. She said he's quite good at it, meaning I'm not."

I don't know what to say.

"Then she tells me not to get any ideas about a divorce; I'm too good a deal and to just get over it."

I shake my head in amazement at the arrogant stupidity of the woman. Her marriage is a funeral pyre, and she's throwing gasoline on the inferno.

The news of their separation stuns the Kaiser cosmos. No one knows what happened. Not even Fran can supply any hot info. It's perplexing and titillating, even more so with Dr. Marshall looking so happy.

I decide it's time to tell my girls about Byrne. They listen intently as I tell them I'm "seeing" a doctor I work with. They're excited when I tell them he has two boys their age. It's enough for now.

We "come out" at a hospital party. Dr. Marshall and I dating is the juiciest piece of gossip to hit Kaiser since one of the OB residents got caught banging a recovery room nurse on the table in the conference room. It's like throwing a firecracker in the middle of a chicken coop—shrieks and ruffled feathers flying everywhere. It's the kind of shit stirring chaos Uranus' wackier side loves.

The day shift eats their entrails in venomous envy, unleashing another round of the Furies upon me. Doris keeps muttering how she thinks this has been going on for a while. Fran's lost huge face at not having the data. My reputation as a *femme fatale* is now set in cement. They don't know me any better than they know Byrne.

The staff doctors gossip about Byrne with great glee. Obviously, the rumors of his harem never reached them. None of them thought he had it in him. The residents are stunned that their lofty director, the epitome of respectability, structure and discipline, is actually capable of human failings, let alone a liaison with me. It's like the Pope running off with a Victoria Secret model.

Stewart congratulates me. "Well done, Constance, I didn't suspect a thing." He's most gracious in defeat. I have been a worthy opponent.

One of the junior residents corners me in the coffee room. He's righteously angry. "So, the whole time Marshall is ragging on me about my infidelity, he's running around with you!" He's referring to his flagrant affair with the OB recovery room nurse while his pregnant wife languishes in humiliating despair.

I stare calmly into his eyes. "Well, he'll just have to live with that, won't he?"

A slow smile spreads across his face. "You're all right, you know?"

April 9, 1977

Neptune's been busy stirring up Byrne's unfulfilled fantasies.
Mars incites a need in him to go for it.

The Cordoba cruises up I-80 to Auburn. Byrne wants to try a new restaurant. He's quiet and subdued. Saturn's about to body slam some hard realities into me.

"I have to tell you something." He plunges on, not looking at me. "I've been thinking about other women. I can't seem to stop. I feel terrible; I don't know what to do."

The words land at my feet like a live grenade; my thoughts explode into a fight or flight response. At the pinnacle of the panic, I breathe deeply and surrender to it. In that moment, a calm envelops me. My intuitive right brain whispers a perceptive truth in my ear. "He needs to do it."

I stare straight ahead, unable to look at him. If I do, I'll burst into tears. "Well, you were married pretty young. You never had the chance to sow any wild oats. Now, you can; it's your chance." I look at him. "I won't lie and say it'll be easy for me, but I don't want you unless you're absolutely sure I'm the one. You won't ever be absolutely certain unless you try this. You have to do it."

"I'm sorry." He sounds contrite and ashamed.

My voice remains soft and calm. "I'll tell you one thing: you'll never find anyone who'll love you the way I do."

"I know that. I feel like the biggest jerk in the world."

We try making small talk during dinner but keep getting lost in our own thoughts. Byrne looks up from his plate, "You're planning on marrying me, aren't you?"

"Probably."

He stares softly into my eyes. "You're the warmest person I've ever known. I've never really loved anyone but you; I'll always love you—and someday I want you to marry me."

I reach for his hand. "Take the time you need. When you're sure you're done, let me know. Our relationship can't move ahead until then."

The possibility of losing Byrne terrifies me. What if he decides he wants children of his own? MJ is the infertile one. He could marry someone who could give him babies. I think how ironic it is he's the one who tied my tubes. But for the first time in my life, I sense the bigger picture. I don't see it yet; I only feel it. What I know is: I love this man more than I've ever loved anyone, and I want him to be happy—even if it isn't with me.

That night, the dream comes:

I was in a very small car driving down a twisty highway with my girls, trying to get to a wedding. As I drove, bombs exploded everywhere, barely missing the car. I was afraid, but I couldn't turn back; I had to get to the wedding. Jerry Brown and Linda Ronstadt were getting married.

We made it to the wedding in time. Relieved and happy, I listened to everyone talking about what an unusual couple Jerry and Linda made. They didn't care what anybody thought; they were ecstatically happy to be married.

I smile widely. I'm Linda Ronstadt and Byrne is Jerry Brown. The dream tells me there will be obstacles, but we will be married. Mrs. Marshall. I snuggle down into bed. Saying the name triggers a cherished teen fantasy. The memory sweeps over me, catching me unaware like a rogue wave.

West Sacramento, California
October 1956

Rheumatic fever confined me to bed for six months when I was fifteen. I filled my hours with fantasies. I dreamed of a tall, dark, handsome man who would be my husband. He looked like Prince Charming from the Disney movie. I ran the same scene over and over every day: I pictured myself as a beautiful, grown woman with a successful career, my husband equally successful. We were deeply in love and happy; I visualized us coming together and embracing. I decided my married name would be Marshall.

I'd totally forgotten about that until now. Was it a premonition, or had I been able to create this somehow? Actually, I did. I wasn't aware at the time but my fantasizing mobilized the law of attraction where my focused thoughts and intention created the reality. And fate also played a part, something I'd never contemplated before. My dream and the old fantasy comfort me in the times coming.

Byrne's obsession with physical fitness inspires me. I decide to take up jogging so I can run the two miles with him along the bike trail on the American River near his apartment. Stacie rides beside me on her bike with training wheels; we take off down the street. After one block I feel like my lungs are exploding; I can barely breathe. This is not going to be easy, but I'm determined to get in shape. He's the catalyst for change on many levels for me. The Saturn energy in my 9th house of broadening experiences inspires me to try new things that will serve me well in the future.

I meet Byrne at his apartment after work. We make love and he holds me tightly.

A tear drops onto my cheek. I look up at him, startled.

"I had sex with the woman across the court last week." He bursts into tears. "It wasn't anything like what we have together. There was no love. I felt so horrible afterward."

I cradle his face in my neck and stroke his hair. "I'm sorry."

"She told me there was nothing but shattered lives here. I think she's right."

This is crazy. He's just screwed somebody else, and I'm comforting him because he's disappointed. I'm not surprised at his reaction. Byrne isn't the casual sex type. He needs to find that out. There'll be other experiences to convince him.

Byrne walks into the workout room at Selby. It's empty except for a young, attractive girl in her early twenties lifting weights. She looks up and stares at him like a panther surveying a piece of raw meat. Her gaze makes him uncomfortable. He feels himself going into an altered hyper alert state like a rabbit confronted by a mesmerizing cobra. They make polite conversation. He's only partially aware of what they're talking about.

She moves slowly toward him, pulling her pants down, the sexual tension claustrophobic. There's no mistaking her intent. She stands in front of him, smiling in anticipation.

'I can't do this," he tells her and bolts from the room. Outside he breathes deeply. As he tells me later, "She's young enough to be my daughter. What was she thinking? I couldn't have sex like that."

Suzanne is a 32-year-old nurse, a babe in her prime: tall with lush, ripe curves in all the right places. She's a major player in the big game hunt for the ultimate trophy—a doctor husband. Her off-again, on-again romance with Dr. Fields is currently off, and she needs new prey to stalk. Her best friend's doctor husband sets her up with a blind date.

They meet at The Ram. Suzanne walks through the door, her friend's words echoing in her ears: "For God's sake don't have sex with him on the first date." When she sees Byrne Marshall, M.D., her knees buckle, and her hormones shoot that resolve deader than a Mayan mummy. She sits next to him, blowing off enough pheromones to sex up an entire city. The prey catches the scent and goes for the bait. They go to her place.

Faces of Love, Death and Transformation:

Suzanne offers a plethora of sexual possibilities. She suggests pot and poppers to kick off the night's festivities. Byrne declines the poppers, agrees to try a little pot, and they get down to business. The act is quick and conventional. Suzanne figures it's the warm up for the long night of hot sex she's planning. It's not to be.

Byrne tells me later he couldn't get dressed fast enough. He told her he had to go because he may have left his barbecue on and he didn't want to burn the building down. He thanked her and made a hasty exit. The pot made him tired, and he lost interest.

Safely at home in his own bed, he drifted off to sleep with a satisfied smile on his face. Since he hadn't any dinner, he tells me all he could think about was the pot roast and gravy I made for him last week. He can still smell the rich aroma. He sighs, thinking about that first bite of mashed potatoes, smothered in perfect, rich, brown gravy. I smile; Suzanne used the wrong bait.

Byrne calls me at work: "Tell me how to make gravy; I'm doing a pot roast." It isn't Wednesday, so I know he isn't cooking for the boys. He has a date. I hesitate then give him careful instructions on how to do it. I hang up the phone and shake my head. I must be nuts. Patience, I tell myself, patience.

In spite of Byrne's desire to experiment with other women, he makes sure I feel totally loved. He still calls me every day at noon and never stops telling me how much he loves me. Our time together doesn't lessen. He only dates while I'm at work. It softens the pain.

MJ contemplates the frightening possibility that Byrne isn't coming back. She panics and invites him over on the pretext of discussing a problem with the boys. When he arrives, she meets him at the door in a sheer, baby doll negligee and stiletto heels, Ready to fight fire with fire.

Byrne recoils when he sees what's obviously on her agenda. Too little, too late. He beats a hasty retreat and leaves her with a feeling of doom and searing humiliation. It's over.

Neptune burst her last illusionary bubble and false feeling of control, flattening the flimsy foundation of her life like a house of cards. Uranus handed her the hammer, and she nailed her own butt to the wall with her stubborn refusal to get real. But, in retrospect, fate really called the shots on this one. She fulfilled her purpose to show Byrne the meaning of emptiness so he could truly appreciate fullness with me. Their reason for being together is over.

I'm headed to the Nursing Director's office again. Both the Director and Assistant Director wait for me. This doesn't look good. I can tell by the looks on their faces the Furies are back. Denny starts, "We've had some complaints about you from the day shift. They say you're leaking information from the doctor's staff meetings and it's affecting morale."

My eyes turn hard and cold. "Let's make this brief. The only reason I'm here is because I'm dating Dr. Marshall. For the record, we have better things to talk about than what goes on at staff meetings. And even if we did, I wouldn't be so stupid as to share that information and betray his confidence." I note by the look on their faces, they aren't used to such a direct response. "You do have a leak," I continue. "It's Dr. Bouchard. He's a notorious gossip. He sits in the coffee room and tells everybody everything that goes on. If you're really concerned, you need to talk to him."

Denny looks at Anita, the Director, for guidance.

"I think we're done here," Anita announces. "Thank you for the information."

I walk triumphantly back to L&D and take report from the day shift who search for some hint at how the meeting went. I smile brightly for one and all. Women can be such bitches.

May 7, 1977

Byrne is incapable of keeping anything from me. He compulsively tells me everything; it never occurs to him not to. I get past the one night fling with Suzanne. He tells me the whole story and how she called him the next morning in hysterics because he might think badly of her for having sex on the first date. He assured her it wasn't a problem. He tells me he thinks she's highly neurotic. He isn't interested in seeing her again.

The tawny haired, dental hygienist Pam, who lives in the next building, is another story. Byrne seems quite taken by her. This is like my dream in the tiny car with bombs going off all around me. I'm on emotional overload; I need space and distance. I tell Byrne I need a break; I don't want to see him for two weeks. I think if I don't see him I won't think about him. It has the opposite effect.

Faces of Love, Death and Transformation:

May 9, 1977

"Dearest Con,

Since we won't be seeing each other for a few days (it won't seem like a few) I thought I'd keep a diary until we see each other again. I must admit that your refusal to see me has been very upsetting and I think that it's because I feel I'm losing you, yet I have no one to blame but myself.

Today felt like a real downer. I feel an overwhelming desire to confess—to my wife, to the women I've seen, and anyone else who might be available. In short, I don't feel good about myself, or about what I've been doing. I know I've hurt you terribly and at present there is no way to rationalize it by terms such as 'sowing oats.'

I love you,
Byrne

May 10, 1977

Dearest Con,

It was important for me to see you tonight at work because I could tell by your eyes that you still love me. You can probably guess that I've been under some stress, but this is something that I'm trying to deal with and hopefully, I can. I hope that you can tell how much I love you when I see you in Labor & Delivery. I'm sure that everyone else can.

My love always,
Byrne

May 10, 1977

Byrne, my love,

It's the second day of not seeing you. I'm really down today—a mixture of moderate depression and profound sadness. I can't really explain it except to say that you are on my mind constantly.

I think we both needed time away from each other. I feel like you need some time to process your guilt feelings about me. I understand how hard it is for you. You're finally getting to do something you've always wanted to do, but you can't enjoy it because of your love for me—and because of the guilt feelings that get in the way.

I want you to know I'm proud of you for sticking to your belief that this is something you have to do to grow and feel better about yourself. I don't think you could have done this six months ago. The first hint of your making me unhappy would have made you give up. Now you realize that you're just as important, and even if it temporarily makes me unhappy, it will be worth it in the end.

So much has happened in the past ten months. Sometimes I'm overwhelmed with the changes. All my life all I've ever wanted was to have someone love me the way you do and to love you back. I'm still having a hard time realizing it's true.

I wish I were better about expressing my feelings. I envy you because you don't seem to have any problem verbalizing your feelings or expressing your emotions. This is one of your qualities that I most love.

I still can't bring myself to cry in front of you. On Saturday, driving to your apartment, I had tears streaming down my face uncontrollably and I knew when I got there, I would take one look at you and burst into hysterical sobs. Instead, as soon as I knocked on your door, something clicked and I couldn't cry. I still have a hard time lowering my defense mechanisms—even with you. I know I would feel better if I could throw myself in your arms and cry, but when I'm hurt, I just find it too threatening. I'm still four years old and saying, 'It doesn't hurt, and you can't make me cry.'

Wonder if I'll ever get over that?

I was so happy to see you on call tonight. I loved it when you ran your fingers down my back at the nursing station. It's incredible that you can still give me the chills when you touch me. I will remember moments like that until I die. I'm glad you can tell by my eyes that I love you. Sometimes, I feel like I'm wearing a neon sign.

I'm going to sleep feeling much better for having spent the evening with you.

I love you, Byrne
Connie

Faces of Love, Death and Transformation:

May 11, 1977

My Dearest Byrne,

I'm still on a high from last night and seeing you at work. It's amazing how good you make me feel just by looking at me.

I have depended on our daily conversations more than you know. Things would definitely be harder for me to cope with if I didn't have you to hold me and tell me you love me. When you have your arms around me, I feel like nothing really bad can happen to me. It's only one of the reasons I love you so very much.

I almost called you tonight. I miss you so much it's an actual physical ache. When I first decided on the two weeks, I was very tired emotionally and slightly numb. I just didn't want to think about everything that was going on. I thought I could put you out of my mind for a while if I didn't see you or talk to you. Instead, I ended up thinking about you even more, as if that's possible. I couldn't pass up the chance to see you after work tonight. The flesh is weak, especially where you're concerned.

I love you.
Connie

May 16, 1977

Hello my love,

I've been thinking a lot about my sister's comment on how everyone has a peak experience in their life, and for us, it's been each other. I know for me it's very true.

I have come to realize in the last weeks that no matter what happens between us, you will always be the love of my life. I don't see how I could ever duplicate the feelings or the intensity. The incredible part is how real it all is. There are no fairy tale fantasies about who we are. That's part of the reason we've never been disappointed in each other.

I had really given up on finding the kind of love we have. Most people never experience even a part of what we have together. I don't want to ever take any of that for granted.

I love talking to you in the morning before I'm totally awake. You have the softest, sexiest, most intimate voice…there are so many things about you that move me…I keep discovering more all the time.

I'm hopelessly in love with you.

Yours, Connie

May 15, 1977

Dearest Con,

It seems so strange to be writing you a letter when I'll be calling you in about an hour, but it's what I feel like doing. I'm really looking forward to "sleeping over" on Wednesday and seeing the girls. Actually, I've missed them. I don't think I'll feel uncomfortable at all and I'll be able to be with you all night long.

Also, there will be no problems next Saturday when we go to the clinic party and screw anybody who thinks badly of me. The important thing is that I love you so much and am proud to be with you as people will be able to tell.

Your letters were just great. We think so much alike it's frightening sometimes.

My love always,
Byrne

May 17, 1977

It's Byrne's first sleep over, a Wednesday night. At midnight, right on schedule, Stacie and Melissa crawl sleepily into my bed as they've done every night since Eddie left.

Byrne rises from his slumber like a groggy Goliath, "What in the hell is going on?"

"Nothing, babe. Go back to sleep."

I scoop the girls up and head down the hall to their bedrooms. It's time to halt the communal sleeping.

It's still the middle of the night when I hear Byrne's eerily alert voice ask me,

"So, how much did you pay for the wine we had tonight? It was really good."

"What time is it?"

"3 A.M."

"Do you always carry on conversations in the middle of the night?" I ask sleepily.

"I'm a light sleeper."

I groan with dread. I sleep the sleep of the dead.

Byrne's wild oats phase fizzled a little before Venus completed her loop, freeing him to move our relationship forward. Pam Pureheart, as I've come to call her, lasted four dates. She tired of hearing how much Byrne loved me. They parted on amicable terms, but not before she gave him a little something to remember her by.

August 1977

Byrne spends all his free time with me. When he isn't with me, he writes me letters of love and longing. I'm never out of his mind. I can tell he's out of wild oats. In five months at Selby Ranch, he's had sex with a grand total of three women. His Neptunian, illusory adventure wasn't meant to last, but it was important for him not to have any regrets.

Byrne's boys are about to meet my girls and me on our first family date. We take our four kids to see Englebert Humperdinck at the Memorial Auditorium and to dinner at the Pheasant Club in West Sacramento. I've been eating at the 'Pheas' since I was a small child. It occupies a hallowed place in my life. Mom and Dad took us to the Pheas every other Sunday for dinner. Mom worked there as a waitress for three years. I went to school with one of the owner's daughters. The Pheas is famous for their steak sandwiches: thin, tender slices of garlic riddled beef piled between two hot pieces of French bread soaked in garlic butter—pure heaven.
My favorite is the oven-fried chicken, marinated in garlic, rosemary, olive oil, and white wine. The baked skin turns a golden, crispy brown. Mama Palmadessi, a hell of a cook, passed her recipes on to her family.

I sit with Byrne and our kids at the table with the red-checkered cloth and feel a sense of wonder at being together. The kids bond quickly, which will prove to be a blessing and a curse. Brett is 9, Darren 7, Melissa not quite 8, and Stacie 5. We're the Brady Bunch.

MJ is apoplectic at losing control. She crawls into a sleeping bag on the dining room floor and stays there until friends take her to Sutter Memorial Hospital and check her into the psych ward for severe depression.

Byrne moves home temporarily to take care of the boys. I don't have much sympathy for MJ. Rich women can afford nervous breakdowns. The rest of us have to get off our butts and go to work to support our kids. I know I'm not being compassionate, but it's how I feel.

October 10, 1977

Byrne's mother arrives from Michigan for a visit and to help him with the boys for a couple of days. I wait for Alyce to deplane with trepidation. She's a formidable woman according to her doting son. Alyce had tuberculosis as a teenager, and her doctors told her if she got pregnant, she would surely die. Alyce, thirty when she married Bob, wanted babies, and what Alyce wants, Alyce gets. She navigated the pregnancy like a woman on a tight rope, putting one foot carefully in front of the other, keeping her eye on the destination. She proved them all wrong, not once, but twice. I like that.

I fret: this is a very awkward situation. Byrne's still married. MJ is in the psych ward, and the "other woman" is picking his mother up at the airport. Alyce and Bob know about me; Byrne visited them in early September to tell them about the impending divorce and being in love with me.

I don't know what Alyce looks like, but I know the small, white haired woman in the designer knit pantsuit is Byrne's mother. She has the same kind of aura: elegant and authoritative. Byrne has her mouth and eyes.

I greet Alyce who smiles warmly at me like a co-conspirator. She tucks her arm through mine: "Let's go get a drink and talk."

It's noontime, but I take her to La Casita where she orders a Perfect Manhattan, just like Byrne. She wastes no time in telling me she never liked Mary Jean—too little and too dark. "She's half Puerto Rican you know," she intones gravely. "She's adopted, so God only knows what else she is."

Alyce studies my blond hair and green eyes. "Now you, you're tall and obviously Swedish, or something splendid like that. You and Byrne would have had beautiful children. Such a shame."

Byrne must have told Alyce he'd tied my tubes and there wouldn't be any babies together. I agree it's a shame.

Alyce's eyes narrow. "I knew there was big trouble last time we visited. Mary Jean stood at the kitchen window for hours staring into space. She got drunk before dinner and passed out."

I plan to drop Alyce at the house and head for work, but she insists I come in to see the horrible decorating MJ's done. We survey the entry hall and the flamboyant foil and flocked wallpaper. "Look at that," Alyce clucks disdainfully. "They should have put that decorator in the insane asylum with Mary Jean. Isn't that the worst thing you've ever seen?" I sense she isn't looking for feedback.

Alyce marches to the master bedroom and starts going through MJ's things, much to my discomfort. "Where is it?" She's rummaging through each drawer until she clutches the prize, a black beaded evening purse. "Here, you take it. I gave this to her years ago, and I'm taking it back." I flash back to Eddie's mother and her list. It must be a mother-in-law thing.

It's an order. I take the bag. She turns and looks at the bed. "How could he ever be a husband to her again after where she's been?"

She doesn't expect an answer. Byrne is right; his mother is formidable.

October 1977

> We're going on a trip. Venus and Mars join us for another romance filled trip. Neptune, the ultimate tropical god, hitches a ride with my Mars. Venus trailing Byrne's Mars, before linking up with Jupiter, promises an orgy of steamy passion and glorious fun. Jupiter, now in Byrne's 7th house of relationships, encourages him to expand and deepen his relationship with me.

All is right in the heavens: MJ's home after three weeks of in-house therapy. Alyce flies back to Michigan. Byrne moves back to Selby Ranch.

It's my last day at work before going on vacation. After report, the day shift lingers, circling like buzzards. "Are you going somewhere on your time off, or staying home?" Fran wants to know. They're all terminally curious about my private life.

"I'm going away."

"Where?"

I pause for effect. "Tahiti."

I savor the profound silence. They know I have to be going with Dr. Marshall. Their long held hopes that he'd dump me have come to naught. I celebrate their bitter defeat.

Los Angles, California
October 15, 1977

The plane lifts off, airborne out of LAX. I'm too excited to think. I'm grateful Christine, my faithful sitter, could stay with the girls. I'm feeling a little guilty about leaving them; I haven't been away from them this long before. I'm on my way to Tahiti with Byrne. We'll have ten romantic days together. I think of it as our honeymoon. We kiss and make out like a couple of horny teenagers all the way to Papeete under the watchful eye of a nervous flight attendant.

The hotel, a fantasy come true, clings onto a cliff hanging over the ocean. Our spacious room and generous balcony overlook Cook's Bay. The spectacular view sparks my senses of sight, sound and smell. I stand at the railing and survey the black sand beach below, smell the salty air and listen to the waves roll toward the shore—the balmy weather perfect for making love.

We waste no time. The headboard bangs loudly under the assault of our enthusiastic thrashing and bouncing, so we pull the mattress onto the floor. We eat Mahi Mahi, drink perfect Perfects and dance. Byrne relaxes his prohibition on my being in his space. The music and the closeness of our bodies arouse intensely romantic feelings between us. We lose ourselves in the erotic energy, kissing briefly, keeping perfect rhythm, oblivious to anything and anyone else.

Byrne teaches me to snorkel and body surf. I shriek with joy as the waves gather me up and race me to shore like an out of control bottle rocket on the 4th of July. I feel like a child again, light, happy, free. We jog barefoot on the black sand beach together and walk miles holding hands.

I sit at poolside watching Byrne. He swims his 100 laps with hypnotic grace. His arms move in slow motion in and out of the water, the strong muscles in his back glistening. The water yields to his movements, barely rippling as he glides through the water. I can't take my eyes off him. I've never felt this way about anyone before. This love between us touches a place so deep in me I never dreamed it existed.

On the flight home, Byrne asks if he can move in with the girls and me—the perfect ending to a perfect trip. He's made it to the bus at the top of the hill.

Chapter 15

January 14, 1978

> **Jupiter visits my 9th house, ruling higher education and universities, encouraging growth and expansion. My Higher Self has my future in mind. Uranus on Byrne's Moon signifies big changes in his domestic life. Venus on my Moon makes it a good thing.**

The wind blows relentlessly under threatening, gray skies. Intermittent showers pelt the ground. Byrne and the four kids drive back and forth between Selby Ranch and the Cruz Way house; it's moving day.

I push myself against the strong wind, working my way across the parking lot at Sac State. I finished my Bachelor's degree last year and now I'm taking the GRE for grad school. I smile, thinking about Byrne's reaction when I told him I wanted to get my Master's degree.

He looked at me in disbelief. "Are you crazy? You'll never have to work another day in your life when we get married. Why would you want to do that?"

"I know, but this is my just in case. If something happens to you, I don't want to have to work weekends as a staff nurse and beg for Christmas Eve off to be with my girls like I did last year. I just need to do this."

He put his arms around me and hugged me. "Okay, Con, sweetheart. If it means that much to you, I'll do whatever you want me to do to help."

"Speaking of marriage, I hope you don't expect me to be a typical doctor's wife. I won't go to teas, join the Cerebral Palsy Guild and do all that society stuff."

"I wouldn't want you to. I'm glad you're not interested in that whole scene. It's all MJ ever thought about. I still remember how upset she was when the Junior League turned her down."

Blending a family is a bloody bitch. The kids like each other, but they're not so sure about our relationship and what it all means for them. Brett, the nine year old, stirs up major shit. Like Uranus, he loves creating chaos. Even at his young age, he has a certain power and presence. Add intelligence and a simmering pot of hostility, stirred constantly by Mary Jean, and we've got the makings of a major uprising.

MJ tells the boys that I seduced their father into running off with me. Like Eddie, she's not big on accepting responsibility for her role in the failure of the marriage. Brett has a right to be angry. His life has been turned upside down. He didn't ask for any of this. He takes up his mother's cause. There is nothing more vicious than a little Virgo on the warpath. I don't take it personally. He directs most of his anger at Byrne.

Melissa likes Byrne until she runs into his Saturn-like discipline and structure side. The karma between them simmers. Byrne is everything Melissa needs and everything she doesn't want. I feel her wrath. She scornfully points out to me that Byrne is too tall, his socks show when he sits down, and if I marry him, she will run away—and not kiss him goodnight.

Darren's mischievous Gemini talks constantly and laughs like Woody Woodpecker. He lives in the large shadow of his older brother, always looking for his own place in the sun. He finds it as a double agent, reporting what MJ says about us. He gives her the scoop on Dad and "that woman."

Stacie loves Byrne from the beginning. She embraces his quiet strength, stability and kindness. He's the father she needs and wants. She loves him for all the reasons her mother loves him.

I think about when Stacie was born: Byrne came into my room the morning after I delivered to congratulate me. Little did we know then he would become Stacie's father.

I work the day shift this weekend, and we have all four kids. It's up to Byrne to ride herd. I breeze through the door at 3:30 P.M. to the sounds of crashing, banging, squealing, screaming and laughing. Byrne sprawls on the couch in the living room with his arm across his eyes. He looks shell-shocked, battle fatigued. "Thank God you're home!" He leaps from the couch and runs to me. "You don't know what it's been like all day—the screaming and noise. It never stops."

Byrne hates noise. He told his mother at age six he never wanted another birthday party because the kids were too loud. Brett's done an admirable job whipping the troops into a major frenzy. The girls adore him, and he's delighted them by punching Darren in the stomach, making him cry.

I cook chicken for dinner. Brett looks at his plate, "Is this what we're having?" he asks with contempt.

Byrne leaps to his feet, grabs Brett by the arm, drags him to Stacie's room and shoves him through the door. "How dare you insult Con's cooking. Stay in there until morning. No dinner!" He slams the door and returns to the table.

Later in bed, we hold each other for comfort like a couple of hostages in a war zone. The three kids raid the refrigerator and smuggle food to Brett. It's their first bonding experience with more to come.

December 24, 1977

Byrne and I have the kids tonight. We know this is an important milestone, spending our first Christmas together. Tension rides high on all sides. Brett sulks. Darren looks wary. The girls wait to see what's going to happen. To Byrne's horror, I hand each child a can of snow. The energy changes instantly. Brett's eyes light up, Darren grins, and the girls squeal with excitement. The chaos begins. They empty the cans. Snow blankets the Christmas tree, the walls, the rug and the kids. I'm smug at my foresight. Byrne thinks I've lost my mind. The kids are happier than I've ever seen them. They will remember this Christmas as their ultimate bonding experience. It becomes a treasured family memory.

January 1978

We're home alone; I'm off this weekend. We've just finished making love. Byrne puts his hand on my abdomen and looks perplexed. "Your uterus is enlarged." He's alarmed. He takes both hands and palpates the large lump. "I want you to go see Bouchard on Monday. I bet you've got some fibroids. Time to get that thing out of there. Tell him you want your ovaries out, too. I don't want anything happening to you."

Bouchard agrees: I have major fibroids. Nothing to be alarmed about, but in time my periods will rival the Jonestown flood. I can wait or just do it now. He mentions he needs to give me a prescription for the hemophilus vaginal infection I have.

I look at him, my mind trying to register what he just told me. "Wait a minute—are you telling me I have a sexually transmitted disease?"

"Ah, yes." He's uneasy. "Lots of people have hemophilus these days."

"Well, there's only one place I could have gotten it." I'm angry. "I told him if he was going to fool around while he was at Selby, he'd better use something."

I burst through the doors between the clinic and postpartum and run into Byrne. He smiles at me and asks how the appointment went.

"What do you want to hear about first? My fibroid uterus or the hemophilus you gave me?" I'm furious.

Byrne looks dazed and utters a contrite. "Oh, oh."

"A little parting gift from Pam Pureheart, I presume?" I leave him standing there.

He's in bed when I get home from work. I don't say anything, settle into bed and keep my back to him.

"I'm sorry. You want me to move out?"

"No, I'll get over it."

Byrne slides himself to my side of the bed and puts an arm around my waist. I wait a few seconds before I put my hand over his. I can't stay mad at him.

Kaiser Hospital
February 27, 1978

The surgery orderly puts me on the gurney. Byrne holds my hand and looks down at me. Tears fill his eyes. He stands in the hallway, watching me as the gurney turns the corner.

I'm in the recovery room. I hear Byrne's voice. I try to open my eyes.

"Con, sweetheart. Wake up. It's me." He kisses my lips gently. "I love you. The surgery's over; everything is fine."

I smile and reach for his hand, then drift off to sleep again.

I'm Byrne's landlady. We agree on four hundred dollars a month for bed and board, sex included, laundry not. He pays an extra hundred to keep his Cordoba in the garage.

We make minor adjustments. After a night on call he needs sex to release the cumulative tension. The residents call it the "after call hots." And he snores from the exhaustion. When Eddie snored, I'd punch him. Once in frustration, I straddled him, trying to stifle the noise with a pillow over his face. With Byrne, I touch his shoulder, tenderly stroke his bottom and say, "Turn over, sweetheart." It works.

I keep the food coming. A typical breakfast includes well-cooked bacon, eggs, hash brown potatoes, English muffins, orange juice and half a grapefruit, polished off with cinnamon rolls and peanut butter slathered over the top. His fried eggs have to be almost well done with just a hint of soft yolk to dunk his toast. His scrambled eggs have to be fluffy. I'm in awe of his appetite, amazed his weight remains at 198. After years of Cheerios on the run while MJ slept, Byrne is in heaven.

I cater to all his culinary quirks. He has to have Heinz catsup, Laura Scudder's Natural Creamy Peanut Butter, Yuban coffee and potatoes—lots of potatoes cooked in every imaginable way. He wants hamburgers once a week and meatloaf the way MJ makes it twice a month. Our double agent finds her recipe, copies it and smuggles it to me. I'm not proud.

And then there's chocolate. To Byrne, there isn't any other kind of dessert; it has to be chocolate. Apple pie is the only exception. I try cherry pie; he looks at it with complete desolation in his eyes. "This is a cruel hoax," he declares.

Living with Byrne is a revelation. He loves helping me and actually enjoys doing house projects together. I marvel at his unfailing good humor and patience. Our years of teamwork at the hospital work at home, too. He loves making lists of things to do together then checking them off—very anal.

We don't agree on television. He doesn't watch it, feels it's a waste of productive time. I argue he needs to learn to enjoy something that's totally frivolous with no socially redeeming value. I force him to watch Laverne and Shirley. To my amazed delight, he bonds with Squiggy and Lenny. I gradually add The Bob Newhart Show, Mary Tyler Moore and MASH. I love hearing him laugh.

I work part time on the day shift now. Fran and her crew are resigned to the reality that Byrne and I are a permanent couple. He comes down to L&D at lunchtime with the food I make for him and heats it in the microwave. The smells permeate the department, inviting hungry queries as to what delicacy I've prepared for him that day. I happily list the menu of the day for the envious residents forced to eat Kaiser food.

July 1978

Byrne and I jog on the levee a block from my house, overlooking the Sacramento River. The morning perspires in anticipation of a sweltering afternoon. The air hangs heavy and still. After two miles, we slow to a leisurely walk to cool off.

"I've decided to resign as residency director."

I stop short. "Why? That's been your baby."

"I know, but I don't want to do it anymore. All that time I spent doing research, publishing, running the residency program, I was trying to fill a void. I don't need it anymore. Now, all I want to do is spend my time with you." He puts his arm around me and pulls me close. "There's something else I want to do," he smiles, kissing my forehead. "I want to go house hunting."

I don't know what to say. The thought of moving makes me anxious. I love my house. The girls wouldn't be happy leaving their friends. "I don't know, honey, If something happened to you, I wouldn't be able to afford an expensive house. I won't move my girls again."

"How about this: I'll take out an insurance policy on myself with you as the beneficiary, say $250,000? Will that make you feel okay?"

He always knows how to make me feel safe and loved. "Remember your birthday dinner when I asked you about starting a retirement plan? What were you thinking when you shook your head no?"

"I was thinking that I'd always take care of you. I'd find a way, no matter what."

I put my arms around his waist and rest my head on his chest. I silently vow to always take care of him, no matter what. I'm not yet aware of the Kentucky life where I abandoned him when he was my father and the karmic debt I incurred. All I know is: I won't ever let him down.

"Sweetheart, as soon as my divorce is final, we'll be married and none of this will be an issue. I want us to have a house that's ours. Prince Charming wants to move Cinderella to a proper castle."

Faces of Love, Death and Transformation:

Chapter 16

Fair Oaks, California
August 31, 1978

The moving van pulls out of the driveway on Cruz Way, heading to Lafitte Court in Fair Oaks, a suburb in the north area. I find it ironic that our new house is less than a quarter mile from the wedding chapel where Eddie and I were married. I pile the four kids in my car and follow. Byrne is working.

As I direct the movers where to put things, a florist van drives up. The driver hands me a bouquet of roses. The card reads: "*To my Cinderella—thanks for taking care of the move. I love you always, Prince Charming.*"

I smile with delighted surprise. I read the card several times, brushing my fingers over the words, letting them sink in. I put the card in my purse and carry it with me until the words blur from my fondling and the paper frays from reading it over and over.

Our new house sits on the crest of a hill in a subdivision called Brittany Hills. It's a thousand feet bigger than the Cruz Way house: two stories, four bedrooms, a huge family room with a 22 foot ceiling, a large stone fireplace and sliding glass doors off the balcony that run the entire length of the house. A loft, with a fireplace and wet bar, sits at the top of the stairs. From the loft, you can see the grammar school a half-mile away. The large master bedroom with a balcony overlooks the bare back yard. The adjacent property in the back, still rural, teems with the neighbor's sheep, geese and chickens. A dilapidated chicken coop adds to the Green Acres ambiance.

I settle the girls into their new rooms. Melissa requires only a kiss goodnight. Stacie demands the same exacting ritual each night. I have to place every stuffed animal she owns in bed with her, each one in their special place. Miss Taurus must have her security objects. With everyone in proper position, I kiss my contented child and say goodnight.

Byrne sleeps. As I slip into bed, he reaches out, pulls me to him and holds me silently. He rests my face in his neck, his hand holding the back of my head. After a moment, he releases me, falling back to sleep still holding my hand. He will repeat this same ritual every night of our life together. It's like a meditation for me. No matter what goes on during the day, the moment he gathers me in his arms at bedtime, everything in my skewed world moves back to a centered peace.

The sound of clanking sheep bells, cackling geese and a crowing rooster wakens us.

Byrne sits up in bed. "What in the hell is all that racket? We've moved to a goddamn zoo."

I smile at my city boy. "Relax. Give it a few more nights and you won't hear it anymore, honey."

I love the house and the neighborhood. We both agreed we didn't want to live in the designated doctor and lawyer ghettos on the American River. We've met our next door neighbors the Berrys, Ken and Sandy. He coaches football at a local high school and Sandy sells real estate. "Coach" beams with delight when he discovers that "Doc" recites football statistics like a pro. We become instant, life-long friends. We were meant to be here.

Stacie and Melissa react differently to moving. Stacie eagerly plunges into this new world. At heart, she's a little princess and feels at home in the castle. She isn't as bonded to the old neighborhood as her sister. Melissa falls into a noticeable depression. She's already unhappy with me for allowing Byrne into our lives, and now this. She determinedly refuses to accept it—any of it. I watch her with a mother's sadness. I know it's traumatic for her to move, but I pray she'll see it's for the best.

I sell the Cruz Way house back to Eddie for less than I could have gotten on the open market. I leave a lot of the furniture, but he's furious I took the refrigerator. He calls to scream at me. I ignore him. I like the idea of the girls going back to the old neighborhood every other weekend. Everybody can be happy. I want so much for everybody to be happy.

September 1978

I get up three mornings a week at 4 A.M., drive downtown to the Greyhound bus depot and take the 6 A.M. bus to San Francisco. It's an hour and ten minute trip, another twenty minutes on the Muni up the hill to UC San Francisco. I'm in grad school. I do this for two years.

I struggle with transient guilt about the time it takes away from the girls and Byrne, but he makes it as easy for me as possible. He never complains. It's Byrne's nature to encourage developing potential; he does it for everyone.

I'm not used to being nurtured. The mornings I'm home, Byrne gets up, makes coffee and brings it to me in bed. He's learned exactly how much sugar and cream I like. He knows I'm a slow starter, so he gently wakens me and sits on the bed with me while I sip my coffee and clear the cobwebs from my sleep drenched brain. He tells me he wakes at night to watch me sleep. I'm so touched by his tender thoughtfulness, I can't do enough for him.

On my school days, Byrne gets the kids up and off to school. He has dinner waiting when I get home. He always greets me with a huge smile and a hug, happy to see me and share our day. It's important to me that we eat dinner together every night. It's the one treasured memory of childhood that stays with me. I want my girls to have those memories. Byrne grew up the same way.

Each night at dinner he asks the girls what was the best part of their day. He has a question every evening, something to do with history or geography, like what's the longest river in the country. Whoever gets it right, gets a prize. At first, the girls moan in agony when he quizzes them about anything. As time goes by, they began to enjoy sharing their day; the days of Eddie's temper tantrums at the dinner table and my endless tears blissfully gone.

The boys come on Wednesdays and every other weekend. We go to the Pheas for dinner, listen to Abba and the Michigan Marching Band on the Cordoba's eight-track tapes. Byrne remains a rabid Wolverine fan after 12 years at the University of Michigan. All things Michigan become a part of our lives. I come to understand the depth of his athletic passion and learn to decipher screams of agony over a fumble from cries of ecstasy over a touchdown.

I couldn't have picked a better role model for my girls than Byrne. Stacie tells me she wants to marry someone just like Byrne: fun, funny, smart, sweet and a little bit out there, but not too far. He takes Stacie to his stylist for a haircut and takes pictures to commemorate the event. He teaches her how to ride her bike. He drives Melissa to modeling lessons and surprises her with private singing lessons. He looks for ways to nurture their special talents. He never forgets an occasion, buying thoughtful presents for each of us that he wraps himself. They look like a first grader did the job, with layers of scotch tape, ragged edges and bows askew. It's endlessly endearing. It makes up for the peanut butter.

Byrne has a major thing for peanut butter. Each new jar demands the same ritual of mixing, a laborious, messy task. The girls dread it, running through the house like Paul Revere announcing the coming of the British: "*Run! Byrne's mixing a new jar of peanut butter!*"

First, he inserts a fork into the morass of oil and peanuts, stirring forcefully. The oil drips over the edge of the jar like lava from an erupting volcano. A knife severs the peanut butter back into the jar; he stirs over and over until the surgery is a success. And, just like a doctor after surgery, he leaves the mess for someone else to clean up. That's the girls' job; it's why they run.

We collaborate on the spaghetti sauce. I have my time-honored recipe from Eddie's Aunt Cassie. A labor of love that requires grinding meat and vegetables and simmering the sauce for hours. Byrne loves his mother's recipe made with Ragu. We compromise and combine the two. Byrne helps by chopping onions, wearing swim goggles to keep the tears away. The kids think we're hopeless.

We furnish our house with amalgamated leftovers that are uncomfortable in their new home. Styles clash instead of mesh. MJ took everything but a few castoffs she didn't want, like the Margaret Keane painting, a large, colorful rendition of three depressed looking, pissed-off teenagers. The kids and I dub it "the ugly picture." Over the years, we come to think of it fondly, but we still think it's ugly. I brought a few pieces from the Cruz Way house, but we are happy to start over together.

August, 1979

MJ moves the boys to Florida to live with someone she met at a Club Med in Cancun. She had her choice of several suitors but we think she chose the one who would put the most miles between the boys and Byrne. This is the consequence for the changes he's made. My heart aches for him, his worst fears realized. Change always carries a price. He's devastated, but he'd been expecting something like this. Still, he wouldn't change all that has happened. It had to be. He believes in fate and that we were meant to be together.

Byrne gets chest pain every day. He eats aspirin like candy. The stress at the clinic builds relentlessly. Kaiser expects their doctors to see a patient every 15 minutes. There isn't enough time; it makes the day frantic. His patients complain they can't get appointments. He resorts to having them send him postcards, and he makes their appointments for them. It doesn't work for him anymore. It's not the way he wants to practice medicine. Uranus feeds his unrest and the need for more change.

I begin to recognize when Byrne is truly stressed: when he can't control the big things, he goes for the little things.

"Mom! Melissa wails in anguish, standing in front of me in a towel, dripping wet. "He put a low flow valve on our shower. There's hardly any water. You've got to stop him. First it's a water saver on the toilet, now this!"

Stacie is equally upset when Byrne puts a timer in the bathroom and sets it for 10 minutes at the commencement of each shower. When the timer goes off, he starts banging on the door. He's putting an end to hour-long showers. I try not to laugh.

I know he's out of control when I find him in the side yard erecting a clothesline.

"We have a clothes dryer; why are you putting that thing up?"

"Because, dryers cost money. It's cheaper to dry things naturally."

Stacie stands behind me with a look of disgust. "All our clothes will smell like dirt. Byrne!" The little princess isn't into conservation.

Fate steps in again and Uranus brings disruption: Doctor Ben Berry's partner dies unexpectedly. Byrne plots his escape. He never considered leaving Kaiser before, but this seems right. A beneficent Jupiter angle to Byrne's Sun brings opportunity. Synchronicity is a wonderful thing.

The move frightens him to the core of all his insecurities about money, change and the unknown, but he knows he has to do it. He tells me as long as he has me, he can do anything.

Byrne and Kaiser never fit well. His peers didn't accept him. They envied and feared his ambition and his intellect. His seminal paper on the dangers of the Dalkon Shield made him a national expert, and they resented him for it. Being the current President of the Northern California Obstetrical Society only added to their ire.

Ten years to the month, Byrne leaves Kaiser. No one gives him a going away party; no one says good-bye. He doesn't notice; he's already moved on.

Ben Berry, M.D. rejoices in welcoming Byrne to his practice. It's a coup and they're a good match. Ben's current wife Donna, the interior decorator and ultimate social climber, welcomes Byrne, too. Me—she's not so sure. She doesn't know what to make of me; I don't fit the doctor wife mold, and I take mild delight in annoying her with my total lack of interest in social matters and keeping up appearances.

Byrne blossoms. The nurses at American River and Mercy San Juan hospitals fall in love with him. He's a good doctor. He's kind and sweet; he loves nurses and he's gorgeous. He treats them as peers; he's totally unlike any of the other doctors. Private practice agrees with him. It's like moving to a new town and starting over as a virgin. The changes he's made in his personal life now move to his professional one. He lets his old reserved persona from Kaiser fall away like the caterpillar emerging from the chrysalis as the butterfly. His transformation continues to unfold under the guidance of his Self and the workings of Uranus.

November 1979

I'm studying for an exam. Byrne calls, "How about if we get married on Friday, December 7?"

"I can't do that; I have class that Friday."

"Do you think you could play hooky one day to marry me?"

I crash land to earth and smile brightly at my unthinking idiocy. "Yes. I'd love to marry you—anytime, anywhere."

"I'll take care of all the details. Keep studying, sweetheart. I love you."

We've waited two long years for Byrne's divorce to be final. It doesn't seem real. I wonder what I've done to be this lucky.

December 7, 1979

> Our wedding day: Venus and Jupiter join each other again as they have in previous memorable events for Byrne and me. Mars occupies the same position as he had that fateful first lunch in 1976, signifying new beginnings. A harmonious Mars link with Jupiter and Venus promises abundance, sex, affection, romance and enjoying life together— diametrically opposite of the planetary energies when I married Eddie.
>
> It's a fortuitous combination, foreshadowing our marriage will be metaphysical, having the elements of intellectual, mental, and spiritual exploration. It's a journey we were meant to share. A Sun-Neptune conjunction in the heavens fuels our relationship bringing a mystical, psychic, romantic, past lives, eternal love dimension that will come into to consciousness over the years.

Judge Puglia, an old friend of Byrne's, marries us at the State Capitol Court House Library. Melissa, Stacie, Joan and her girls, my brother Graydon and his fiancé Barbara witness our long awaited special day. The cavernous, wood paneled room and soaring ceiling echo with our vows. I cry through the ceremony. Byrne smiles through his tears; we hold hands tightly as we exchange vows. It's been a long journey. We go to the Pheas for dinner afterward.

The next day, Byrne coordinates the reception at our house. He arranges everything: music, dancing, food, friends, neighbors and family. We dance in our unfurnished family room. Guests roam the newly landscaped back yard with its sparkling pool and sports court.

The girls didn't want Eddie to feel left out so I invite him. I invite Richard, too; we'd made peace with each other the year before. He called and said he wasn't coming because he "had things to take care of." It doesn't occur to me it might be too painful for him. Karen makes the trip from San Diego to be here.

We didn't plan a honeymoon; we don't need one. Nothing could top our trip to Tahiti two years ago. No honeymoon could be more perfect than that.

Faces of Love, Death and Transformation:

Fair Oaks, California
June 1980

Summers bring mixed blessings. I don't have school, and the boys are with us for the entire summer. Byrne obsesses over food even more than usual. He's sure MJ isn't feeding the boys enough. His noon phone call always starts with questions about what the kids had for breakfast and what's for dinner. And will there be enough potatoes? He wants me to weigh them weekly to make sure they're gaining weight. The eating contests they hold nightly guarantee it. Watching them eating their way through a mountain of tacos, or a mile high pile of mashed potatoes swimming in gravy makes their father a happy man. For Byrne, food is love.

Brett is already tall for a 13 year old, gangly and gawky. He's extremely self-conscious and sensitive. His biological father, a college basketball player, destines Brett will be even taller than Byrne. He has a strong face that will ultimately be quite handsome: an aquiline nose, full lips, expressive brown eyes and thick, curly, light brown hair. His fiery temper lends a penchant for violence, usually directed at his smaller, younger brother.

Darren is almost pretty. His blue eyes, curly lashes, fair skin and baby fine dark blond hair make him look like a kewpie doll. Considerably smaller than Brett, he's a fearless risk taker, constantly looking for attention, always ready to do what no one else will, like jumping off the Berry's roof into a pile of sand in the driveway. He takes great delight in provoking Brett to overt hysteria, even though he knows he'll take a beating for it.

The four kids make an interesting mix: Brett and Stacie bond immediately. Brett declares himself Stacie's protector. No one messes with Stacie or they face the wrath of her "lawyer," as he refers to himself. Melissa loves Brett. He makes her laugh raucously and often. The three of them conspire, and Darren often ends up odd man out.

Starved for attention, Darren has learned how to be charming and ingratiating with adults. He's also devious, secretive, frequently untruthful and prone to petty thievery. The kid has some serious character flaws, but I optimistically think with some guidance he can be steered in the right direction.

Much to our dismay, the four kids refuse to play with anyone else but each other. They prefer to stay in the house, causing constant pandemonium. After several weeks of daily non-stop chaos, I order them outside with instructions to wait out there until Byrne gets home, then lock the door. On arrival, he finds Stacie and Brett stretched out side-by-side on the lawn in a crucifixion pose; Melissa curled up on the doorstep in the fetal position, and Darren lying in the gutter. They all brandish their most pathetic looks.

"Dad!" Brett whines. "Con wouldn't let us in the house. We've been out here for hours in the heat. Can we come in now?"

The four kids run into the house ahead of Byrne, whooping and laughing at Brett chanting "Ancient Chinese Urn." It doesn't matter what he says, the other three think it's hilarious. He's like an evil monk with supernatural powers.

I look at Byrne wordlessly.

"I know, sweetheart. I know," Byrne says hugging me. "You are so wonderful. God, I love you."

I melt and cling to him. He's irresistible.

"Come on. I'll make you a perfect Perfect, my love. The world will look better. I promise."

Faces of Love, Death and Transformation:

Chapter 17

August 1980

> Saturn passing over my natal Neptune pushes me to get serious about my spiritual progress.

The high of finishing grad school wanes quickly. I have a new yearning, not unlike when I wanted to have babies. My experience of love yearns to expand. Byrne's love healed my father issues and filled the void in my heart. Being a mother and my girl's love healed my mother issues. Now, I'm longing to forge a connection to a greater whole, to experience love at the transcendent, spiritual level. My search for cosmic unity begins when I have my natal chart done by Charlsie Gillespie of Atlanta, Georgia. It changes my life.

I know nothing about astrology, so the process is a total mystery. I don't understand about planets and what that all means, but Charlsie's soft, Southern drawl leads me down a path I find fascinating. This woman seems to know exactly who I am, never having met me or talked to me. She describes my childhood experiences and my parents with eerie accuracy; she talks to me about my past lives, my lessons for this life, the challenges and the opportunities, and my destiny. Some of it makes sense, some of it doesn't.

"Your chart is the most spiritual one I've done in a while, and I am deeply aware of your space. Only an old soul would be allowed to take on the challenges you've chosen for this life. You have the opportunity to attain the Christ-like consciousness in this life and escape the wheel of karma.

You came into this life with a unique combination of very powerful creative and healing energies. You have a quintile in your chart, a planetary aspect that the Greek mystery schools used to identify gifts a soul brings in with them from past lives to use in this life. It's more than just a talent; it's a creative artistry of the soul. These latent gifts don't become available until the person reaches a certain maturity, discovers what they've come to do and heed that inner calling.

This gift will have you dealing with those energies in a way uniquely your own, working with the deepest forces of transformation, growth and individuation—the Phoenix-like Pluto transformative energy that's very powerful at an intellectual level, delving into the mysteries of life and understanding the dynamics between people. You have the ability and potential power to deeply impact people's lives.

Water is symbolic of emotions, and you have no water in your chart, so the challenge to learn certain emotional lessons is in place and critical to your growth on a soul level. The mental and emotional makeup in your chart is very challenging for someone whose chief lesson is to learn compassion. Aquarius has a humanitarian, global kind of compassion. As an air sign, it's mental, rather than heart centered. Compassion requires a heart connection; not an easy task for someone who comes in with the confidence you have, the strong judgments, an intolerance of other's shortcomings and the sharp-tongued impatience of the Capricorn/Sagittarius connection. The dark night of your ego will not go quietly into the light,

Your house of children is badly afflicted. One child will cause you great stress, wanting you to give and give and not appreciating it. There will be major challenges there.

Venus in Capricorn gives you wisdom beyond your years. You take relationships seriously. There's a great aversion to rejection, so you're cautious not to let your feelings be known until you feel safe emotionally

In 1974 or 75, you went through something that was very difficult. That happening had to do with ages 5 to 10 and 12 to 13. The event might have been different, but it dredged up a childhood situation of something you couldn't do anything about, so when 1974 came along, you had the same type of reaction, pain and stress.

From past lives, you came with a great deal of authority, creative talent, confidence and determination. In past lives, you didn't appreciate what people did for you. Karmically, you've received, now you have to give. You're learning to sacrifice yourself for the needs of other people. Now, you've got to balance how it feels to give and receive. Your role for this life is to be a kind of fairy godmother, instilling confidence in others so they can develop themselves. This fairy godmother type energy in your 10th house demands you give service to others. If you try to use it for your own self-gratification, it'll cause you pain and trouble.

The hardships and loss you experience in this life have to do with the father, causing you to pull men into your life to resolve this father situation. The men would be difficult and cause you pain and suffering. At some point in your life, you could become the sole provider for the family, being both mother and father to your children. The disharmony in your 7th house means more than one marriage, but before you die, *there will be a very spiritual marriage with someone like a minister or a doctor.*

In this incarnation, you've come to deal with writing, the public and publishing. People will be more receptive to what you have to say when they see it in books as opposed to telling them.

Well, darlin', I wish you good luck on your journey and send you love and light."

I listen to those tapes numerous times, taking notes. I don't get the spiritual part; I'm not religious, but it's the only kind of spirituality I know at this point.

Her comments on 1974 relating to ages five, ten, twelve and thirteen give me chills. My Gramma died when I was six and my other grandmother when I was thirteen. I found her dying in the bathroom of a massive stroke, major trauma—then Bobby dying in 1974. How could she know these things?

The emotional aspects she describes are dead on. The past lives thing is intensely intriguing. I'd like to know more about that. Little do I know then that past lives will play a major role in my search for Spirit.

The writing and publishing thing I discount. I don't see the prenatal book I wrote for Byrne's practice as a career. I'm not interested in that; I see myself as a nurse, not a writer. But in time, her prediction pans out: my prenatal guide, From Here To Maternity, ends up selling over 2 million copies without being in bookstores by finding a niche in the healthcare and insurance industry. Other books follow, and I make the transition from nurse to writer.

The spiritual marriage is obviously with Byrne; I'm impressed it shows up in my chart. It only validates for me the special connection we have. I see the father connection with both Richard and Byrne. Like my father, I couldn't breach Richard's emotional wall, but it's different with Byrne. In him, I see that part of my father who wasn't loved or appreciated by the woman he was married to—a man who desperately wanted to be loved. I couldn't do that for my father, but I can for Byrne. He's given me the opportunity to heal that part of myself, and him in the process.

The difficult, unappreciative child is Melissa. She's a handful and becoming more so all the time. I'm dreading puberty.

The pieces to my life puzzle are there; I just have to connect them to get the big picture, to find my way to that connection, the ultimate love I yearn for.

Faces of Love, Death and Transformation:

Chapter 18

I've always believed in past lives. Pluto in my natal 8th house makes the concept irresistible as Pluto loves to dig and probe and the 8th house is about the mystery of death and what lies beyond. As a child, I read Greek mythology and religions of the world. Reincarnation made perfect sense to me. It's time to explore.

Sacramento, California
April 21, 1981

My new job as a Clinical Specialist at The Perinatal Center requires I spend a week in orientation, enduring the boredom of visits to all the departments in the hospital. I'm one of a small group of new employees touring the personnel department.

My mind wanders. A calendar on the wall catches my eye. The picture jolts me. It's the picture of the house I saw in my mind when Richard and I played that game in 1974. I ease my way over to the calendar and look at the name: My Old Kentucky Home—Federal Hill. It's the John Rowan house. I have to find out about that house.

Sacramento, California
September 1982

I'm at a Learning Exchange past life regression seminar with a certified hypnotherapist. Eleven people relax in chairs and on the floor. In the preliminary introduction, the hypnotherapist disclaims any belief in past lives but acknowledges that many of his patients seem to have them when he hypnotizes them.

I doubt with my strong personality and control issues I can be hypnotized, but I'm going to try. The therapist's voice moves through the induction. I slip into an unfamiliar state of deep relaxation, floating in a warm cocoon. I can hear what he's saying, and I'm vaguely aware of my surroundings. It's nice. It isn't anything like I thought it would be.

The therapist moves us back through time until we connect to a memory. He directs us not to question what we experience just let it flow.

I see a young girl of about 18 walking down a wooden walkway. She's angry. It has to do with shopping, a dress she wants for a party. The girl's name is Mary Suellen Atcheson. I experience her as willful and spoiled. I sense I'm that girl. I live in Frankfort, Kentucky, and it's 1860. That's all that comes to me. I want to know more about this girl, but that's all I get for now. Past lives are like a puzzle; you get bits at a time until a whole picture emerges. I'm intrigued.

Sacramento, California
April 1983

My next journey into the past takes me to an all day regression session at an old church on Auburn Boulevard. Some thirty-odd people mill around, clutching their blankets and pillows. A middle-aged man with bright blue eyes talks intimately with an attractive young woman of about twenty. She's pleading with him. I move a little closer to eavesdrop.

"I want you to astral travel with me to another planet and have wild sex."

He shakes his head no.

"Why can't we?"

His head touches hers. "If we did that, we'd never want to come back, and we have work to do here." He's trying to discourage her, but he's obviously enjoying her attentions. I'm amused at the conversation and the naiveté of the young girl.

The class starts. The middle-aged man I observed earlier and the hypnotherapist are one and the same. I'm not impressed at this point.

"My name is Dale Snook, welcome to the seminar. I'd like to tell you a little bit about how I got into past lives."

He taught art and history at the high school in Susanville. He involved himself in past lives to disprove they existed. He became a convert and now does regressions for a living. He shows some self-portraits he's done of himself from his previous lives. The first one gives me chills as he talks about his past life in Kentucky in the 1800s. He came from a well-to-do family, but his adventuresome streak compelled him to seek his fortune out West after the Civil War. He died of a gunshot wound in a fight over a card game in Arizona Territory. I get the feeling he's tied to my Kentucky life somehow. My mind whirls and a mild anxiety seizes me.

The first session begins. I float through time and space to find myself back in Kentucky. More pieces come together. I'm standing in front of the house where I live, open the door and enter. The large entry hall leads to a winding staircase to the upper quarters. A room on the left reveals a massive fireplace and a long table in the middle. A bank of windows with cushions look out onto the front. The room obviously has something to do with food, but there's no stove or anyway to prepare it. I sense this is the room where the food sits before being served. My logical mind wants to find the kitchen, but it isn't there. I move on.

The room on the right of the entry shows me a beautiful living room with another fireplace, rich carpets and drapes, a piano and couches.

The dining room sits on the left, adjacent to the room with a long table. A strange looking, ornately carved, wood contraption hangs from the ceiling. It seems to be a fan of some sort. The large room exudes warmth and grace; family paintings adorn the walls. A bank of windows overlooks a garden of forsythia and azaleas.

The story unfolds. Byrne was my father in that life, Dale my cousin and Eddie my husband. I died in childbirth. The session ends.

Dale comes over and kneels down in front of me. He smiles, mischievously. "Hi, Cuz."

I pretend not to understand.

"We were cousins in Kentucky."

"Where in Kentucky?" I'm not going to make this easy.

"Frankfort."

The second session begins. I'm looking at dishes made of pewter. They belong to my family. I don't like the feeling they give me, a sense of foreboding. This isn't a happy life but I don't know why. I'm a male of about nineteen, a drunk who works as a handyman for an inventor. The town is Midland, Pennsylvania. I've never heard of it.

I see myself come out of a saloon drunk and unable to walk steadily. I pitch off the wood walk and fall into the street on my face. A coach runs over me and breaks my neck. I can feel the mud squishing in my ears.

Dale's in front of me again. "How's your neck feel?" He already knows the answer. "Must hurt having the coach break your neck like that." He leaves without waiting for a reply. He's enjoying himself.

Past lives give me a powerful affirmation of connection to a greater plan, purpose and destiny. I'm a thread in the cosmic tapestry, and my lives are woven into the whole.

I bemuse Byrne with my new interest. He doesn't discount past lives, but he isn't quite into it, either. Charlsie impressed him with her reading for him, and he's willing to let Dale hypnotize him. I love that he's open.

I invite Dale to come and do a regression session for Byrne. He goes down like a stone and loses himself in the deep relaxation. He plunges right into one of his more traumatic lives where he was a cave man. We huddled together, starving in a cave in winter. The others in our group died days before. I knew death awaited us, too. I wanted Byrne to stay with me so we could die in each other's arms, but his sense of responsibility wouldn't let him. He left to find food, fell off a cliff, broke both legs and froze to death. I died alone.

In the next life, he went to England in the early 1800s. Together again, we lived in the country, where he practiced medicine. We lived idyllically with Melissa as our daughter, and we expected our second child. I died in childbirth and Byrne, grief stricken, killed himself, abandoning Melissa. Now I know why he worries so much about something happening to me and why he and Melissa have issues.

I experience past lives from a very detached point of view. I don't feel it; I only see it. Byrne feels everything as if he were still there. He sobs with pain and despair. It's wrenching, but each life teaches us something about ourselves: how we've come to be; who we are and why we're together.

Chapter 19

Fair Oaks, California
August 1984

> Since September of 1979, Saturn's been moving through my 10th house of career and recognition and 11th house of goals, hopes, and wishes. He's rewarded me handsomely for all my hard work

I'm living that fantasy of my fifteen-year-old. I have the successful career I dreamed about and I'm married to the successful, handsome man I love madly.

Byrne's practice flourishes and he's Chief of Obstetrics at American River Hospital. My star is at its peak professionally. We are the golden couple: respected, admired, envied.

It's been a wild ride working at The Perinatal Center at Sutter Memorial Hospital. My boss, Jack Schneider, M.D., is an eccentric, charismatic, larger than life character with a huge ego and heart to match. He's fun, hard-driving and wild.

Jack recognized my talent and potential from the start and he pushes me to excel and challenges me continually in my stressful, high profile job as a Clinical Nurse Specialist.

I'm a role model and clinical resource for the nurses at Sutter while teaching classes on the care of high risk obstetrical patients all over Northern California. And I'm part of a multi-disciplinary team of doctors and nurses doing on-site evaluations of hospitals in our designated region. We are the go-to experts in our field. This job is why I went to graduate school.

My first month on the job Jack tells me if I'm going to teach fetal monitoring, I have to pass the rigorous exam for the Advanced Fetal Monitoring course he's co-teaching in Napa with Freeman and Garite, the nationally known experts in the field. Their new textbook has become the bible for obstetricians.

Byrne and I sign up for the course, along with 250 other doctors and a few brave

Faces of Love, Death and Transformation:

nurses. Byrne reads the textbook on monitoring; I devour it. The majority of the doctors I work with at Sutter are here.

The atmosphere for the seminar remains relaxed and casual until the instructors post the results of the test. I rank fifth and Byrne number twelve. The other doctors we know place somewhere in the bottom half. They're in shock.

Byrne ponders the results. I'm waiting for his reaction. "You know, a lesser man would be pissed, but I am so proud of you." He hugs me. I think there is no one like this man.

I now have the solid credibility I need to deal with the doctors at work. It makes me more effective and my reputation grows.

I have a natural talent for teaching. I can take the most complex subject like diabetes in pregnancy or preeclampsia and explain it in terms anyone can understand. My classes are extremely popular and I love seeing that "aha" look in my student's eyes when the information clicks for them. I find myself a popular speaker at national obstetrical conferences in spite of my fear of public speaking.

Jack wants even more from me. He says I must "publish or perish." I write articles for nursing journals and chapters in textbooks. He insists on reviewing whatever I write. He's peppered the pages I have in hand with florid scrawls of BS, HS and MS in the margins and a terse note, "See me re."

I stand in front of his desk. "Okay. I know BS is bullshit and HS horseshit, but what's MS?"

"More shit."

I try not to laugh. I love that his favorite word is shit. "You're supposed to be giving me constructive criticism. Writing bullshit, horseshit and more shit isn't it. You're going to have to do better, Jack."

"Marshall, only you would have the balls to critique the critic."

We have a sometimes contentious, competitive relationship, but we love and admire each other.

I'm thrilled to be part of the State of California grant team writing the manual for Diabetes in Pregnancy for healthcare providers. I also write the patient booklet.

This is meaningful work that helps a lot of people. I'm grateful to Jack for giving me this job.

Jack preens in pleasure when the Governor of California appoints me to the State Board of Medical Quality Assurance. The Sacramento Bee publishes the names of the new appointees. Eddie tells the guys at work I got the appointment because I'm a Commie, pinko liberal.

My accomplishments these past few years have been rewarding, but I'm burnt out as Saturn moves into my 12th house of karma and the unconscious. I need to turn inward.

I tell Jack I'm quitting. I see shock and panic on his face. He tells me I can't do this; I'm irreplaceable. I tell him I'm tired and I don't want to do it anymore. He wheedles and cajoles, but my mind is made up. He's not used to people telling him no.

"You'll be back, Marshall. You know you love this shit."

I did; I don't anymore. I have bigger things on my life agenda.

May 8, 1985

> When adventuresome Jupiter and inventive Uranus link in the heavens, they love to explore the edge of possibility. This night they connect my natal Mercury and Venus, opening new doors of perception for Byrne and me.

It's a Friday Orgy Night. Alone, we devote these nights to hedonistic pursuits: champagne, romance, sex and gourmet food. It's my turn to orchestrate the sexual theme for the evening. We've vowed never to let our relationship slip away from neglect. This is one of the ways we stay on track and keep the romance alive and the fires of passion burning.

Byrne sits on the couch with a mischievous grin. I appear in my costume: a pleated skirt, sweater and bobby sox. It's a departure from the leather hot pants, low cut bustier, fishnet stockings, blindfold, bondage and feather tickling of our last Orgy Night.

Faces of Love, Death and Transformation:

"Okay. I'm a junior in high school; you're a senior, and we're on our first date. We're going to make out, but you can't touch any vital parts. This is the fifties, and I'm a good girl."

Byrne's eyes light up. "Just like high school."

We kiss until we're in a frenzy. I keep saying, "No, no, don't. Stop! We can't." I push his hands away from forbidden territory.

When I feel I've tortured us enough, I let him feel my breast. He moans the appropriate amount of appreciation. I take his other hand and put it up my skirt. I don't have any underwear on, and he falls on me like a Cossack with the after battle hots. He needs release. I want it. We roll around on the floor in ecstatic abandon. I'm on top, looking down at him—shocked at what I see. He's turned into an 18 year-old boy with black, curly hair. It's the Greek life I haven't seen yet. The apparition dissolves. I don't tell Byrne what I've seen; I'm still dazed by it.

Later, we're in the spa sipping champagne and gazing at the richly colored sunset over the trees. The sky explodes in smoky blues and florid pinks. I move my back against the jets and feel the warm water massaging my muscles.

"I'd like to go to San Francisco to that OB meeting."

"I don't want to go." He sounds uneasy.

"Why?"

"I don't know. I just don't like San Francisco."

"Well, let's find out why." I look into Byrne's eyes. "You're in the clouds, floating. You're very relaxed."

Byrne's eyes close and his head drops. He's ridiculously easy to hypnotize. Stacie frequently does it at the dinner table to amuse her friends.

"In the clouds is a hole. Look for it. Let me know when you see it."

Byrne nods his head.

"Okay. Go into the hole. Slide down—follow it, down, down, down. You're there. Where are you?"

"It's foggy and cold and—Oh. Oh, my God! It's terrible, terrible!" He trembles and shakes his head trying to clear what he's seeing. Tears brim.

A picture flashes in my head. I know what he's seeing has to do with me. I've done something really bad. This isn't something I should be fooling with. Dale needs to handle this.

I quickly put my hand on his shoulder, "Blue skies. Blue skies. You're back in the clouds. Three, two, one—you're back."

Byrne opens his eyes; they're filled with panic.

"What did you see?" I put my arms around him.

"I couldn't see anything, but something really terrible happened."

"We need to get Dale here to put you down and find out what this is."

The next afternoon, I meditate. I put myself in the clouds and find the hole.

San Francisco, California
1888

I'm Edna; the last name eludes me. At eighteen, I left my father's house in Sacramento for employment in San Francisco. My mother died six years before.

I rented a room in a boarding house. One of the female boarders befriended me and introduced me to a life of sin. I became a well-paid lady of the evening. I did well in my chosen profession. After several years, I retired to find a suitable husband. I cast my eye on a shy banker named Albert DeWitt—Byrne. He knew nothing of my sordid life.

After a suitable courtship, we married. I counted on Albert to be successful, demanded it, but he disappointed me. I made him feel inadequate on as many levels as possible. My constant criticism and rejection made him sexually impotent.

I viewed a scene where we rode in our buggy. I berated him for his lack of ambition and success. Stone-faced, he slouched in misery. The look of abject pain on his face made me wince at my deliberate cruelty. Edna reminded me of Mary Suellen.

Faces of Love, Death and Transformation:

One night after a particularly heated exchange, I told him about my past. Then I delivered the last insult I'd ever hurl at him: I told him he was the worst lover I'd ever had. As soon as I said it, I knew I'd gone too far. His eyes turned cold and vacant. His mind snapped. My heart raced, my feet frozen to the floor.

He went to the mudroom, got his axe, chopped me into pieces and buried me in the basement. He told the neighbors I'd gone back East to visit family. I was 35-years-old that year of 1905—the same age we got together in this life.

When the earthquake hit in 1906, workers, clearing debris, discovered my bones. The court committed Albert, quite insane by that time, to an institution where he hung himself.

No wonder he was so upset. Then, my excitement soars. This would be a true test of the validity of past lives. I write the story down in my journal and call Dale. I tell Byrne, and Dale, nothing.

Fair Oaks, California
May 14, 1985

Dale puts Byrne down. They go to San Francisco.

"What year is it?" Dale asks Byrne.

"1905, I think. Connie is my wife. She's a buxom, handsome woman. We're standing in the living room of our house. We're fighting; I don't know about what. She's terribly angry. Oh! God. She tells me she was a prostitute and that I was the worst lover she'd ever had! My mind just snaps. Oh. My God! Oh, God! I go to a small room off the kitchen and get an ax. I kill her! I kill her!" He's sobbing. "I chop her into pieces and bury her in the basement.

Sometime later after the earthquake, they find her bones and put me away in an asylum. I hang myself. I'm so guilt ridden for killing her, I just don't want to live anymore. I loved her in spite of how she treated me."

I am stricken with waves of powerful chills during Byrne's recall of that life, especially when he describes that his mind snapped. I can still see the vacant, chilling look in his eyes. There's no lingering doubt in my mind about past lives. This is a powerful affirmation for us. I put my arms around him and hold him close. "I'm so sorry. What a vile bitch I was in that life. You were so sweet; I didn't deserve you." I kiss his cheek. "I guess this time, I have to be nice to you to make up for that life."

"You're doing a great job so far." He nuzzles my cheek. "God, that was a nightmare."

I have come to deal with the karmic lessons of the Kentucky and San Francisco lives. But it will be a couple of years before I know how that will manifest. We're on a mysterious journey through time and love.

Faces of Love, Death and Transformation:

Chapter 20

A novel configuration of Venus harmoniously angling Mars links with opportunity laden Jupiter in mystical Pisces, Neptune and Pluto to form a perfect fusion of deep altered states and intimacy.

San Jose, California
April 7, 1986

It's a three-hour drive to San Jose. I'm excited and nervous. I'm going to a four-day healing class, taught by Ethel Lombardi, the woman Charlsie told me about. Ethel, one of the original Reiki masters, teaches a condensed form of Reiki, a Japanese inspired healing method of working with the energy field in the body. She calls her method MariEl. There are 15 people in the class: two men, the rest women.

Jennifer—a tall, bosomy brunette with masses of curls falling around her face like a Botticelli angel— hosts the class in her home. Her aura of strong sensuality and mischievous smile give the impression she's up for just about anything. She has that same kind of strong Leo magnetism Richard does.

Ethel looks like a typical grandmother type with her reddish hair bound in a plain bun, a comfortable, generous body and green eyes that glitter with excitement. Her presence commands attention and respect.

Ethel explains we all have energy blocks in our bodies that hold memories at a cellular level; memories that need to be acknowledged and healed so that we can rebalance our energetic fields. Each of us will have our crown chakra at the top of our head attuned to their higher consciousness, allowing the divine energy to come through. Now, we see how the energy works. She looks around the room; everyone looks away, hoping not to be the one picked. I already know what's going to happen.

When Charlsie visited us last year, she said she wanted to show me something, instructing me to lie down on the floor.

Charlsie put a hand on my solar plexus. Waves of emotion hit me like a runaway train. To my abject horror, I heard gut wrenching sobs welling from deep within me, the cold energy gripping me like a vice.

"Who's in there, Connie?"

"My Gramma. My mother said she killed herself because of me." I was out of control. The pain crashed over me like pounding surf.

"See your Gramma in a bubble; she's waiting for you. Get in the bubble and ask her if that's true."

I put myself in the bubble. My Gramma looked really happy to see me. She said it wasn't true. I gave her the only happiness she ever knew. She loved me, and she was always with me.

"Give her your love and cut the string holding the bubble here. Watch her float away; she'll take your pain with her."

I did what Charlsie told me: the coldness left me and so did the tears. I felt light and free. I had been given a powerful sample of how energy works.

A large, blonde woman named Stephanie quivers in a corner, trying desperately to be invisible. Ethel beckons her to lie on the floor in front of her. Stephanie's eyes close in terror. Ethel rests her hand a few inches above Stephanie's solar plexus and she immediately begins shaking, sobs welling from deep within. It's her grandfather who died last year. She didn't get to tell him goodbye. Ethel leads her through the process of letting go and Stephanie moves back to her corner with a relieved smile and an aura of radiant peace.

The intense weekend unleashes powerful emotions: tears, fears, hope, joy, laughter. Ethel wields her power with calm, loving assurance. The woman is as mesmerizing as any rock star, as powerful as any evangelist.

She attunes my crown chakra. I feel waves of loving energy coursing through my body. Ethel says it's like tuning a radio to a certain frequency. The person becomes a conduit for the energy. She makes it clear that the energy comes from and is directed by a Higher Power, not by the individual—to think otherwise invites disaster. We must use the energy wisely and only for a higher good.

I experience a powerful connection to all spiritual energy through Ethel. I'm in awe of the potential. My mind churns relentlessly on the drive home. How am I going to explain this to Byrne? What's he going to think? He's gone along with the past lives and the astrology, but this may be too much. He's quite mainstream medicine, as I have been until now. I'm making a radical departure from our shared belief system.

Byrne and Stacie sit at the dinner table when I arrive home, eating barbecued burgers, his favorite. He hugs me enthusiastically. I hold onto him like a child needing comfort.

"You're different; what is it?"

He amazes me, always so tuned into me. I tell them about the weekend. They listen without commenting. I keep waiting for some kind of response. I know it sounds pretty bizarre. "Do you think I've gone round the bend this time?"

He smiles, "Con, honey, if you think there's something to it, there must be. I have absolute faith in your sanity. Have some fries."

I think how happy he makes me. Stacie keeps her thoughts to herself for now. She accepts I'm not a normal mother. She humors me. Melissa is at the age where she thinks I'm border line goofy and completely clueless.

I have a new passion, this journey into the unknown. I need to practice what I've learned. I'm connecting with that quintile I have in my chart, those special gifts and healing energies. It's all making sense.

I have Byrne on my new massage table, ready to experience the MariEl energy method. I put my hands on his head and light the energy lines in his body. He drifts into a profound state of relaxation. I move my hands over his body, feeling for imbalances in his energy field, hot or cold spots. At his pancreas, the site of unfinished business, coldness hits my palm.

I pull at the energy with my left hand, and it unwinds like a ball of twine. Byrne gasps.

Give yourself permission to see whatever is there."

"There's a dark tunnel, but I can't see anything," he says.

"Look at your feet. Tell me what they look like." Sometimes that triggers the memory.

Faces of Love, Death and Transformation:

"I can't see anything. It's totally dark."

I'm frustrated. And then it comes to me—he's dead.

"Oh. I'm dead," he says.

"Why are you still there?"

"I'm waiting for you. I can hear you screaming. You're on a rack. They're pulling your body apart. It's my fault. I'm waiting for you to die so we can leave together." He's crying, overwhelmed with feelings of helplessness.

In a flash, the story comes to me. It's the 1400s during the Spanish Inquisition. Byrne broke his vow of celibacy as a monk. I abandoned my destiny as a healer to pursue my passion for him. He tried resisting me but failed. We were found out and arrested. My servants warned me the authorities were coming for me, but I couldn't leave Byrne. I wouldn't. We paid the ultimate price for not living up to our life contracts. I have him send the guilt and pain out of his body.

"Wow. That was really something. Look at the hard-on I've got. Tell me again what this energy does?"

I shake my head in mock disgust, "Scorpios and sex. I swear to God, honey, you'd follow me into the burning fires of Hell if you thought you'd get laid."

He grins widely, "Looks like I already did."

I'm resisting, but I know I have to do it. I can't work on other people until I clear my own stuff. I see it like a door with demons waiting on the other side, all the old pain and wounds waiting for me.

Jennifer makes countless trips to Fair Oaks to work on me, helping me to confront and explore every dark place my Higher Self lights for me. I spend hours upon hours in the bubble talking to everyone and reliving endless past lives. I cry and cry, release and release. It feels like an emotional root canal without anesthesia. Each session leaves me exhausted but lighter. I'm peeling myself like an onion, one layer at a time.

As a result of our experiences, Byrne and I see life differently than we did before. To us, everything means something. We look for the real reason things happen, the how and why. We've come to understand the importance of releasing old patterns, letting go of guilt and pain. We've come to know the reasons for our deep connection, and that makes it even stronger. It's good we're on this journey together.

Faces of Love, Death and Transformation:

Chapter 21

This energy of 1987 body slams the bunch of us. A difficult Pluto angle to my Sun delivers a serious health crisis, and a strong Uranus hard angling my natal Neptune puts me in touch with the mystical and psychic realms I've come to experience.

Eddie's powerful transit of Saturn and Uranus holds his Sun in a death grip, ready to shake his tree of life.

Richard's energies force him to confront his relationship and commitment issues. Uranus delivers dramatic change and deals him an unexpected and painful loss.

In January, three hard angles assault Byrne's natal Neptune, the kind that literally knock you out of your body. It's a hell of a year for all of us.

Fair Oaks, California
January 15, 1987

Byrne comes down to breakfast. Stacie meticulously eats the poached eggs on toast I fixed for her. I have a way of cutting the toast and eggs so that it remains in precise squares, each one with a piece of egg on it, nothing out of place. They're perfect. She and Byrne are a lot alike. They have endearing quirks I'm happy to indulge.

"Stac, look at my outfit." Byrne stops and poses. "The blue and pink tie, the matching pink shirt, and the blue blazer to complete the ensemble. Am I stylin' or what?" He's one of those happy morning types. I don't want to utter my first word until sometime around 9 A.M. Melissa is the same way.

"Byrne." Stacie giggles. "You look great. I love that shirt."

I love this morning ritual between my husband and daughter. They entertain each other, leaving me to start my day in low gear.

Byrne gives Stacie her usual ride to school on his way to the hospital. I sit at the window overlooking the pool, sipping coffee and enjoying the solitude until the hospital calls. "Mrs. Marshall, this is the ER at Mercy San Juan hospital. We have Dr. Marshall and your daughter here. They've been in an accident."

I don't wait for any other information. I fly out the door in a controlled panic.

The ER buzzes with activity and people milling around. I walk past the ER desk to the holding room. I can't think, my mind frozen in time, not knowing what to expect. Curtains shield two beds. I draw the nearest curtain. Stacie sits in bed looking dazed. She's all right. The beginnings of a bruise show under her right eye, and her nose is swollen, probably broken. "Oh, sweetheart," I put my arms around her. I don't want to cry and scare her.

"I'm okay, Mom. The impact knocked me out for a few minutes. When I came to, Byrne told me what happened. We'd been hit head-on by another car."

"Where's Byrne?"

"He's over there in that other bed."

The blank look on Byrne's face tells me he's still trying to comprehend what happened. I throw my arms around him. I cry with relief he isn't seriously hurt. "Oh, honey. I was frantic."

"We were really lucky; we could have been killed. You should see the car. It's totaled."

The ER nurse brings me the release papers to sign. "They can go home. They have some bruises, but everything else looks good."

I start for home, but Byrne stops me. "You have to take me to American River so I can make rounds."

"Rounds! You can't do that. You need to go home and get into bed. You're still in shock." I'm also in shock, realizing how close I came to losing them.

"I have to make rounds."

I know better than to reason with him.

January 26, 1987

Richard calls: "Constance, I have some news. You know that girl I dated? Vickie? She's pregnant. She doesn't believe in abortion, so we're getting married."

Unexpected tears spring to my eyes, startling me. I struggle to keep my composure. "I don't know what to say."

Richard reacts to the emotion in my voice, "I told Eddie I wanted to tell you myself. I didn't want you hearing it from anyone else. It surprised the hell out of me. I thought I'd been shootin' blanks all these years." He's trying to lighten the mood. "I want Byrne to be Vickie's doctor."

"I'll tell him. He'll be happy to do it."

It's funny—the way I feel about Richard is totally separate from how I love Byrne. They occupy parallel spaces in my heart. Byrne, vulnerable and emotionally open, inhabits the joyful, safe places in my heart. Richard, deep and inaccessible, lives in the wild, untamed parts of my heart. I feel a sense of ownership regarding Richard; I still feel like he's mine.

I occupy a similar place in his heart. No other woman will ever know him the way I do. The life changing experiences we've shared over the years bind us tightly with entwined memories and shared pain. We have more to come.

Sacramento, California
February 22, 1987

> The planetary energies on my wedding day to Eddie were wild; Richard's are worse. A number of highly problematic angles trigger his relationship issues. Venus drifting in the heavens and not connecting to other planets, as on this day, isn't a favorable time for marriage. Saturn and Uranus also make a difficult angle to his problematic birth pattern between Venus and Neptune. Making this relationship work will be like paddling upstream against tidal waves.

After a private ceremony, two hundred people attend their wedding reception. The whole gang gathers for the occasion. Filben jokes that Richard will be so old when the kid graduates from high school he'll have to go in a wheelchair.

I haven't seen Patrick and Nancy in awhile. I don't recognize Patrick. He has a long Fu Manchu beard moustache combo and unkempt long hair. He sees the shock on my face and tells me he's in disguise. He still works for DEA and a Mexican drug cartel has a contract out on him. I don't want to think about what could happen to him. The whole scenario is too unreal.

After the first dance with his new bride, Richard takes my hand and leads me to the dance floor. His cheek brushes mine. "I love you, Constance. I always have, and I always will."

My brain freezes. I'm speechless for a long moment. "Me, too."

We part without looking at each other. It wasn't necessary for him to reaffirm our strong connection but I'm touched he felt compelled to do it.

I'm well into my transformative process, meditating two hours a day, going into deep states of consciousness. I ask to talk to one of my guides. In my mind's eye, I see a big round rock and lean against it, waiting. Down a narrow path come two men. I recognize Bobby. Tears fill my eyes. He looks happy and healthy with rosy cheeks and that mischievous smile on his face. The man with him dresses like a medieval monk in brown robes. Bobby tells me his friend's name is Eric, and he's a teacher. Eric doesn't speak, just raises his hand in greeting.

I ask Bobby if he has anything to tell me. He does. "We love you." They turn around and walk back down the path. I break into tears of joy.

It's 3 A.M. Byrne's left for the hospital to deliver a patient. I drift between the sleep and awake state, resting in neither one. I hear a sound coming from outside on the deck. I listen carefully; it isn't like anything I've ever heard before, an unearthly vibrating sound, like a thousand voices humming in perfect pitch, the sound of souls. I listen in awe until silence comes. I move into a profoundly relaxed state and hear a voice say to me, "You need a good purging."

A strong, insistent energy enters through the top of my head and plunges through my body like a bolt of electricity. The energy shakes me violently, the heat intense. I clutch the bed, afraid I'm going to fall off. The energy leaves as quickly as it entered. I smile, murmur thanks to my visitors and fall into a deep sleep. The paranormal is becoming quite normal. My connection to the divine grows.

Fair Oaks, California
April 1987

The old gang sits around our dinner table drinking copious amounts of wine before, during and after dinner. We reminisce and regale Byrne with our youthful indiscretions and their work related escapades. I'm grateful to Byrne for accepting and even embracing my old friends.

With Eddie as the exception, the guys have successful careers. Eddie's perpetual contempt for all authority keeps him at the entry level rank of Special Agent I where he started and will ultimately retire. He doesn't care; a desk job would take away the power that has come to define him and the high he still gets from being on the street and kicking down doors. His career highlight came two years ago when he helped investigate the Leonard Lake/Charles Ng serial killings. He won't be happy when Filben, now a Special Agent in Charge, becomes his boss at the Bureau of Investigation in four years.

Patrick, now clean-shaven, sits next to me. I assume the threat against his life has passed, but he never discusses his job in any depth. Patrick is a legend in law enforcement circles, featured in a new book called The Underground Empire by James Mills that chronicles Patrick's work with Centac, the elite drug conspiracy unit. He's also become an expert at dismantling methamphetamine labs. He's lost partial hearing in one ear from years of guns going off close to his head. When Byrne asks him if he likes to hunt like Eddie, Patrick replies that he doesn't hunt animals anymore because after you've hunted people, animals are no challenge. He's still the enigmatic Scorpio.

Richard moves steadily up the Department of Justice hierarchy. He's worked Narcotics and Organized Crime and is currently Filben's boss as Chief of the Major Fraud Unit. He will go on to be Chief of the Forensics Lab and Chief of Security for the State Lottery. I'm proud of my boys.

Richard smiles wistfully through our journeys to the past. I catch him giving me that look of love, longing, admiration and regret. Something isn't right with him. He doesn't act like a newlywed; he's ignoring his wife and looking troubled as the evening wears on. He gets up to pour himself some coffee and misses the cup entirely. He's crossed the line of good cheer into shit house mouse land. Time to go home.

I put my arm around Richard's waist to steady him. He puts his arm around my shoulder, pulling me close in a brief moment of intimacy. We walk to the curb. Vickie leans in the car window talking to Nancy, Patrick's wife. Byrne, Patrick, Filben and Babycakes linger at our front door. Eddie left earlier.

"Patrick, I love Constance. Don't you love Constance, too?" Richard shouts. He turns to me. "Things aren't going well. I need to talk to you. Can I talk to you?" He sways drunkenly, hanging on to me. "Is that permissible?" It's more a challenge than a question.

"Sure." It's the alcohol talking. He'll forget about it in the morning. Richard doesn't "talk" about things.

He pulls me close. "God, I love you!" His lips find mine in a passionate kiss.

I don't know what to do. I pull away, hoping no one noticed, especially Byrne or Vickie. Byrne's never shown any hint of jealousy and he's quite fond of Richard but having his tongue down my throat might be pushing the envelope.

"I have to try, don't I?"

"Yes, you do," I reply firmly.

Sedona, Arizona
June 1987

We're going to Sedona with Jennifer and her boyfriend Dan, a black Irishman with a mood to match. Jennifer and I explored the famous vortices in Sedona in April the previous year. We want to go again. I'm busy doing some preliminary packing. Byrne calls. "My back is going out on me; I don't know if I'm going to be able to hike around any hills." He sounds miserable.

"You don't have to do that, honey. You can stay at the motel and rest." My instincts tell me the back thing is a past life surfacing.

Sedona, a leisurely two-hour drive from Phoenix up Interstate 17, wends its way through the arid sagebrush and cactus landscape, slowly changing to cooler and greener scenery as we veer north on Highway 179. Monolithic red rocks appear like apparitions on the horizon, stunning the eye with their improbable beauty and immensity.

Our rented car makes the steep climb off the main road to the Airport Mesa Hotel. Byrne gets out and stretches. "Hey, my hands and feet are tingling; what's going on?"

"We're in a vortex here, feels good doesn't it?"

"Will it give me a hard-on?" He's smiling in anticipation.

"Oh, stop! This is supposed to be a spiritual experience."

We decide we should visit Courthouse Rock first thing in the morning while it's still cool.

"You want to stay here and rest, honey?"

Byrne's distracted, a distant look in his eyes. "I have to go with you. I don't know why; I just do."

I smile. Something is up.

During the night Richard's voice wakes me, "Come home. Come home now; you've done enough."

I lie there and wonder what in the hell that was all about. I turn over to go back to sleep, and I see a male figure dressed in overalls floating through the room, exiting through the wall. He looks like a handyman of some kind. Someone told me the veil between the dimensions grows thin here; it's easy to see ghosts.

We make the drive down the dusty, rural road to Courthouse Rock, ending at a rusty iron gate. None of the vortices post signs to identify them. The location and directions come from various metaphysical sources passed on to seekers through the grapevine. None of the locals admit to any knowledge of their existence.

Courthouse Rock towers above us, a massive, mystical mural of shape, form and color. We trek closer to the base.

Byrne gazes up at a distant ridge. "Look! Look! A deer."

We look up; there's nothing there.

Byrne falls to his knees. 'My back!" He's clutching his lower back.

"What is it?" I'm kneeling beside him.

"I've been shot in the back with an arrow. I'm being left here to die. I can't move; I'm paralyzed."

"Okay, this is past life stuff. Let's see what it is," Jennifer tells him. "This is why your back went out." She puts both hands on his lower back.

"I'm an Indian, an Apache, I think—the chief of the tribe. I'm supposed to marry Con when I get home. She's a shaman. I'm here on a vision quest with one of my warriors. He brought me here to kill me. He wants to be chief, and he wants to marry Con. This is his chance."

"Is it important you know who it is?" Jennifer asks him.

"Yes. It's Richard. He leaves me here. I have flies all over me. It takes me days to die. Con goes to the edge of our village and drums herself into an ecstatic trance, helping me cross over to the spirit world. She stays there three days, then Richard comes for her and says, "Come home. Come home now. You've done enough.""

Chills ripple through my body. Those are the words I heard last night. The rest of the story comes to me. Richard and I married after he became chief. I enjoyed sharing his bed—the sex was wonderful—but my heart always longed for Byrne.

Byrne gets to his feet and tells me, "I hope Richard doesn't get any similar ideas in this life." His face shows shock and disorientation at being thrown back into that past life experience, trying to shake the vivid memory.

"How's your back now?"

"Actually, it feels much better." He puts his hands on his lower back and stretches.

I'm amazed at how these experiences seem to bubble up from deep within us, those ancient memories still there to be accessed.

Jennifer wants a rock, not just any old rock, but a special one she's envisioned, a large malachite and azurite stone to use in her healing work. She instructs Dan to drive up the hill to Jerome, an old mining town now inhabited by a few metaphysical shops selling crystals and other New Age trinkets. We browse through several shops until she gets the "message." Her rock waits for her in a shop across the street.

It's there: a five-pound malachite and azurite stone with enough vibrations to levitate a couple of swamis. Jennifer inquires as to how much the shopkeeper wants for it. The woman looks puzzled. "I don't know. I hadn't thought about selling it like it is. Actually, I was going to take a hammer to it today and break it into pieces to sell individually. For some reason, I haven't gotten around to it."

Jennifer smiles enigmatically, "That's because it's meant to be mine. The angels made you wait until I came for it."

They settle on eighty dollars. Jennifer thanks her profusely and tells her it will help heal many people. The woman gives her one of those indulgent smiles people offer to the demented.

Jennifer and Dan go off to explore Oak Creek Canyon. Byrne's napping. I've borrowed the stone: I place the heavy rock on my abdomen at my second chakra, the site of creativity and sex, and feel a strong tingling sensation. Deep into my meditation, an orgasm shakes my body and a strong, urgent, pulsing energy rises from my second chakra and propels itself like a bullet up my body to my brain. I feel a massive explosion in my head and hear a loud pop.

Oh, shit! I've blown my brains out. I'm lying there in post orgasmic disorientation, waiting for something else to happen. I take inventory, putting my hand to my head; it's still intact. I can move and everything seems in one piece and functioning. *That is one hunk of cosmic rock.*

We need supplies for breakfast. I'm off to find Byrne's peanut butter. He goes to find his powdered donuts. Jennifer and Dan wander the aisles. I find the peanut butter but lose Byrne. I find him sitting in the car, and he's majorly pissed. "What's the matter? Did you get your donuts?"

He turns to me with a fierce look. "No, I did not get my donuts. I had them in my hand and Jennifer took them, opened the box and tasted one. She said they were stale and put them back on the shelf. I want my donuts."

I sigh and head back into the store. Jennifer has to learn never to get between Byrne and his food. He'll never forgive her.

Faces of Love, Death and Transformation:

**Sacramento, California
June 16, 1987**

Eddie's doctor admitted him to the hospital. He thinks he has pneumonia of some kind. I go to see him; he looks forlorn and frightened. Eddie's been depressed ever since Richard married and moved out. They'd been roommates for two years, and he's in deep mourning, his drinking out of control. Melissa's been staying with him and tells me she finds him frequently passed out in the hallway leading to his bedroom. He's been sliding down a slippery slope for a long time.

I've cultivated an amiable if not entirely friendly relationship with Eddie for the girls' sake. I'm determined they won't suffer the slings and arrows of outrageous divorce, caught in the crossfire of bitter post divorce battles.

It wouldn't have been so amiable if I'd known he took them to bars when he had them for his weekends, turning them loose with a few dollars to feed and amuse themselves while he drank himself into a stupor, frequently getting into fist fights before driving them home. The girls knew if I knew, Eddie wouldn't be allowed unsupervised visits; they adopted a code of silence, not telling me until they were grown. I get sick every time I think about what could have happened to them.

Byrne has been extremely tolerant of Eddie and doesn't mind he's spent the last seven Christmas Eves with us. It makes the girls happy. Byrne continues to be unfailingly gracious to both Eddie and Richard when they visit.

Eddie greets me listlessly and reaches for my hand; we make polite small talk. I don't like the way he looks. The orderly comes for him to take him for a bronchoscopy to look at his lungs. I wait in the room for him. They bring him back to his bed and his eyes exude pure rage. He looks at me and gives me the finger as if what he just experienced is my fault. His anger bubbles constantly just below the surface.

That night he goes into respiratory arrest. He's in the ICU and hasn't regained consciousness. The doctor isn't optimistic he'll live. Dread passes through me like a dark cloud. Byrne tells me I'd better go stay with him; he needs me. I burst into tears at the thought of another death vigil.

The ICU resounds with the efficient din of respirators and other equipment hissing and beeping. I approach Eddie's bed. He's unconscious and on a respirator. I put my hands on his head and feel cold emptiness. He isn't there. I light his energy lines to bring him back into his body and anchor him. It's difficult and I'm not sure it will work. Wherever he is right now, he's deciding whether to live or die.

Richard joins me. He tries to look calm, but his face betrays his fear Eddie is going to die. We embrace quickly. We know this could be a repeat of Bobby's death.

"Constance, I had a dream last night that I came to visit Eddie in the hospital, and it was you in the bed, hooked up to all the tubes and machines. I was so relieved."

He doesn't seem to notice the shock on my face. I know he doesn't wish me on death's door; it's just a reflection of his belief I'm strong and can take it and Eddie can't. It still hurts that he would gladly sacrifice me for Eddie.

We talk quietly. I move to Eddie's feet and put my palms a few inches away from his soles and wait. I feel energy move, then his toes wiggle.

"Geezus Christ, Constance, what are you doing? His toes are moving! Are you some kind of white witch or what?" Richard smiles in amazement.

Eddie's doctor stops by and inquires as to our relationship to his patient.

"I'm his ex-wife."

"I'm his best friend and her ex-boyfriend."

"What is this? A "Big Chill" kind of deal?"

"Something like that." Richard smiles.

"We're a very incestuous group," I tell him wistfully.

We take turns staying with Eddie. Richard and I do the day shift and Patrick spends the nights. We do it for three weeks.

I try to be hopeful for Melissa and Stacie when they visit. Emotions run high, and I find myself weeping periodically when I'm not doling out emotional support to everyone around me. It's not that I'm attached to whether Eddie lives or dies, I think it's more of a reflexive action, reliving my father's and Bobby's deaths. I'm here for the girls and Richard.

Eddie decides to live. I'm hoping this near death experience changes him, and makes him a nicer, kinder soul; maybe, he will find new meaning in his life.

That hope vanishes when he regains consciousness.

The Filipina nurse on the day shift adjusts his IV. The look of hatred in his eyes would chill the fires of hell. He stares hard and unflinchingly at her. She ignores his gaze and finishes her task. Eddie's irrational hatred of all ethnic groups and religions remains intractable. He's hopeless. I don't understand why he decided to live.

After Eddie's release from the hospital, he goes to Eureka to visit friends. He gets drunk and sleep walks off a second story balcony, falling into the canyon below. He breaks his hip and lays there all night until his hosts find him in the morning. He'll be spending several weeks in the hospital there.

Richard calls me with the news. He's driving to Eureka. I am disgusted and sick of the drama. I tell him I'm done. Enough is enough. I'm out of the loop.

Sedona, Arizona
August 16, 1987

Sedona bustles. The Harmonic Convergence, a New Age mystical carnival, convenes. People from all over the planet come here to pay homage to the Hopi prophecy known as the 13 Heavens and 9 Hells. Today is the end of the 9th Hell, heralding the New Age of Peace.

I get a room at the Airport Mesa Hotel. Right before sunrise, my friends and I join a large group of people in a circle on a bluff adjacent to the airport. We stand silently, watching the horizon for the first signs of the sun. Someone drums; the sun slowly rises amid spectacular colors. The chanting begins and increases in fervor, reaching a crescendo as the sun comes fully in view. And it's over. Nice energy, but the earth didn't move.

Byrne calls me at the hotel that night. "Something really bad happened."

My heart freezes. He sounds terrible.

"Richard and Vickie's baby died. She couldn't feel it move; I told her to come in for an ultrasound. There was no heartbeat. I'm inducing her now."

"Oh, God." I feel the blood drain from my face. "How's Richard doing?"

"He's doing a good job supporting Vickie; he's pretty stoic."

"How are *you* doing, honey? This has to be horrible for you."

"I find myself crying. This is so terrible; I feel so badly for them. I'll be glad when you get home tomorrow."

I'm calm as I walk into the hospital room. I'm here to offer support; I'm the cool professional. I've done this before. I know all the right things to say and do.

I walk past Richard and go to Vickie and put my arms around her. "I'm so sorry. I know what it's like to lose a baby." That's not what I intended to say. I feel the tears start. All the suppressed pain from losing my first baby wells up and overcomes me. I feel Vickie's pain; I know it well. I'm overcome with compassion for Richard. I know him. He'll do what I did: he'll bury this overwhelming pain with all the others he's accumulated over the years, unable to deal with it any other way.

I turn to Richard and throw myself into his outstretched arms, bursting into uncontrollable sobs. We hold each other tightly; I feel his body shake as he sobs with me. "It's okay, baby. It's okay." He says it over and over as we hold each other. "I knew you'd be as upset as we are," he tells me.

Vickie watches us. Shock registers on her face. Until this moment, she didn't fully realize the strong emotional connection between us—a painful reality. Now she knows why she's never felt comfortable with my relationship with her husband.

Byrne and I are quiet through dinner that night. He's in a rare dark mood. We haven't talked about my latest Sedona trip. "So, what's it going to be now? We've done astrology, numerology, reflexology, Tarot, Runes, past lives and MariEl. What's next?"

His intense Scorpio side just zinged me. I figure that the stress of Richard and Vickie's baby dying weighs heavily on him even though nothing could have predicted or prevented it. My not being here to emotionally support him made the experience more difficult. Byrne is feeling abandoned by my spiritual pursuits. He does this every once in a while, like when he gets paranoid about my spiritual evolvement reaching a point where I won't want to have sex anymore. Experience should tell him that will never happen. His condemnation, however mild, hurts me. I go to bed with my mind in turmoil, questioning my sanity.

Faces of Love, Death and Transformation:

In the middle of a dream, I'm pulled up and out of my body to an elevator; I sense two beings on either side of me, but I don't see them. The elevator opens into a cavernous round room. Small groups of people congregate in tight knots like a classroom with small seminars going on. I sit on a raised platform, waiting for what I don't know.

A hand touches the back of my neck. I instantly fill with an energy that moves through my entire being, lifting me into what I can only describe as a pure state of ecstasy, an indescribable feeling of love and joy. I look up; a man stands in front of me, tall with a long, steel gray beard and black robes. He smiles and puts his arms around me, filling me with love and peace. I thank him with great humility and my spirit plunges back into my body with great force. The mysterious being gave me Universal love and support just when I needed it. I say my thanks again and drift back to a bliss-filled sleep.

Chapter 22

Pluto's been squaring my Sun since 1986. It's a tough energy. A new moon in Phoenix-like Scorpio in my 12th house of karma fuels the energy, along with unexpected change Uranus in a difficult angle to Neptune. In a year of crisis, chaos, death and near death, it's my turn in the tank.

Fair Oaks, California
November 20, 1987

More strange experiences visit me: I've been meditating with a dark quartz crystal Melissa found on a rock hunting excursion with her school. It has three perfectly formed pyramids on its face. My research tells me it's a record keeper, a crystal with a story or history embedded within it. I want to know the story. My first visits to the stone during meditation yield fleeting pictures of symbols and the face of a blond man. One symbol stands out: it resembles the bottom half of a rectangle, bisected from right top to bottom left.

I dream of the blond man that night, the symbol etched on the left side of his cheek. I sense that it's a karmic mark of some kind. Nothing else comes to me. In meditation, I ask about the symbol and I'm told, "It's God's knife." It doesn't mean anything to me at the time.

November 26, 1987

I double over when the severe shooting pain hits my stomach and travels to my rectum. I feel like someone jammed a cattle prod up me. I think it's my Kundalini energy awakening. I've just finished a book on the subject, and my symptoms are similar. I decide to ride it out.

It's 4 A.M. and I can't sleep. My stomach burns so badly I'm afraid to move.

"You're awake, aren't you?" says Byrne.

"Yes."

"You still have that pain?"

"Yes."

"Get your clothes on. I'm taking you to the ER. I know you think you can handle this yourself, but you can't. You scare me with your high pain tolerance. You should have been a lab rat."

I'm not arguing anymore; Byrne is right. I walk to the car doubled over.

On Thanksgiving Day, and instead of turkey, I serve the surgeons a badly infected, stone-filled gallbladder. In my absence, Eddie comes to the house and cooks a turkey dinner for Byrne and the girls.

When I wake up after surgery, the sun shines through the window, reflecting on the closet door in front of me. The shadow forms the mysterious symbol of the dark quartz crystal in perfect detail. I smile to myself and drift back into drug induced sleep.

The surgeon comes into my room the day after surgery. "Sweetheart, why didn't you tell us you were so sick? I've never seen a gallbladder like that; it was ready to pop. Byrne probably saved your life, insisting we do the surgery right away. That man sure loves you."

I smile at the surgeon and express silent gratitude to Byrne for loving me and taking care of me. I wasn't ready to die yet.

I'm at the point in my spiritual evolution where I need to figure everything out. Why something happens. The reason. The lesson. The message. It's clear to me: the symbol has to do with healing. According to the MariEl theory, the gallbladder is the site of unfinished business and unhealed wounds. I've spent nearly two years working on myself to heal those wounds. I've done the intellectual, emotional and spiritual releasing. The body heals last. This is validation for the work I've done. I decide it's a good thing.

Lima, Peru
October 2, 1988

> **Mystical Neptune harmoniously angling my natal Jupiter deliver a significant spiritual journey for me that will give me new levels of faith and understanding of myself.**

I've never had any desire to go to Peru, but I'm compelled to go now. Jennifer and I will be gone for two weeks. Byrne doesn't like the idea, but when I tell him I have to go, he surrenders. He knows how much my spiritual journey means to me.

Jennifer made the arrangements through a travel company specializing in metaphysical tours. We spend the first night in Lima, and now we're boarding a rickety boat that reminds me of the African Queen. We putt three hours down the Tambopata River, a tributary of the Amazon, deep into the jungle to stay at a famous botanical reserve, The Explorer's Inn.

Somehow, I didn't know about this part of the trip. My great fears have to do with snakes and creepy crawly things that go bump in the night. There are lots of those here. We spend four days without electricity, phones or hot water. Our guide tells us if we get sick, we'll have to be evacuated by helicopter to Lima. How fortunate I just had my gallbladder out. I give my guardian angels high marks for thinking ahead.

The other people on tour with us are friends and acquaintances of Jennifer's. Charles and Karen are married. Scott and Carol are not and they have noisy, robust sex every night to the amusement and envy of the rest of the group. Newlyweds Schoen and John Henry hope to conceive their first child on this trip. We're a compatible group, having taken the MariEl class together.

We sleep in a long grass hut with thin walls separating the rooms. We hear Scott and Carol thrashing and moaning from three rooms away. Charles snores loudly. Moths as big as my hand fly around during the night, brushing my face with their wings.

We sleep fully clothed with long sleeves, applying liberal amounts of Skin So Soft on all exposed flesh to keep the fierce mosquitoes at bay. Jennifer and I are deathly afraid to get up to pee at night. It's pitch dark, and we're convinced there's a boa constrictor hiding in the toilet. Jaguars scream somewhere in the jungle around us. Some unknown creatures gnaw loudly at the thick poles supporting the huts.

Faces of Love, Death and Transformation:

We're told they're bamboo rats—big as pigs. It's a toss-up which strikes more terror in my heart, rats or snakes.

Our first night, we're invited to go cayman watching. I think cayman are monkeys. Six of us sit in a long canoe, rocking to and fro perilously in the darkness. As the guide's flashlight dances over the dark, piranha-filled water, we see tiny eyes flashing, illuminated by the light. Crocodiles float partially submerged like fallen logs. After snakes, I'm terrified of crocodiles. I'm mentally whipping myself for not checking the itinerary before we left. I harbor deep fear I've come here to die.

We walk miles into the jungle each day, admiring the flora and fauna of this famous reserve where biologists and botanists from all over the world come to study. I'm becoming more comfortable with my surroundings. I know I've conquered my fears when I walk into the dark jungle alone on my way to the river to find Jennifer. Until now, I've been in a mild state of panic, thinking about all manner of creatures waiting to feast on my flesh. I decide this experience is about conquering the fear of dying and of the unknown. Now, we're off to the next adventure.

We land in Cusco at an elevation of 11,000 feet. Kika Caballero, our guide, warns us of pickpockets. She tells us, "They will be waiting for us and they have knives to slash open your backpacks. Keep your backpack in front of you with your arms crossed over it. I will make a scream to distract the pickpockets; when I scream, you will run for the bus.

Kika then warns us about the altitude, saying we won't be able to breathe at first but not to panic, which isn't easy when you can't get your breath. I think this must be like having emphysema, slowly suffocating from lack of oxygen. She gives us hard candy to suck on.

We get to the hotel where they sell small canisters of oxygen but Jennifer and I pass and tough it out. We have a room on the second floor of the Royal Inca hotel. We take one stair at a time, stop, rest, breathe and move to the next step. It takes fifteen minutes to work our way up to our room. We drink coca tea to fend off altitude sickness. I don't know if the tea is actually made from coca leaves, but it kills my appetite and leaves me light headed. We have our first hot shower in five days and clean hair. We're in heaven.

A special guide takes us to the ruins of Sacsuyhuman, a sacred Incan temple built on 150 ton rocks placed together intricately. The Incas used this site as a healing place. A medicine wheel sits strategically in the middle of the high bluff. I step inside the circle and feel a hollowness inside my body. I speak, and the sound reverberates throughout my body with a strange power. My voice transforms into a low vibration like a man's. I imagine this is how Moses must have sounded when he came down from the mount. I step outside the circle, back into reality. Somehow, the Incas knew to create a profoundly healing place on this site.

Next, we're riding a bus to Olantyambo and Pisac to visit the Valley of the Moon. I'm uneasy. My stomach roils. The group sets out on a 90-minute trek up the mountain to drum and meditate. I know I can't make it. I stay on the bus by myself. I lie down to keep from vomiting. A strong energy moves into my body, and I start to shake. Intense heat rages through me like a high fever. I feel like I am outside my body. It's a past life I had here: Someone poisoned me and I died in convulsions. I'm reliving the experience. The powerful energy goes on for an hour before I fall into a healing sleep.

Our train to Machu Picchu brims with armed, uniformed guards. Rumors circulate that the Shining Path terrorists plan to blow up the train. Kika doesn't seem nervous, but the rest of us perch on the edge of panic. At worst, we could be killed; at least, we could be stranded at Machu Picchu for an unspecified period of time while the railroad is being repaired. In this country, it could take months. I miss Byrne and the girls terribly.

Our spacious room at the hotel seems like paradise compared to the places we've been staying. Glass patio doors bring the colorful garden indoors. We find it idyllic until Kika tells us that this month heralds their earthquake season. More death fears punch our emotional buttons.

Later, we sit on a high rock platform in the surreal, moonless night, meditating. I want to reach out and touch the stars shimmering through the clouds that hang over us like a thick fog, lost in the wonder of it all. I've never done acid but I think this must be what it's like.

Deep in sleep, an explosion rocks my bed. I lay there motionless, trying to decide if it's a Shining Path bomb or an earthquake. Jennifer and I don't speak. The next explosion comes, shaking everything in the room—it's only thunder. The high altitude magnifies the sound and fury. I gratefully go back to sleep.

Lake Titicaca in Puno, the deepest lake in the world, is home to one of the most powerful energy fields on earth. We glide through the frigid water in small boats to the island of Taquillui. The Indians who live there have three rules they live by: don't lie, be lazy or steal. Unfortunately, they forgot cleanliness. We eat off used plastic plates, hastily washed from the previous user. I have a premonition this meal will come back to haunt us. The ride back proves arduous. The boat leaks. One Indian guide bails water while the other siphons gas from an open bucket with a plastic tube. We inhale the fumes for three hours. I have the worst headache of my life and a stomach that wants to turn itself inside out.

Jennifer wakes up in the middle of the night and runs for the bathroom; she doesn't make it. The explosion blows out the seat of her pants. She collapses in the bathroom sobbing. I hold my nose and go back to sleep. I'm ready to go home.

Back in Lima, the rest of the group is ready for their trip to the Nasca Lines. I say farewell and crawl into my bed. I plan to sleep until midnight when my plane leaves. I end up in the bathroom with raging diarrhea and puking my guts out. I perfect the art of vomiting between my legs. I sob uncontrollably and pray this is the last great cleansing before I leave. Gratefully, I finish by the time the driver comes for me. I intend to be on that plane, no matter what.

I call Byrne at the airport to come and get me. We've never been away from each other this long before. I realize, even more, how deeply I love him.

Our car pulls to the curb, and Byrne bounds out, smiling. He takes me in his arms and bursts into tears. He's been frantic with worry having me so far away in a country with terrorists and no way to communicate. I feel like I never want to go away again, but I will.

Cairo, Egypt
April 1990

Jennifer and I wing our way to Cairo with several of our MariEl and Peru buddies. Carol of the noisy lovers in Peru, now married to Scott, sits with Jennifer and me on the plane. I have my favored window seat so I can sleep. It's about 18 hours to Paris and then on to Cairo. Directly in front of me sits a young Frenchman. He's unkempt, wearing a soiled tank top. He reclines his seat so his head is nearly in my lap. Periodically he raises his arms to stretch, transmitting the worst body odor I've ever had the displeasure to smell.

I force myself to sleep and drift into a dream that takes me to an Egyptian temple where I participate in some erotic ritual, bringing me to a glorious climax that wakes me with a shudder. I look at Jennifer and Carol to see if I've given myself away. I'm embarrassed. The dream had taken me back to a time I will later revisit at one of the temples.

Cairo, a sprawling, noisy city vibrates with chaotic energy. Donkey carts and cars vie for space on the congested streets, dodging and weaving in a ruthless game of chance, fueled by testosterone rage and animated blaring horns.

Our hotel room at the Mena House in Giza faces the Great Pyramids. I'm relieved to be out of the city in a more tranquil setting. It's Ramadan, the Islamic holiday of month long prayer, fasting and charity. Loudspeakers blare the call to prayer three times a day. I love the chanting, even in the middle of the night and early morning hours; the sight of the sun rising over the Pyramids at dawn humbles me as I ponder their ancient mysteries and massive, stark beauty. I can't believe I'm here—again.

Our Egyptian tour guide, Abbas, gets us into sacred sites we wouldn't ordinarily see by bribing guards and officials. We enter the Queen's tomb after dark when other tourists must leave for the day. I meditate, sensing a past life tied to the tomb. I, and another young girl, served the Queen. I don't know her name or the time. We lived extravagantly as part of her entourage. We had pledged to be buried alive with her when she died. I remember the tomb being sealed, feeling quiet resignation; the air thinned and the slow suffocation began. My tomb-mate, not so stoic, cried and screamed to be set free. Our local Egyptologist tells us servants were not routinely buried with their mistress as we may have heard. I don't know if that incident was unusual, but I know what happened. I have no strong feelings about this life, either good or bad.

A group of us descend into the chamber where the dead were prepared for their journey to the afterlife. Getting there requires crawling on your stomach through a hot, pitch-black tunnel that's so narrow I think it must be similar to the birth canal. Jennifer leads and then stops in the middle of the dank, almost airless space. She entreats us to breathe; I hear panic in her voice. Someone orders her to move ahead and she does. We exit into a cavernous space that echoes with the sound of our voices. We form a circle and chant. The air charges with energy, and I feel it move up through my body from the earth, vibrating as it moves through me. I sense it's changing the energy in my body somehow. Immense power pervades this space. Each temple has a different energy to it.

We sail to Elephantine Isle on a Falucca, an Egyptian sailboat. We were told to bring something we no longer want in our life, something that no longer serves us. We also have to bring something we want to keep and nurture.

Faces of Love, Death and Transformation:

My trip to Peru conjured my fear of dying; Egypt connects me to my fear of living. I think about what I own that symbolizes what I need to release. Suddenly, it occurs to me that I have to throw away the diamond ring I've worn since I was nineteen, a gift from my first husband, the tree frog. The thought shocks me, and then makes perfect sense. That ring symbolizes all the pain and anguish of my early years and symbolizes the person I used to be.

I tell my fellow travelers what I intend to do. Celia, a woman who loves and collects jewels and furs, looks at me like I've lost my mind. She bursts into tears and pleads with me not to throw the ring away, but I'm determined.

I stand at the edge of the Nile River with the ring in one hand and a pen in the other. I state my desire to let go of all my past pain and sorrow and throw the ring into the dark water. I hold the pen as a symbol of the creativity I express through my writing. I feel exhilarated and liberated.

One of our tour guides Mary, an astrologer, knows a lot about symbols. I ask her if she's familiar with the one I saw in my dream on the blond man's face. She tells me it's the trinity of spirit, mind and body, aligning and connecting the energies of those three parts of myself. My gallbladder held all my anger and sadness, the obstacle to unifying the trinity within me. It had to come out—made perfect sense.

I feel a strong energetic connection inside the temple of Isis at Philae, one of the many temples on our itinerary. I find a corner to sit and meditate in. I go to the place I visited in my dream. I'm a temple priestess here. We're responsible for the fertility of the earth, closely linked and connected to the spirits of rain and other deities responsible for the well-being of Mother Nature. Annually, we join with the priests and perform our fertility rites, symbolizing the planting of seed. A priest and priestess engage in intercourse while the others watch and chant to the gods for abundance. I recognize Byrne as one of the priests. I smile. Another life together.

I see myself standing in a field, gazing at the sky. I raise my left hand, point my index finger to the sky and command the rain that begins immediately. Then my attention shifts to the temple where the priestesses gather. I'm lying on a rock platform, naked. The other ten or so priestesses gather around me and begin pleasuring me. I'm shocked at the scene, yet fascinated. We only see the priests once a year, so the rest of the time, we take care of each other.

With this trip to Egypt, I feel a shift in my vibration, my consciousness and my energy field. I keep asking the Universe for growth and change for the better in my world and the world at large.

Chapter 23

Monterey, California
April 3, 1992

A Uranus-Neptune conjunction transiting my Venus brings erotic breakthroughs on the frontiers of sexual exploration.

Marriage is never perfect, but Byrne and I have been unusually fortunate. We do have a recurring problem. Over the years, Byrne has short, but intense periods of performance anxiety that interfere with our usually rich, adventuresome sex life. His need to please me and his perfectionist personality short circuit his sex drive. It's frustrating for us. I can usually pull him out of it by the sensual massage techniques our friend Ned, a sex therapist, taught me and by denying Byrne any access to my body for a couple of days. But, we'd like to find a permanent fix. We're continually on the lookout for ways to deepen our connection and keep the passion alive.

Sixty people attend the weekend Tantra Yoga seminar in Monterey with Charles and Carolyn Muir, who have been teaching Tantra for years. Most of the married couples verge on divorce and are desperately making this one last effort to salvage their relationships.

Byrne and I listen to the stories of couples who've never experienced true intimacy, sexual or otherwise. One single guy moves Byrne to tears: he's an overweight, double amputee who's been to several of these seminars and never found anyone to be intimate with him. Several of the single women struggle with their personal history of molestation. We feel decidedly out of place.

We enjoy the exercises, like kissing in the "yab yum" position. We sit facing each other. Byrne sits cross-legged; I'm astride him with his thighs supporting my weight. My legs wrap around his waist with the soles of my feet touching each other. In this position, we experiment with different kissing techniques, focusing on the sensual sensations of tongue, lips and the ways to stimulate various parts of the inside of the mouth. We learn the importance of "soul gazing", looking into each other's eyes and maintaining prolonged contact. We establish a deeper connection, focusing only on each other.

Now, we're ready for the heavy stuff—the G-spot. I've heard of it, but have no idea what it is or where it is. Byrne knows what it is but doesn't know exactly where it is. Massaging the G-spot heals sexual issues in both men and women. In women, access is vaginal; in men, it's rectal. Charles makes the point that a man has to be very comfortable with, and confident about, his sexuality to allow his partner to explore that area. The buzz of male murmurings to their partners says he's right.

The Muirs give us a live demonstration of G-spot massage. Carolyn, wearing a semi-sheer negligee, lies down on a raised platform in front of the class. Charles kneels beside her, gazing into her eyes. He tells her how beautiful she is, how much he loves her. His middle and index fingers inside her, he massages her G-spot, located up and behind the pubic bone. Her body quivers and her back arches. Within minutes, she reaches climax. The shocked look on Byrne's face makes me think that maybe this was a little too much for him, but I'll find out later that I'm wrong.

Our homework assignments for the evening require the man to please his goddess by doing whatever she wants him to without intercourse. He gives; she receives. Tonight, each man must search for that elusive treasure the G-spot and heal his goddess. Byrne's excitement grows.

Charles asks the single people to come to the front. He clusters the men together, and the women make a circle around them. He asks the women to choose a partner to pleasure them that evening. This is optional, but no one opts out. One adventuresome young woman chooses two guys. I like her style.

I luxuriate in the tub, preparing my goddess body. Byrne prepares the temple, lighting candles and burning incense. We're in the spirit of things. I appear in a sheer negligee and offer myself to him for my pleasure.

We assume the "yab yum" position and stare into each other's eyes without breaking contact. We breathe in synchrony. As I breathe in, he breathes out. I can feel the energy whirling around, heating up the room, just like it did in the Japanese life with Richard.

In spite of my misgivings, Byrne finds my G-spot. It's a different sensation, an urgent burning, itching feeling together with intense pressure and the urge to urinate even with an empty bladder. At some point, I feel out of my body and lose all sense of time and space. At climax, I crash back into my body, totally disoriented. Byrne asks me if I'm all right. I am more than all right.

The next morning we were encouraged to share our evening with the class. The arrogant, single guy who declared he could go into any bar and get laid within five minutes is first up. A plain, slightly overweight woman his age chose him. He seems transfixed as he tells us he's never experienced anything like it in his whole life. He'd never experienced such joy in giving to a woman and expecting nothing in return. He declares himself forever changed. He gets it, and we're all thrilled for him.

The ménage a trois sends us into fits of laughter with their tale. The two guys, friends, brought a juicer and a crate of oranges with them for extra energy. They took turns pleasuring their goddess with all sensual delights, except intercourse as instructed. In the morning she wanted another go-round; so, while one of them pleasured the goddess once more, the other one juiced. He also called the front desk for a late checkout. He speculates with great hilarity on the clerk's reaction to hearing the powerful juicer, and the screams of their goddess blending in ecstatic synergy. It's a wonder the clerk didn't call the cops.

Many of the married couples recounted the joy of experiencing true intimacy, and not just sex. They now had hope of saving their marriages. It was inspiring.

Byrne and I didn't feel the need to share our experiences, which seemed tame by comparison. We thought it more important for the troubled couples to share and revel in their success.

On the drive home, we agree it was a great experience. We welcome anything that brings us even closer. I feel incredibly lucky to have someone willing to share these experiences with me. I don't think many men could be married to me. I think my emotional intensity and unquenchable thirst for personal growth and adventure might prove too daunting for most men.

Sacramento, California
May 18, 1993

> Change oriented Uranus and Neptune pass over my Moon bringing restlessness and domestic changes.

Faces of Love, Death and Transformation:

The kids have their own lives now. Stacie is in her junior year at UC Santa Barbara. Darren chose the University of Arkansas so he could run track. Melissa works in an office for Kelly Services while she searches for her true path in life.

In the life reading Charlsie did for Brett when he was thirteen, she predicted that at age nineteen Brett would have something happen that would change the course and direction of his life. Getting married and starting a family certainly qualifies. He and his wife have a three-year-old and newborn twin girls. They've taken on huge responsibility with great tenacity and persistence.

We weathered the angst, rebellion and assorted hi-jinks of the kid's teen years with no major casualties. The family unit holds strong, bound by shared experiences and cultivated memories. Byrne and I have done a good job blending our family. Now, it's time for new adventures.

We're restless and need change. Byrne and I are moving to Little Rock, Arkansas, where he accepted a position as an assistant professor at the University of Arkansas Medical School. He wants to leave the stress of private practice behind and teach medical students. It seems a good way to wind down his career in medicine.

I smile when I think about Charlsie's predictions last year of a move for Byrne and a new career where he would be helping poor women. At the time, he totally rejected the whole possibility, saying, "Why would I want to do that?" It did seem pretty improbable. But now, he's to be the director of the new women's clinic at the University in addition to teaching. She hit the mark, as usual.

Sacramento, California
August 1996

> Pluto moved into my 1st house of self in 1995 to begin the 14 year transformation of my self and my entire personality. My strong natal drive to be in control will be assaulted. Uranus in my 2nd house of values works with Pluto to bring drastic change to my life, showing me the areas within me I need to reform
>
> Neptune brings confusion and uncertainty. Saturn brings the safe structures of my life crashing down.

> **The related energies of the San Francisco and Kentucky lives ready to reveal the immense challenges that will show me the way I can balance those experiences with this life and learn surrender and compassion, my life's greatest lessons.**

I've been thinking about writing a book, chronicling the story of the group for a long time. I promised Bobby I would do that someday, which was odd since I didn't think of myself as a writer at the time. That long-ago planted seed now pushes its way to the light.

I think about the possible consequences of revealing the secrets of the past in telling our stories, the reactions to it. That night I have a dream that banishes my fears:

I stood on a vast, grassy savanna out of Jurassic Park. Prehistoric beasts roamed freely, challenging each other. I watched them fight and kill each other, nervously fearing for my safety. I was in an extremely vulnerable position. A strong voice said to me, "If you tell the truth, they can't kill you."

I'm back in Sacramento for a visit and I use the time to interview Richard. I want him to tell me the reasons for the decisions he made regarding our relationship back in the 60s. He reveals himself only when he's well lubricated with spirits.

I buy a bottle of Seagram's Crown Royal and invite him to Filben's, where I'm staying, for dinner. He arrives from work, looking harried and nervous. After the second Perfect, he loosens up. By the time we finish the bottle, the shit house mouse has us in his back pocket, but I haven't asked the crucial questions yet.

I walk Richard to his car. "You know, it wouldn't have killed you to marry me for a couple of years and let me have my babies."

He stops and grins. "I was too young and stubborn. I wish you'd have gotten pregnant; we could have gotten married and had a couple of kids."

He's just blindsided me again as he did at his wedding. I don't know what to say. If he believed in fate and past lives, I could explain to him why that didn't happen. But he doesn't. I was meant to be with Byrne and experience the deep connection we have. I couldn't have grown into the consciousness I have without Byrne's love, support and nurturing.

It's really late. Richard glances at his watch. "I'm going to catch hell from Vickie being out this late. I don't know what it is, but she's really jealous of you and she's not the jealous type. She's never had a problem with anybody else. She doesn't understand why I still see you. I told her you've been in my life forever and you always will be."

I don't tell him about the look on her face in the hospital when we cried over their baby. I know exactly why she feels the way she does. I can't blame her.

We talk more about old times. "If you had tried to marry anyone out of the group, I would have come down here and torn the place apart."

I smile at the thought, Richard's personal version of "The Graduate." He stops talking and looks at me intently. "Look at you: you're still a beautiful woman. Can I kiss you?"

I'm human. Stroking the bones of the old feelings we've disinterred tonight makes me naturally curious. I say yes.

We kiss. It's as passionate as ever; our bodies coming together like two pieces of a puzzle, fitting perfectly—time and space of thirty years disappear. Richard holds me tightly and sighs deeply. I feel the intensity of his regret for what might have been. "I love you, Constance, always have, always will."

"I love you, too," I tell him. And I do, as ever, and it still doesn't have anything to do with how I love Byrne. Richard will always have that special place in my heart that belongs to him, but we're in silent agreement: we are merely reaffirming our timeless connection to each other. It doesn't go beyond that.

Little Rock, Arkansas
February 1997

> **Uranus sits on my Sun, bringing shock, disruption, traumatic change, demanding I be strong.**

Byrne's always been the absent minded professor type. We all have endless stories affectionately recalling his quirks and lapses of memory. It's part of his lovable persona. I'm desensitized and all the subtle signs don't register.

I'm waiting dinner while Byrne has his annual physical. The doctor calls me to alert me that he'd found some disturbing signs while doing a routine neurological exam. He wants a full work-up done. My heart sinks; I know something isn't right. Things are falling into place in my brain.

The exams completed, I'm driving Byrne home from the hospital. We have the diagnosis: Alzheimer's disease. Profound shock rocks us.

We sit on the couch in our family room and look at each other in desolation. Collapsing in tears, we hold onto each other. Byrne says, "If something bad had to happen, I'm glad it happened to me; I couldn't bear it if anything happened to you." We break down in tears again. "When I get really bad, just put me away somewhere and leave me."

"I could never do that, sweetheart," I sob. The Universe tests my vow to always take care of him, no matter what.

"Well, I'll have more time to work out at the gym. I'll be buffed, but brainless. Light's on, nobody's home." We burst into nervous laughter.

I'm on the verge of panic. I don't want Byrne to know, so I go upstairs to my walk-in closet and let the feelings overwhelm me. I fall to my knees and beg God, "Please don't take him away from me. Please!" The panic subsides, and I know my plea is fruitless. I do the only thing I can to survive—I shut down emotionally. I go into battle mode; I'm going to fight this with everything I have. No surrender.

I call Charlsie. She hadn't done Byrne's progression for the year as yet. I tell her the news. She tells me she'd written on the front of his file for this year "nervous disorder." She didn't know how that would manifest, but Alzheimer's fit the category. Charlsie expresses her heartfelt sorrow that we have to experience what's coming. She knows I'm inconsolable and no words will help.

Byrne's been trying to hold himself together for so long, he deflates like a worn tire. I want him to fight, but he doesn't have the energy. He turns everything over to me in passive surrender to whatever comes. He resigns from the University, and we put the house up for sale. We have six months of alone time to try and adjust. I can't bring myself to tell anyone yet.

I spend hours on the Internet researching Alzheimer's, looking for something to help him. Anything. I try and make sense out of what's happening. The best I can do is venture that it's karma. This is how I can balance my lack of compassion in the Kentucky life when Byrne became senile, our San Francisco life when I drove him mad. Now I have to watch him lose his mind, and this time I have to take care of him, be good to him, be compassionate.

I don't know what karma he's working on, but I take some solace in knowing that we've agreed to do this for our souls' growth. I'm terrified of what the future holds. I know, no matter what happens in this life, that we'll be together again. We just have to get through this. We joke that compared to the Spanish Inquisition life, this is a piece of cake. At least we aren't being drawn and quartered. But emotionally we are.

Santorini, Greece
April 1997

I meditate and focus on my spiritual beliefs to comfort me, in order to rise above what's happening and find some meaning and peace. I fixate on the Greek life. I want to find that beach to reconnect to that experience and the happiness of that life. I book a cruise to Greece and Turkey.

I know the beach exists. After I first saw it in my past life recall, a brochure came for a trip to Greece. On the front there was a picture of the beach. Elated and stunned, I vowed we would go there someday. The photo identified the beach as being in Santorini, one of the stops on this cruise.

A tour takes us through a recently rediscovered ancient city in Santorini that's being restored. I don't feel any connection as we walk around. I know this isn't it. We were wealthy back then and lived in a small town a few miles outside of Santorini. But it's not here. I'm more than disappointed; I feel let down by the Universe at a time that I need comfort.

The ship sets sail. We sit at the bar; I'm morose. Gwen and Bernie from Boca Raton invite us to join them on deck for champagne and caviar. Ordinarily, I wouldn't go on deck because of the wind—I hate it—but the champagne sounds inviting.

I settle myself in a deck chair, and Bernie hands me a glass of champagne. I look up and I see it—the beach. We're sailing past it right at that moment. A minute later, I would have missed it. It's where I thought it was, a few miles outside of Santorini; It's called Oia. I'm speechless. Profound joy moves through me as I stare in wonder. I thank my guides and ask forgiveness for doubting. They've given me what I asked for.

Little Rock, Arkansas
October 1997

Life gets more complicated. Melissa calls to tell me she and her live-in love of five years are getting married. She's pregnant and can I put together a wedding in two weeks. I'm thrilled about the baby and marriage, but I tell her it's impossible for me to do a wedding right now. Melissa says they can't wait, so they'll get some friends together and go to Nevada. I'm really sad I won't be at my daughter's wedding, but I have no choice.

I pack my blue Jaguar tightly, every space filled. The seat belt in back secures a covered litter box. Food and water for our cat Matty, the stray orange tabby that adopted us last January, sits on the floor. We look like the Beverly Hillbillies as we set out for Gig Harbor, Washington, our new home.

I drive, and Byrne bears the long hours in the car stoically, waiting for the Perfect Manhattan that awaits him at the end of each day. Matty quickly adjusts to the car, roaming at will from the back to the front as the spirit moves him. He's delighted to be included.

When we stop for lunch in Russell, Kansas, the transmission goes out. Jaguar sends a tow truck. The driver looks like a mountain man type with shaggy hair and beard, flannel shirt and a beer belly. It's Saturday, and he's pleased at the prospect of double time. He loads my Jag on the flatbed truck. Matty and I huddle together in the well behind the driver and passenger seat holding Byrne. We set out for Denver, Colorado, the nearest Jag dealership, stopping at a McDonald's drive-thru on the way. It's a three-hour drive; I'm hanging onto my sanity by a thread.

We have to be in Gig Harbor by Tuesday when our furniture arrives. We can't wait until Monday when the mechanics are back on duty, so we make a deal, swap cars and hit the road in a red Jag. I promptly get ticketed for speeding. I curse the color red. I can't find the registration in the mess; the trooper peers into the car and surveys the chaos. He tells me he'll wait in the patrol car until I get myself together. Matty tries to escape, but I grab his tail in the nick of time and haul him back inside. I can only imagine what the trooper is thinking.

Faces of Love, Death and Transformation:

Gig Harbor, Washington
March 1997

I picked Gig Harbor because Filben and Patrick live here, and I like the idea of living on the water. It's a small town across the Narrows Bridge from Tacoma. I think it'll be good for Byrne to be in a quiet, small town setting. Now, I realize I'm here to hide. We'll be here four years.

I need alone time, always have. Now, I have none. Byrne and I are together all the time. Patrick and Filben help by taking turns staying with Byrne for a few days at a time so I can get away and visit Melissa and my new grandson Tanner. I devote my monotonously regimented days to cooking three meals, helping Byrne do all the things he can no longer do, and taking over the functions he used to perform, such as handling finances.

I'm forced to learn about IRAs and stocks. My stress levels mount every day. I alternate between feelings of altruism and anger, faith and hopelessness, I wrestle with the guilt for not always being patient and unfailingly compassionate with the person I love most in life. I curse my weakness and pray for strength.

Alzheimer's affects each person differently. Byrne's primary symptoms involve a badly altered visual/spatial perception. I think it must be like living in a house of mirrors where nothing is really where it seems, everything off kilter. His motor skills persistently deteriorate. He walks like someone with 10 martinis on an empty stomach. It's indescribably painful to watch someone who was once so dexterous that he could remove ovaries through an endoscope now fail at buttoning his shirt or zipping his pants. Byrne's speech slurs, and he frequently forgets words that will complete his sentences. He can't read because he doesn't recognize some of the letters anymore. He picks clumsily at his beloved guitar but can no longer tune it. I learn to do it for him. My duty roster grows each day with frightening speed.

The most painful loss for him is sex. Next to eating, having sex with me is what has always given him the most pleasure in life. Now, he can't get an erection that works. At his request, I take him to a urologist, and he gives us a prescription. I have to inject his penis with Papaverine before making love. We do that for a couple of months, but the act is impossibly awkward and frustrating; Byrne has forgotten how to do that, too. Instead of kissing me, he pecks at me like a bird and licks my face like a dog. I finally tell him I just can't do it anymore; it's too emotionally painful to bear, even more than the look in his eyes when I tell him.

We look forward to cocktail time. We share a Perfect and watch Seinfeld reruns, laughing even after seeing each episode numerous times. We hold hands.

But I haven't given up entirely. I enroll Byrne in a drug trial program at the University of Washington in Seattle. I pray he's getting the research drug and not the placebo, but he is. I stuff him with organic food, vitamins, herbal products and anything else anyone suggests. It's time consuming. I'm tired and discouraged. I meditate and ask for some sign to tell me what to do. The dream comes.

Byrne and I were at a remote resort on the shores of Lake Michigan, having dinner at a lodge. He wanted to walk by the water. We strolled a quarter mile from the lodge, coming to a large, round pool of deep water. I turned to look at the lake. The weather dark and ominous, the wind whipped large waves into froth. I told Byrne we shouldn't be there. When I turned back, he'd disappeared into the pool of water. I saw his hand reaching up as it slipped beneath the dark water. I fell to my knees in a panic, plunging my hand into the water; I reached for him, but I couldn't find him. I knew if I jumped into the water, I'd die with him. I stood up, sobbing and wailing in anguish. I knew it was too late; no one could help him now. A voice said to me, "Let him go; he's better off, and so are you."

I have my answer: surrender. I stop torturing him with all the remedies, potions and pills. I go back to feeding him the kind of food that makes him happy, and I work at surrendering. We both now have a measure of peace.

Faces of Love, Death and Transformation:

Chapter 24

Granite Bay, California
March, 2001

> Over the years, I've revised my understanding of karma and the role of astrology in my life. I've moved past the idea that karma is punishment for past misdeeds. I see it as balancing feeling and experience, the opportunity to grow spiritually. In the Kentucky life I experienced receiving, in this life giving. Astrology, a blueprint of the past and the possibility of the future, sets nothing in stone. As Yogananda's teacher, Sri Yukteswar, explained to him, *"The message boldly emblazoned upon the heavens at the moment of birth is not meant to emphasize fate—the results of past good or evil—but to arouse man's will to escape from his universal thralldom. What he has done, he can undo."*

It's clear to me this life has been about undoing the karma from the Kentucky and San Francisco lives. I have a choice: I can wallow in the pain, or I can connect with the Higher Power that helps me rise above difficult experience, to see meaning in suffering, and give it purpose. If I hadn't reached this point of understanding, I wouldn't have survived the last four years. The stress, pain and bitterness would have killed me, and I would have to come back and have another go at it.

I've moved us home, close to where we lived in Fair Oaks. My sister Joan was right when she told me I couldn't do this by myself, that I needed to come home. I need to be closer to her and Melissa, my brother Graydon and old friends like Ken and Sandy who lived next door to us on Lafitte Court. And our grandkids Tanner and Hannah, Melissa's kids, are here. They bring Byrne and me such joy.

I've always believed that even the worst events have something positive come out of them. In this instance, the family grew closer, coming together with love, compassion and support for Byrne and me. Old friends didn't desert us. I appreciate how blessed we are.

Some days I can barely understand Byrne when he talks, so we play our version of

Clue. I ask him yes or no questions, trying to figure out what he wants. It's frustrating, but we manage for a time.

We can't sleep together anymore. I miss that, but he gets up countless times during the night, disturbing me. I have to have sleep or I can't function. I dread waking up each day, knowing what awaits me. Each night, I tuck Byrne into his bed like a small boy and crawl alone into mine to fall into a fitful sleep.

I enroll him in daycare three days a week at Somerford Place, an Alzheimer's care facility two miles away. I know the day will come when I won't be able physically to take care of him anymore. I'm preparing us.

I think about the people who lack the resources that we have enduring and navigating this disease. I count my blessings. Things could be worse.

I try to train Byrne to sit down and pee. I'm not having much luck. He misses the toilet completely and pees on the floor. No matter how many times a day I mop, the smell of urine overpowers the bathroom.

I wake to a new smell. I lay in bed, dreading getting up. I find Byrne in the bathroom standing in his own shit, his hands covered. The mess is all over the floor and walls. He's trying to clean it up, but making the mess worse. He looks like a small boy, terrified his mother will be angry. I don't know where to start. I wipe his feet and walk him to my shower. I get in with him and scrub him clean. It takes me two hours to clean the bathroom. I'm overwhelmed, crying and gagging. I realize that we're moving into a new phase of the disease. I don't know who to feel more sorry for—him or me.

March 2002

I'm waiting for a sign, dreading it. I don't know if I have the courage. The patient coordinator at Somerford calls me to tell me they have an opening for Byrne. She tells me it's better to move him when he's still oriented enough to make an easier adjustment. It'll be much harder on him further down the line. I know she's right.

He takes the news with quiet resignation, telling me he'll do whatever is best for me. It's killing me, but I'm on the verge of a breakdown. We hold each other and cry. I promise him I won't desert him; I'll bring him home for dinner and cocktails every other night. That consoles him.

As I leave him that first night, I'm in so much emotional pain I can barely see to get out the front door. I go home and sleep 12 hours straight.

Byrne does well with the structured routine at the home. They have coffee waiting for him, no matter what time he gets up, and give him whatever he wants for breakfast. He enjoys the food and the social activities. The staff members love him. I keep my promise to bring Byrne home every other night. He thanks me for making the transition so easy for him. I feel like I've weathered a major hurdle, but problems still challenge us.

I'm with Byrne every other day, but when I'm not there, he's convinced I'm dead. When he sees me, he bursts into sobs of relief. His pain is so real my heart breaks. This goes on for several weeks. We're emotionally exhausted. I try to make him understand. I sit on the couch with him and hold his hand. "You've got to stop doing this. I'm not going to die before you. I promise. And even if I did, I wouldn't leave without you. I'd come and get you. I'm not going anywhere without you, sweetheart."

Something clicks in him. His eyes tell me I've hit the right note. "You'll take me with you?"

"Yes. I promise. Remember? We always go together."

He sighs with relief and that crisis ends. We move on to the next one.

Now he's in love. His brain seems to be at the 12-year-old stage. He has a crush on Maria, the new, young caregiver on the day shift. He tells me she's coming on to him and they've been kissing. I know that's impossible.

"I think she wants to marry me."

"Have you forgotten that you're already married?"

"Oh, my gosh." Bewildered, he thinks for a minute. "Is there any rule that says I can't have two wives?"

What the hell, I decide. "It's okay with me. Just remember, I don't do trios." He laughs. It amazes me that the part of his brain that rules humor still functions. It's not supposed to.

His 12-year-old gets up the courage to ask Maria if she wants to have sex. She tells him he's too old for her, and he's crushed. He was sure she reciprocated his affections. He's oblivious to his inability to perform, to the depths of his delusion. I console him and try not to take it personally. He's not in his right mind.

August 15, 2002

Richard calls. We've had no contact since our move back to Sacramento. He knows through the grapevine I moved Byrne to Somerford. He wants to see him. I give him directions to the home. I can tell he's confused. He says he wants to see me, too. I tell him I'm busy. I'm unhappy that he's waited so long to call.

That evening he calls again. "Ed and I had lunch with Byrne today. Boy, it's really tough seeing him that way—but I don't have to tell you that. It's hard communicating with him, but he can still eat up a storm. I am so proud of the way you've handled this whole thing. You've really been through it. There's no way you could keep taking care of him. You're a real trooper, Constance."

I don't appreciate his kind words. I resent his marching into the trenches of my life like a general visiting the troops on the front line, giving a pep talk and marching out again. I don't react to his praise and change the subject. I know he'll disappear again and he does. I still want more from Richard than he can give me. I need him to be present in my life, not an infrequent visitor.

September 10, 2002

> A powerful Venus retrograde loop in Gemini in my 7th house challenges me to reflect anew on my relationships. I'm pitched into emotional territory I've avoided for a long time. The Venus energy makes me realize I have to face to my fears and connect with my feelings, despite the pain.

I'm going through the motions. I spend time with Byrne, but I'm distancing myself emotionally, and he feels it. I'm protecting myself, but it's time to release the emotions I've suppressed. Before I can be whole again, I have to walk through my grief, and own it.

I subscribed to an e-mail astrology service several months ago. Chris Hedlund, the astrologer, explains how the Venus loop energy works:

"Venus's retrograde loop to Scorpio offers us a chance to create a richer, deeper, wiser, stronger presence of love in our lives.

It is likely to make us scrutinize the exchanges we have in play with important others in our lives and perhaps "fix" ones that aren't satisfactory, and that may be important to do; but it also should make us scrutinize how much we expect to get from outside versus how well we realize that we must create love from within.

What it's really about is moving to a place where we have greater love within ourselves, and thereby create greater love around us."

His words on Venus trigger insights. I haven't allowed myself to grieve over what used to be with Byrne. The pain terrifies me, and I'm already emotionally exhausted. I've almost forgotten what it was like between us, the love and passion, the emotional connection, the joy of being together. I have to reconnect with that again before Byrne dies. I have so much I want to tell him. He needs to know how he healed my heart with his unconditional love, and how no one will ever be able to break it again. We were better people for having loved each other, much better together than we were apart. We enriched each other in such unimaginable ways.

Our children grew up experiencing our love, respect and support for each other and for them. When Eddie's wife once asked Melissa and Stacie what kind of relationship they wanted when they got married, they both said, "Like Mom and Byrne's." The boys feel the same way.

I make him an album of our Wonder Years. I sift through the mountain of pictures we've collected over time and pick out the ones that show the love between us— the fun, funny, poignant, romantic ones that illustrate our deep bond. I can't find one photo where we aren't touching. I think about how affectionate Byrne was. If he could reach me, he had to touch me in some way—a brief kiss, a caress, a squeeze of my hand, running his hand down my back as he passed by me. If we were out to dinner, his hand always found mine and he held it throughout the meal. It was so natural and instinctual to him. He relished our connection and his frequent gestures of affection showed me how much it meant to him. I loved it and I never took it for granted. It's what I miss more than anything. It's one of the first things Alzheimer's took away from us.

I take out our old love letters and read each one and sob, remembering those wonderful feelings we shared. I play all the old Englebert Humperdinck songs we love until my heart is back in that loving place. I walk through the pain and find the joy still there, waiting for me.

I bring Byrne home for dinner and tell him what I've done. I tell him how much I love him, how much I miss him. I tell him how wonderful he is—the best person I've ever known, my hero, and that he will always be the love of all my lives.

The love in his usually vacant eyes warms me. He cries as I kiss him. I'm so ashamed I couldn't do this sooner, and grateful I have now.

Our evenings together now are different. We talk about the good times, our early days together, and how much we love each other. We laugh. We still don't have sex, but I make love to him, and it's good. I have some peace.

I'm trying to do what the Navajo Indians do, which is to walk in beauty. No matter what's happening in your life, you find the good, the beautiful, and you live with gratitude.

I'm overwhelmed at times by the kindness and compassion from family and friends. I'm grateful for the kindness of the caregivers like Pam, who buys me presents on special occasions from Byrne and cards that tell me how much he loves me. I'm grateful to Joann, who talks to him about me and cooks him the special things I bring in for his breakfasts. I'm indebted to Cindy who fusses over him. I promised Byrne in one of those black humor moments that I'd hire a pretty blond with big boobs to take care of him. Cindy fits the bill. It takes a special kind of person to do the work they do with such compassionate, loving commitment.

February 2003

> **Saturn returns to my 8th house of sex and deep relationships again until fall of 05. Richard returns, forcing me to revisit our relationship. I have to deal with those deep psyche issues I've avoided until now—face those hidden parts of myself as I did in 1976. Parts of me will fall away, opening new doors when Saturn moves into my 9th house.**

I've finished the first, rough draft of this book, and I need feedback. Richard is the obvious choice, but I'm hesitant to make myself so emotionally vulnerable.

Richard recovered slowly from Vickie leaving him for another man four years ago. I talked to him about the breakup at the time. He professed shock and proclaimed he didn't see it coming; he thought they had a good marriage. I didn't have the heart to tell him: if he didn't see it coming, it's because he wasn't paying attention. Women don't leave "good" marriages. I always felt Richard committed to the marriage but not to the relationship—big difference. I'm surprised it lasted as long as it did. He has that same stubborn will that I have.

He's excited that I've finished the draft; I want him to read it and tell me what he thinks. I want him to come and stay with me for two days. I don't want him to tell anyone in the group about the book yet. He says he'll let me know when he can come.

A month goes by and he's made several excuses for not coming. I know he's not being truthful. I'm mad. I e-mail him and tell him if he isn't going to be there for me when I need him, we can't be friends, and I'm ready to banish him from my life.

That evening, Richard calls. He just read my e-mail. "I don't know what to say. You know I'm not good at—communicating."

"I know, but try."

"I don't want to lose you. I can't lose you. I can't imagine us not being close and being in each other's lives."

He's not making any sense. We haven't seen each other in two years. "I need you to help me with this project. I've done everything I can to get you here, except promise you sex. I'd throw that in, too, but I haven't had any in six years, and you wouldn't live through it. I need you alive." I'm trying to lighten the mood.

"I thought about what would happen if we were alone. With our strong chemistry, one thing would lead to another—if Eddie ever found out we were together, he'd be devastated. We're so close. I can't do that to him; I won't! It wouldn't be right, you know?" He's pleading for my understanding. "We can't ever be alone." There's genuine panic in his voice.

"Eddie? Eddie's married, now. He doesn't care about me. It's always about Eddie," I fume. This doesn't make any sense.

Eddie remarried about ten years ago to a nice woman with a drinking problem equal to his. Right after she moved in with him, he put her in an alcohol rehab unit to dry out. Eddie called me and told me, "It's funny. Even after being married and having two kids, I never knew what love was until now—that feeling of the other person being more important than yourself, you know?" It was a nice speech and I hoped it was true.

Until recently, Eddie and his wife remained on the wagon. But I know he's drinking and smoking again, despite having several heart attacks requiring stents to open narrowed vessels. He seems determined to kill himself.

I've become friendly with his wife who tells me she's in counseling and on antidepressants. She says, matter-of-factly, that Eddie's an emotional abuser. I agree with her. He doesn't treat her any better than he treated me—so much for the true love speech.

In spite of the facts, Richard obviously believes Eddie still has feelings for me. I think he's projecting on to Eddie how he felt when Eddie told him we were getting married. Richard's never gotten over me and he doesn't think Eddie has, either. Richard's perception they share the same pain makes a strong bond.

Richard still plays into that Virgo martyr trap, still willing to crucify his happiness on the cross of friendship. His stubborn Taurus need to do the right thing is more important to him than being happy, still trying to protect Eddie from himself.

"Life isn't fair," Richard adds. After a brief silence, he shifts gears. "It's funny; every woman I've ever been with has hated you on sight. I've tried downplaying the whole thing, but it never worked. Women must have some kind of intuition about these things. I can't lose you."

"What you're saying is: we can only see each other at weddings and funerals." Richard doesn't seem to have any idea how irrational he sounds. He doesn't want to lose me, but we can't see each other alone. He wants me to honor our close connection, but at a safe distance. The forbidden sign at his lake warns me away once again.

I capitulate. I don't agree with his thinking, but I have to accept it. I get that Eddie is the most important person in Richard's life—the child he will never have. He dotes on Eddie, protects him, rationalizes his bad behavior and gives him unconditional love. It's disturbing to me Richard doesn't realize that his years of enabling Eddie have helped keep him a child, not in his best interest.

I don't think it's all about Eddie. Like my father, Richard chooses safety on the shallow shore of his emotions. He's terrified of my luring him into deep waters that will swallow him. He knows that's where I'd surely take him. His engulfment fears still live large in his psyche.

I finally agree to send him the manuscript. Two weeks later, I realize it was a big mistake. He doesn't like it. He thinks the whole focus should be on Bobby and he thinks I made too big a deal about his mother sending him away.

We have decidedly different artistic visions of this project. I'm furious, not so much at what he said, but at all the things he didn't say. I expected him to be moved emotionally, but if he was, it's not apparent. I fire off another e-mail, raging at his monumental insensitivity, and how he's unworthy of my friendship. I even use the "F" word in my fury, telling him what he can do with himself. I tell him when it comes to relationships he doesn't have a clue and never will. I order him out of my life forever more, or similar words to that effect. Richard still has the ability to make me totally crazy. I sob and scream for at least an hour to purge the rage and frustration I'm feeling. Then I call Karen to tell her my tale of woe. She laughs, tells me that we've always fought and we always make up. I assure her, I'm serious this time.

"You know I adore Richard; I love him, but I hope you don't get romantically involved with him again. He broke your heart. You deserve someone like Byrne. You're fun, smart, don't need his money and you're gorgeous. Richard's an idiot. He doesn't know how to do those little things that make a woman happy. He isn't good at relationships and that isn't going to change."

Family and friends that know both Richard and me echo Karen's sentiments. It's unanimous.

Chico, California
July 2003

I've been adrift since my close friend and astrologer Charlsie died three years ago. To me she was the mother I never had, and I deeply miss her. I'm a spiritual orphan in need of sustenance. I read *Destiny of Souls* by Michael Newton, PhD. His book documents thousands of hypnotic sessions with people who traveled to the space where we go between lives. This is the place where we evaluate how we've done in our current incarnation and plan the next one. In the book, all the subjects reported similar experiences and understanding of how the process works when we go to the place between lives. I found it enlightening and comforting. I want to experience it for myself, so I make an appointment to take my trip to the netherworld.

I settle in the soft recliner and close my eyes. David, the hypnotherapist, begins the induction, and I slip down into that familiar place.

"Where are you?"

My voice, soft and slow, sounds like I'm on the verge of sleep. "I'm back in the Greek life, 5th century B.C. I see a fountain. I live in a very big house. There are children running around, very happy; they're my grandchildren. It's a normal day in the household. Life is good. The best life my husband and I ever had together. He's teaching right now, teaches math and history, a renowned teacher. I've been madly in love with him since I was 16, very happy together. I'm about 55 now. House full of guests, learning things.

"Move forward to an important event."

"I've just died, my husband died the day before. I'm going up and there's this big white light. He's coming to meet me. We explode in the light and the feeling is indescribable—the love. I see us the way were when I was 16 and he was 18. We're crossing over to the other side together. It's like the heavens open; you go through the opening and it closes. Everything else is gone; the connection to the life is gone. We're just back as energy together. I see a table and it's full of food."

"That's unusual."

I laugh. "Not if you know my husband. He loves to eat; I swear. We're celebrating a life where we weren't brutally killed, where we died within a day of each other. That life was like taking a vacation. We learned a lot and taught a lot. Now, we're back to see where we go next. We're enjoying a life well lived.

Now, I see a waterfall; we're under the water and letting it run over us. It's a cleansing thing, a rebalancing of energy, part of the re-entry process. We just sit under the waterfall, like it's washing away residue and we're just enjoying being together, like coming home after a long journey. It was good, but it's always better to be home.

Now, we're at a place with intense lights of different colors, coming from all directions, like it's doing something to our energy fields. It's kind of interesting because I sense that you don't usually do this with someone; most other souls do it solo; for some reason, we're doing it together."

"You're quite right. That is unusual."

"We're just very bonded. We've been that way practically every life we've had. I keep seeing this intense red energy that connects us. I have no idea what that is. It comes out of our sides and connects from under our arms to our hips, so the torsos of our bodies are connected by this intense red color."

"Move into the red color and describe what you know."

"It's a kind of oneness. That's the only word that comes to me. A total blending at the center of the energies, a bonding."

"Is this connected to what Connie needs to do for Byrne?"

"No, it just is. It's just a part of us, a part of our energies together."

"What are you experiencing now?"

"What's come to me is that it represents the bond between us. It's so strong nothing could ever break it—nothing. I get the feeling that there's some kind of important progression in our souls' growth—at our level of being that is ready to shift after this incarnation. I don't know if it means we don't need to come back again. It's like there's something different, like graduating to something else. As usual, he's going to die before I do, which he almost always does. I have to finish what I've come to do, then we can move on."

"In the spirit world, what do you call him?"

"Atarax." I start laughing. "It sounds like an antidepressant. That's a screwy name. My rational mind is going, Oh, no!"

"Will you allow him to speak through you."

"Of course. I've never done that before."

"Atarax, why Alzheimer's?"

Faces of Love, Death and Transformation:

"I needed the experience. I needed to know what it was like to be taken care of."

I'm weeping now. That made perfect sense. In all his lives, he always took care of everyone, being responsible.

"Is there anything else Connie needs to do for you as Byrne?"

"She's done it. She's loved me. She made me happy. She helped me grow. Just taken care of me. We were gifts to each other. I love you, and I miss you. I'm always with you. Always."

"Breathe, Connie. Go back to the lights and rest. Rest in each other's company. Balancing. What color are you seeing?"

"Blue, bright blue. The lights are turning us blue."

"What do you notice about the red energy that connects you? Is the color and intensity shifting?"

"We're just one blob of blue. Together. It's like the guides, they humor us." I'm laughing. "They think we're like a couple of teenagers, joined at the hip. But they indulge us and let us do what we want to do. We've had that kind of relationship in this life; people just couldn't get over how different we were from most other people—our relationship, how close we were."

"What do the guides say now?"

"Time to move on, whatever that means. To the next level. The word that comes is teachers. We both did that in this life in various capacities. I get the feeling we're going to be allowed to just be for a while after this incarnation. Take a long spiritual vacation. Do fun things and get ready for the next experience, kind of like going to Europe after graduation, one of those coming of age things."

"What's going on now?"

"I was just thinking I really don't want to come back again. Rather do something else; I'm tired. He's telling me we might have to. I don't know, like it's up in the air."

"Rest, and know things will take care of themselves. How many souls know they are truly loved."

"I do."

"That's right. Now, feel the blue color and what it means."

"It's a very light energy, very light. Like shifting to a higher gear."

"How does it feel in your nervous system?"

"Peace. A calm knowingness."

"From here in the spirit world, as you look forward to Connie's life, what do you see?"

"I see lots of good things. Got a lot of good years ahead."

"What do you notice that's different about her?"

"No expectations. A total surrender to what needs to be and not trying to make anything happen. Just do what I know needs to be done, let the Universe take care of it and do whatever it wants with it, like finishing the book I'm writing."

"From here in the spirit world, what do you see that you need to do for yourself?"

"Have fun. Yeah, have fun. Enjoy what I have. And I do, even now."

"The guides are telling me that Bobby's here."

"Yes, he is. I asked him to be here. He's telling me he loves me. Outside of my husband, I know he's part of my spirit group. He was the one who originally planted the seed for my book; although it's not what it originally was going to be, he approves."

"Is it time for a council of wise beings?"

"Yeah, I'm always up for that."

"Find yourself at that place."

"Just a group of people at a long table, it isn't straight, and it isn't semi-circle; it's different, and they're very pleased with me."

"How many are there."

"A lot, the number 12 comes to mind. Huge gathering it seems like. My primary guide is right beside me on my left; he's purple light. They're telling me that I took on a huge load of lessons and I did it. I did it; I pulled it off. I'm dancing around ecstatically. Yahoo."

"Now, go to another place in the spirit world that's important to you."

"I'm in the library where the records are kept. I need to spend a lot of time here when I go back, because I get to try to be a guide, kind of a low level guide, entry level, and I can stay on that side if I want to and just help from that side. See how that fits and learn the rules of engagement, the ones about not interfering, not saving. It's about just giving support and planting seeds and hoping that they take. Letting people be accountable for what they do, otherwise they won't learn the lesson. Kind of like what Bobby's been doing for me on the other side. When I do deep meditation, he shows up in a short white robe, and he has a guide with him, looks like a medieval monk; his name is Eric. Bobby hangs around with Eric, his teacher. I don't know what I'm going to do.

I was really afraid in this life that because I'm an older soul than Byrne is we might not be able to stay together after this life. But it's come to me that he's just as advanced; we can do what we do and do it together. He won't have to come without me if he doesn't want to. If he had any sense, given our past lives, he'd never come back with me. Poor guy."

"What does Eric say about your book?"

"He says it's going to change people's perceptions of reality. Which is good, because that's what it's meant to do. He says, 'And the sex helps, too.' We both burst out laughing. "He has a sense of humor."

"Before we leave the spirit world, is there anything else you'd like to know?"

"No, I think that does it."

Experiences like this one sustain me, recharging my spirit with hope and purpose, making my connection to the divine stronger and more vivid.

Lake Tahoe, California
September 13, 2003

It's Stacie's wedding day, a bright, warm day, the sun creating prisms of dazzling color dancing on deep blue water. Stacie declared at age 10 she wanted to be married on the deck at Sunnyside, a popular restaurant and lodge, overlooking Lake Tahoe. Joan and I convinced her adored husband, Bob, to become a minister of the Universal Life church for ten dollars so he could marry them. He's the titular head of our family since Byrne had to abdicate, and Bob's a natural choice to be our spiritual leader as well. Stacie wanted someone special to marry them, and Bob is the one. She's thrilled that he's agreed to perform the ceremony.

Everything waits in perfect readiness. I'm an emotional wreck, terrified I'll do nothing but sob the whole day. Stacie wanted Byrne here to walk down the aisle with her and Eddie. I cry when I think about all the times the three of us talked about Byrne dancing the first dance with her, a waltz. I'm in a panic, hoping he won't fall and hurt himself. He can barely walk now, but it's important to Stacie he be here. Maria from Somerford is driving him up from Sacramento.

I reflect on the men my girls have chosen to marry. They've done a remarkable job given the father they have. I credit Byrne for modeling what a man, husband and father should be. They've both married men who are like him: smart, kind, stable, responsible and who make wonderful fathers. I am as proud of them as I am embarrassed for me. In spite of my belief that we choose our parents, I'm not pleased Eddie is their father. I'm grateful they are more mindful of their choices.

Brett is here from Florida with his family. I'm so proud of him. In spite of the odds against them for marrying so young, he and his wife grew and matured together. Brett has a Master's in psychology and his wife is a school principal. Their three daughters are happy, well-adjusted teenagers.

Brett's been a God-send to me today, helping me with Byrne and staying by his side to see that nothing happens to him. He's grown into the kind of man his father is: strong, loving, loyal and compassionate. Darren is another story.

My early optimism that Darren could overcome his personality flaws waned over the years. Darren fell into a distinct pattern of neglect about two years after Byrne was diagnosed with Alzheimer's. We only heard from him when he wanted money. Eventually, he ignored Byrne's birthdays, Father's Day, and Christmas. It hurt Byrne terribly. I couldn't stand by any longer; I tried to talk to Darren about the importance of family and being there for Byrne. My plea fell on deaf ears. Darren reacted with a blistering rebuttal that ended communication between us.

Darren is here alone. He's tried to be charming, acting as though nothing has happened between us. It isn't working. I feel sorry for him, but I have no patience for his bullshit and I can't forget how he's treated the one person in his life who has loved him unconditionally.

Richard will be here. I plan to ignore him, and I'm sure he'll do the same to me.

To my great relief, Byrne makes it down the aisle. Everyone is in tears. Eddie does the first dance with Stacie, then she leads Byrne to the dance floor. I look at Joan and say, "Kill me; just kill me now and get it over with." The next song is Unchained Melody. I dance with Byrne and bury my face in his chest and sob for the way it should have been. He's oblivious, enjoying the dancing. When he's tired, Maria takes him back to Sacramento.

I take a deep breath, get a big glass of champagne and rejoin the festivities.

Richard grabs my hand and pulls me onto the dance floor. I'm surprised. I thought he'd leave me alone, but he seems determined to get back in my good graces.

"Constance, you are smashing!" There's genuine admiration in his eyes.

"Yes, I am; I'm still mad at you, and you're still a shit."

"No, I'm not—you really hurt me!"

"You hurt me; you need to tell me you're sorry."

"I'm sorry; I'm sorry."

"So, what part of what I said hurt you? Tell me." I'm looking into his face. He's avoiding my gaze and hesitates several times. I can see his mind working frantically to find a way out of answering my question.

"Constance, you're a handful, always have been."

I knew he wouldn't tell me. We dance a few more times as Richard looks for reassurance he's not banished from my life. When I give it to him, he kisses me quickly on the lips with a relieved smile. I silently chastise myself for abandoning my resolve so easily.

Granite Bay, California
December 1, 2004

Eddie calls: "Do you know of any rest homes around here? Richard needs to find a place for his mother. He wants her in Sacramento. He's on his way from Fort Bragg."

"I know of a couple of places. If he wants, I'll go with him."

We visit several homes, and make small talk to banish our nervousness. At one stop, Richard jokingly suggests we put our names on the waiting list. "Remember? We're supposed to end up in the same place." He rubs my arm like he used to years ago. The old intimacy feels good.

We had this conversation when Bobby died. Richard wanted me to find a place for the three of us. I didn't like the idea then, telling him I knew how it would be: I'd be cooking and picking up after them while he and Eddie would be in the activities room playing pool and looking up the skirts of the more attractive ladies. There's no way in hell I'd spend my declining years with Eddie, not then, and certainly not now.

Richard declares he's had enough—too depressing. He says he needs a drink. I take him home and make two Perfects that dissolve any remaining tension between us. We slip into that comfortable space of intimacy. We talk about traveling and all the exotic places we want to visit before we die. I can't remember the last time I've seen him this animated and happy.

It's right during rush hour, so I suggest he stay for dinner until the traffic to Eddie's house lightens up. He nervously accepts but tells me he'll catch flak from Eddie for staying. During dinner, we talk about Byrne and remember how he used to be. We touch on the ancient history of my divorcing Eddie. Richard tells me he understood immediately why I had to do it. I thought about asking if he understood why he abandoned me, but I let it go.

We talk about Richard's mother and her health problems. I'm touched he's been with her for over a month, taking care of her and I sense how stressed he is. His mother's a nurse and an Aquarian. I wonder what else she and I have in common besides loving her son. He thanks me for helping him and tells me how much it means to him.

Unthinkingly, I blurt out, "I love you," in explanation of my motivation. I attribute it to the second bottle of wine that I'm not more horrified at my indiscretion.

Richard drops his head to his chest, trying to compose himself. "You are so special to me." His voice cracks on the word special.

"See, we can be alone and control ourselves," I declare. We grin at each other.

I shouldn't let him drive after all the alcohol he's consumed, but I know it's futile to try and stop him. As he leaves he tells me, "I'll catch hell from Ed, but I'm so glad I came."

At this point, Richard stands at a critical karmic junction in all of his relationships—his main lesson in this life. He has all the heavy change planets lined up: Uranus moving into his 8th house of death, intimate relationships and the deep psyche; Neptune in his 7th house of partnerships and relationships, getting ready to dissolve old barriers and boundaries and encourage him to merge with a greater whole; Saturn in his 12th house of karma and the unconscious, stirring up the past, pushing him to let go of false values and attachments, the end of a cycle.

Pluto sits in his 5th house of romance and emotional needs opposing his Venus, encouraging him to discover parts of himself unknown before and change his value system. Uranus opposes his Moon, representing the health problems his mother currently experiences. The energies plan to shake up his reality and bring dramatic changes to his life. He can try to hold the old way of being together, but it's like standing next to a tornado. I pray he'll come through the other side of the challenges with some new insights and philosophy of life. I hope he nails that bloody nun to a cross and walks away, free to be who he really is and be happy. I figure if I can overcome the challenging side of my Venus in Capricorn, he can do the same with his Moon in Virgo. We're not that much different.

I call Eddie to be on the alert for his arrival. "Richard's flying high, and he shouldn't be driving. And no—we did not have sex."

Eddie laughs, a short, nervous burst. I couldn't help myself. I'm grinning as I hang up the phone.

April 2005

I was never comfortable around the residents at the home that first year. I looked at them and could see where Byrne would be in time, and I couldn't bear it. I would breeze in and take him home for his visit, limiting my time and contact with the other residents. When he couldn't walk well enough to leave anymore, I had to face spending time there.

I hate sitting around. I help by serving the food at lunchtime, setting the table, helping get the residents seated. I become part of the daily routine. I come to know each one and see the humanity that still lives behind vacant eyes and mute tongues. I learn to cherish the occasional smile and brief moments of connection. I learn to connect with them emotionally where they are now. I find compassion without drowning in the emotion of it.

I haven't been able to bring Byrne home for at least a year now. He can no longer talk, feed or dress himself. He's in diapers and a wheelchair. He smiles when he sees me, reaching out for me as he's always done. I sit with him and hold his hand. I kiss him. His vacant eyes look somewhere in the distance. I wonder what he's thinking, where he is. I once asked him, when he could still talk and he had that faraway look, "Where are you?"

"Out there."

"What's it like out there?"

"Nice, really nice." I'm comforted that he's happy out there.

Austin, Texas
July 17, 2005

I have a deep longing to connect with that doorway in my 8th house. I'm compelled to attend a workshop on shamanic journeying. I'm not sure why, but I'm here for five days to drum and journey to meet my spirit helpers, my angels on the other side.

The instructor, Hank Wesselman, PhD. an anthropologist, teaches at two of the local community colleges in Sacramento. His workshops guide the student in experiencing ancient methods of achieving mystical states pioneered by traditional shamans, bringing connection to inner sources of wisdom, power and the spirit helpers and guides that connect to our life goals.

I'm amused that I've had to travel all this way to meet him. Until a month ago, I'd never heard of him. He's been practicing shamanism for 24 years. I've read the trilogy of his mystical journey: *Spirit Walker*, *Medicinemaker* and *Vision Seeker*. But it was *Journey to the Sacred Garden* that intrigued me the most, a do-it-yourself book on connecting with spirit helpers on the other side.

I wanted to know if my mother made it to the other side. I followed the protocol in Hank's book: set my intention, meditated to the drums, asked Spirit for help and set off on my journey.

I found her watering the red geraniums in the backyard where she killed herself. I called to her. Excitedly, she hurried to my side. "Where have you been? I've been waiting for you. How do I get out of here?"

I put my hand on her heart and visualized the hole filling with love. She seemed oblivious, being in a hurry. When I felt her heart fill, I called for a spirit helper to come and take her to the other side. I asked for an eagle, but a griffin came instead. I helped her mount the giant beast and told her I loved her. Daddy, Pop and Gramma were waiting for her. She didn't acknowledge me, looking upward. The griffin took flight. An opening in the sky appeared; the griffin flew through, and the opening closed abruptly. I felt an exquisite peace.

I'm excited to see what further connections and adventures I can conjure for myself. Last night, the sound of drums awakened me twice. I feel the energy gathering.

There are six of us in the class, unusually small for Hank's workshops that customarily have 30 or so participants. I'm not fond of large groups, so I thank the spirits for this gift.

We sit on the floor ready to begin our first journey as Hank shakes a rattle. He tells us the drum and rattle cue our Ku—subconscious—to open the door to the other side. I'm aware of someone standing directly in front of me rattling. I open one eye and see Hank still across the room; it isn't him. I conclude it's coming from a spirit, joining Hank in the rattling. I smile; this is going to be good.

Each of us must create our Sacred Garden, a place of refuge and renewal where we can commune with our spirit helpers. If we've already done that, we look to see if anything has changed since the last time we were there. I created my Garden several weeks ago after reading *Journey to the Sacred Garden*. It's a replica of the place Byrne and I go to between lives, the place I visualized in the between lives regression session. It's the same except for a rainbow hovering over my waterfall. My lion greets me affectionately. When he first appeared in my Garden, I asked him what he represented. He told me he was love. A voice called him Richard the Lionhearted. As a rule, entry to the Garden requires an invitation. I don't understand how he found me, but I'm happy to see him.

I tour my vegetable garden, find a few weeds and pull them. I plant a cherry tree and some sunflowers. I go to my room of lights, lie down naked and let the colors dance over my body. I rebalance my energy. My lion comes and lies on top of me like a giant cat. His energy merges into mine.

The afternoon session begins with group drumming and rattling to cue our Ku. I hear a loud droning noise in my left ear, women chanting in my right ear. Hank wants us to find a spirit helper who has a special gift we can access. I want divination. I go to the luxurious bedroom in the house of my Sacred Garden. At the foot of the bed is a round pool of water, looking exactly like the pool Byrne fell into in my dream. It comes to me that it's my access to the middle world where we go when we first die. That's what the dream was telling me: Byrne was moving into that world. I descend into the water, taking Nanya, my Apache Indian helper with me. We glide effortlessly through the water until I see a tunnel, and I go through. A leprechaun waits for us. I expected an animal of some kind. I ask the leprechaun if he's there for me. He bows in assent. I ask if he's to be my divination helper. Again, he bows. I ask his name, and he refuses to tell me. I ask how I'm supposed to call him when I need him. He points to his forehead, tapping his fingers to it. I ask if there's anything he needs to tell me. "You're safe," he replies.

I smile. "Is there anything you want to show me?" I ask.

He takes my hand and leads me through a dark cloud into a bright new world. I see beautiful mountains with snow that feels warm; I slide down one of the mountains like a kid. I'm filled with joy as I fly through a star filled sky in bright daylight. All these things I'm experiencing symbolize a lighter future of joy and love. As I hear Hank's drum change rhythm, the call back, I thank my new helper and return.

The second day, Hank wants us to invite an ancestor who loves us unconditionally into our Sacred Garden. I already know my Gramma will come and she does. She's waiting for me. We have a joyous reunion. I see another figure coming down

Faces of Love, Death and Transformation:

the path, an Indian woman. Excitedly, she waves to us. Aniwa is a Cherokee medicine woman. She's from my father's family several generations back. I'd heard about her when I was a kid. She tells me she's been waiting for me to open up so she could have access to me. The three of us join hands and jump up and down, screaming with glee at our reunion. My spirit helper group grows.

Our next assignment requires enlisting a great shaman to be with us. Hank starts his drumming, and I find myself on the bank of a stream. An Indian sits in front of his teepee. He has on an antler headdress, the sign of a high shaman. He's swaddled in a bison skin, completely alone, no sign of animals or humans. I ask if he's there for me, and he says yes. I ask his name. "Manitou," he replies.

"Isn't that the Indian name for God?"

"We are all God." He then takes me to a canoe, and soon we are sailing through a dark sky, filled with stars; we're in outer space. We swoop down back to earth and fly over a great plain of green absent of trees. I wonder where we are and a voice tells me Ohio. Back at his teepee, we dance together, and he tells me we will have great adventures. I thank him for being part of my spirit helper team and heed Hank's call back.

I'm not satisfied with the God answer Manitou has given me. During discussion, I ask Hank if Manitou is the Indian word for God. He tells me that Manitou really means Spirit. The Jesuits changed the meaning when they converted the Indians to Christianity. The Manitous, mystical, spirit beings to the Algonquin Indians, could assume human form. That makes sense.

Hank discusses the condition of "soul loss." This can occur when we suffer a trauma of some kind. We lose part of ourselves, and that's when disharmony in the form of disease can result. If we die in this state, we can bring that back with us to another life; it's stuck in our energy field.

I think about Byrne. I know after his car accident in 1987, he was never the same. And he's lost his mind in several lives, a recurrent pattern. It comes to me: Byrne's suffering from soul loss.

I haven't been able to figure out why he's been hanging on to this life, and now I think I have the answer. He doesn't want to die with a fragmented soul again. He's waiting to get the pieces back. Now I know why I'm here in this class. I'm overcome with emotion. I tell Hank what I think. He smiles at me and says, "Go find it and bring it back to him. You're very connected to him; you're the person to do it."

I skip lunch and go back to my room. I have to do this. I go to my Garden and call all my helpers. I tell them our assignment. They agree to help. I ask the leprechaun to find the missing piece of Byrne's soul. We find it in a life where he was a sea captain, a drunken, violent man incapable of love. He'd been physically abused and sodomized by family members as a small boy. He mentally escaped to survive. That piece of his soul hides there in that little boy. I call for Manitou to help me bring the little boy back. We find him in a black bubble, whirling in the cosmos. He refuses to come out. Manitou scares him. I call for the leprechaun, and he coaxes him out with a shamrock and a promise of a ride in the canoe.

Byrne waits for us in the Garden. Manitou takes the energy of the little boy and blows him into Byrne's heart and through his head. I see cords of white light connecting each of the lives during which he lost his mind and I see their aura expand. I smile in gratitude as Mary Suellen's father, Albert DeWitt and Byrne become whole again. I ask all my helpers if it worked, and they agree it has. They cheer delightedly.

Joy and peace overwhelm me. I take Byrne to sit under our waterfall together. We hold each other. I know this is where he will be when he passes, and I can come to the Garden whenever I want to be with him. I ask him where he spends his time right now. I laugh when he tells me he's in Detroit with his mother, living in his beloved childhood home. He tells me he's happy. He doesn't want me to be sad. Everything's all right. We'll be together again.

Esalen Institute
Big Sur, California
September 26, 2005

I'm attending the Vision Seeker 3 class taught by Hank and his wife Jill Kuykendall. She's a beautiful, warm and charming woman with an infectious laugh; I see why Hank loves her so much. She co-teaches with him and does soul retrieval work. I know I need to have a session with her at some point in time.

At lunch, Hank asks me how Byrne is doing. I tell him he's unchanged and I'm perplexed at why he's hanging on. He tells me if I want to know, invite Byrne to my Garden and ask him. Sometimes, things really are simple.

I journey to my Garden. Byrne stands on the beach next to a moored boat. I ask him why he's hanging on. He tells me he doesn't want to leave me. He seems surprised when I tell him I can't bear to see him the way he is anymore; it's too hard. I break into sobs; he holds and comforts me. He promises to try and let go.

October 5, 2005

The ballet dancer life as Leah Strom nags at me. I have the feeling she's hanging onto a soul part—a piece of my heart she vowed never to give to anyone again after Richard died in that life. I journey to retrieve it.

I ask Aniwa, my Indian ancestor, to go with me. We find a forlorn Leah sitting in the middle of a darkened stage; her head bowed. A spotlight shines on her dejected figure. She wears an apron with a big pocket on the front.

I approach Leah and tell her who I am. I ask if she has something of mine. She nods yes. I tell her I need it back to help the man she loved in his current life. If I'm to help him, I need my whole heart to do it. She reaches into her pocket and pulls out the piece of my heart. Aniwa steps forward and takes it. I thank Leah and bless her.

Aniwa and I fly back to the Garden where my spirit guide waits. Aniwa gives him the soul part and he blows it into my heart. I feel it expand and warm.

October 10, 2005

The nurse from Somerford calls to tell me Byrne isn't able to swallow anymore and they've put him on hospice care. I'm in shock even though I've expected this. I knew that this fall would be the likely time for Byrne to go with Saturn moving out of my 8th house and into his 8th house, just the way it did back in 1976 when we first got together. Our lives changed drastically during that time, and now it's time again.

I make the calls to tell the family Byrne is dying. Brett and Stacie want to come immediately. I discourage them. I don't want them to see him the way he is, and I don't know how long it will take Byrne to die. I'm not thinking clearly. They tell me they're coming anyway. I'm glad.

A million things whirl in my brain like a cyclone until that evening when my mind becomes still and I know with great clarity what I have to do. I have to bring Byrne home to die. When I tell Melissa what I'm going to do, she cries with relief and affirms I'm doing the right thing. He deserves to die in our bed, in my arms, in our house surrounded by the family and friends who love him. Euphoria and dread fill me. I move into that altered state that helps me survive—a focused numbness fueled with adrenaline.

Melissa and I meet with the hospice nurse at Somerford that morning. She tells me they are available to me 24 hours a day, 7 days a week. Sounds good. She tells me the plan is to give him Ativan suppositories to keep him comfortable and she will get the doctor to write the prescription.

The staff cry when I tell them I'm taking Byrne home. They want some time to tell him good-bye. I know how hard this is for them. We all hug, and I head home to get ready.

The ambulance brings him home that afternoon. I have our bed waiting. I tell Byrne he's home in our bed. I can't tell if he understands what I'm saying. My heart breaks at what this disease has done to him. He weighs 140 pounds, so skeletal and fragile he looks like a soft breeze could shatter him. He holds his arms and legs stiffly, unyielding to movement. His breathing is shallow, rapid and ragged. His eyes stare vacantly into space.

Byrne needs the Ativan. He's struggling and anxious. He's been without food and water since Sunday. It's what he wanted: no extraordinary measures like intravenous or tube feedings to prolong his life. The hospice nurse on call doesn't know anything about his medication; she can't help me tonight. I have to do something to help him. I take some old Vicodin I've had around and crush two of them, mix it with a little water and draw it into a syringe. I hold Byrne's head and dribble the mixture into his mouth slowly so he won't choke. He calms, but he's still not comfortable. I do this through the night.

When I reach the hospice nurse in the morning, she apologizes for the mix-up and tells me she'll get the Ativan today. It doesn't arrive until 5 P.M. The doctor prescribed a half a milligram every six hours. The amount is insufficient and given too infrequently to help him. I'm frustrated and the on-call nurse says she can't help me. I give him the Ativan every four hours, but he has a restless night.

I've been without sleep for several days. I lie down for a nap while Joan sits with Byrne. She comforts him with a cold cloth and massages his head.

The hospice nurse pays a visit and "assesses" Byrne. She tells Joan his blood pressure and pulse are high, his respirations fast and labored. It all indicates he's anxious and uncomfortable. She does nothing.

The family fills the house all six bedrooms are occupied. We prefer being together, so some have to sleep on air mattresses on the floor. We are holding an old fashioned vigil, the way it used to be done. The somber mood of death lightens with the sounds of two babies and three kids playing. Seven-year-old Tanner and five-year-old Hannah know Poppa Byrne is dying and we're sad, but we also celebrate his life by talking to and about him and the wonderful times with him. I'm glad they're experiencing the love, compassion and support we give each other. It's a good lesson in love and in how the circle of life works.

Stacie, Melissa and Brett help me change Byrne's diapers and turn him. Ken and Sandy bring food. Ken and Byrne had a special relationship and I know it's hard for Ken, but he brightens when Byrne responds to his voice. I leave them alone so Ken can say his goodbye privately.

I make a batch of Perfect Manhattans and we all gather on the bed with Byrne and tell Poppa Byrne stories. We laugh; we cry. I dab his mouth with a swab dipped in a Perfect. He smiles slightly when he recognizes the taste. Rylee, Stacie's four-month-old daughter, sits on my lap, reaches over and touches Byrne's face. Her tiny fingers stroke his cheek. I'm sad she'll never experience his love except through those of us who did..

October 13, 2005

I can't bear to see Byrne have another restless night. I tell the on-call nurse that evening I'm furious and frantic. She understands and shares my frustration, but the doctor on-call will only allow him one milligram of Ativan. This isn't the way it was supposed to be. I have to face that I'm on my own.

I gather an assortment of medications from everyone here: Valium, Seconal, Ambien, Percodan, Vicodin. I divide them into equal piles and crush them. I don't know the dosages or what all he's getting; I don't care. He's dying, and I won't have him suffer anymore. I think I have enough to last him through the night until I can get someone at the hospice program to help me in the morning. The medical system he so dearly loved has failed him, but I won't.

Every two hours I dribble the mixture into his mouth. I crawl into bed with him, lie next to his stiff body and listen to the rhythm of his breathing. It progresses from the ragged, sonorous struggle to a quiet, shallow cadence. I can tell he's deeply relaxed. About 4 A.M. his breathing slows and I know it's almost over. I lay my head on his chest and whisper for him to let go. I stroke his head and feel my fingers glide through the soft silkiness of his hair. I kiss the bridge of the nose I love so much. I'm crying quietly. The last breath comes. I lie there for a while, waiting for one more, but he's gone.

I call the hospice nurse and ask her to come pronounce Byrne dead. I don't want to wake the kids yet. I move quietly into Joan and Bob's room and tell them he's gone. Joan reaches out and pulls me into her arms and rocks me as I sob. She puts me between them, and the three of us hold each other until dawn, crying and talking softly.

The days since Byrne died move in slow motion. We all reflect on his death in our own way. Certain memories trigger tears, others laughter. We all gravitate to Rylee, taking comfort in holding her even the men. I hold her and cradle her face in my neck, feeling the warm softness of her baby skin and the smell of her. My depleted heart fills with life.

My brother makes spaghetti for the friends and family who fill the house. He wants to comfort me and this is how he does it. I know how difficult this is for him; it's like reliving Dad's death, but this time he's part of the experience, not cut off and alone. In some way, I know this is healing for him.

Richard and Filben drive 12 hours from Gig Harbor to be here to honor Byrne and support me. I love them for being in my life and being here when I need them.

October 22, 2005

We're having Byrne's memorial service at the Northridge Country Club. The large room's crystal chandeliers dazzle, vast expanses of glass overlook the trees and rolling grass. It's perfectly Byrne: elegant, serene and expansive. A classical guitarist plays Byrne's favorite pieces. The bartender readies to make Perfect Manhattans in honor of Byrne after the service.

We all agree this is better than the church service we originally planned. That plan fell through when several churches rejected us because the focus of the memorial service would be on Byrne rather than Jesus Christ as our personal savior.

Bob leads the service. The kids each eulogize Byrne in touching ways. The boys talk about what Byrne taught them about being a man, the value of honor, honesty and loyalty. I lower my gaze and bite my lip during Darren's speech, cringing at his hypocrisy.

The girls focus on what he gave them as a man and father. Melissa relates how Byrne treated both Stacie and her as his own, and how funny, loving and even a little goofy he was. I break down when she tells us, "And I loved how he loved my Mom."

Stacie tells everyone how she was drawn to Byrne's warmth from the beginning. She said, "You don't know how it makes an eight-year-old little girl feel when someone like Byrne brightens every time you walk in the room, says your name and puts his arms out to you." She said that when she went looking for a husband, she went looking for Byrne: someone sweet, smart, funny— and rich. That gets a little laugh.

I wonder what Eddie is thinking through all this. My sense is he's okay. Byrne stepped in and relieved him of the fathering role he didn't want and I think he's grateful to him for that. He should be.

Writing about my relationship and marriage to Eddie has been difficult, dredging up unresolved feelings of anger for the way he treated me, and the kind of father he's been. Stacie got off easy; he ignored and neglected her while she was growing up. But she's his trophy now that she has a Ph.D. and teaches at the University level.

Melissa didn't fare as well with her father. Her teenage rebellion and irresponsibility reminded Eddie too much of himself. He unleashed all his self-hatred on her, inflicting as much emotional damage as he could. He knows she wants his approval and he deliberately withholds it even though she's matured into a model wife and mother who makes me proud. It still hurts my heart to think of him shoving a loaded gun at our troubled sixteen-year-old daughter and telling her to blow her brains out because she was stupid, useless and didn't deserve to live. Melissa's forgiven him for that and much more. I admire her courage and compassion.

I struggle. I forgive him for being incapable of truly loving anyone, for choosing to remain a child. I have compassion for the hell on earth and the terrible karma he's created for himself in this life. The cruelty I can't forgive or forget.

I am immensely grateful my daughters have come through the challenges of the years whole and happy. They tell me frequently how important a positive influence and role model I've been for them and I see it reflected in their choice of husbands and the joy in their children's eyes. No mother could ask for more.

Brett and I have remained close. He's been a loving, caring son to Byrne and I am grateful to him for showing his father how much he loved him these last difficult years. We've shared this pain together.

I've been kind to Darren these past days, hoping in vain to see some sign of contrition. I have to accept he lacks the ability to connect emotionally. It's why he's never had a successful long-term relationship and remains single at thirty-five. He had the greatest role model in the world on how to be a man, but he's only able to live for himself. It's why he's alone. I feel the same compassion for him I have for Eddie.

Bob shows a 20-minute slide presentation of Byrne's life from childhood to the end. It's filled with joy and love, and touching pictures with those of us who shared his life. I know that Byrne's spirit is here and he's pleased.

The reception is warm and relaxed, fueled by an open bar and beautiful food. The Perfects are perfect and popular. The kids take their shoes off and slide across the slick floor with delight after Bob tells them Poppa Byrne would approve.

We all feel relief. Christine, my niece, comes to me in tears. "Aunt Connie, you've shown our men that no matter how bitchy and difficult we can be, we won't desert them when they need us." I know this has been an important family experience. I'm so proud of all of us.

Richard tells me Filben worries about me, but he told him not to because I'm a survivor. I tell Richard I'm much more than that.

November 7, 2005

I don't want any loose ends. I have an appointment with Jill, Hank's wife, for a soul retrieval session. I'm covering all my bases. If there are any soul parts floating out there, I want them back. I keep thinking about the connection between the Japanese and ballet dancer lives and how those affected the Kentucky and San Francisco lives. I know there's a connection and pattern there that needs to be broken.

I tell Jill about those lives and how I shut down emotionally in the last two past lives. I tell her of my connection to Richard in the dancer life and his uninvited appearance in my Garden.

I lay on the massage table and go into a receiving mode as she sets out on the journey for me with her spirit helpers and guide. Jill begins her detailed narrative:

"I'm encountering the past life as the dancer Leah where she experienced the great pain and made the silent decision that created a kind of personal curse. Instead of protection, it created an emotional paralysis. My guide explains to Leah a little bit more about the current situation; we're here for the next stage of healing for the person now known as Connie. She has contacted you and you have afforded each other a certain amount of resolution.

Suddenly, a vision of your heart appears. It's as if the front and back parts of your heart have separated with a space between. This is the result of the decision she made, so if they weren't together she was no longer vulnerable to the kind of wounding and pain she suffered. But you as Connie can't completely heal that until they do come back together. The guide tells her if she doesn't have the soul part, could she direct us to whomever does. Leah listens intently. She seems greatly relieved as she points up.

We start to go up and find ourselves in the presence of the energetic field of your over-soul. An auric field forms around your over-soul. Between that auric field and your over-soul an object, a spool of golden thread rests, a symbolic presentation of the soul part that left and the thread that will sew the two parts together again. We put out the call and one of your guides comes represented as two arms and hands. It creates a wave-like motion that moves the golden spool to the surface where we can reach it. I bring it into my heart for safekeeping.

We take off again and we're standing in front of the spirit of Richard. My guide tells Richard we are here for the soul part that belongs to Connie. Our man Richard has your soul part and he gave you one of his. That's how he found your Garden, through that soul connection.

Our man Richard has a little courage issue. Change requires a certain level of courage vibration in order to make any changes. It's easier for you than it is for him. I put out the call and a lioness comes and imbues courage into him. He reaches into his heart and here comes this beautiful ball of light, pure essence, hands it back, participates in the releasing and very pleased to be of service. It's all good and positive."

I'm dumbstruck by the session, but not surprised. This is how I end that karma with Richard. Jill points out that this is just as much about my releasing his soul part as getting mine back. It puts things back so we can really meet at our own personal boundaries and be of service to each other. For a real true relationship you have to have boundaries.

She emphasizes his life essence can only serve him and mine me. For people to really know each other they cannot be holding onto each other's soul parts. She tells me it's a common thing for lovers to exchange in that way when there's a deep connection that they feel has to be sustained. I have my assignment.

I want more information about the soul parts before I release Richard. I want to know what we gave each other. My guide tells me I gave Richard my capacity for joy in the dancer life. He gave me his trust in the goodness of life—makes sense.

I prepare the soul release ritual by lighting a candle. I state my intention to release Richard's soul part. I journey to my Garden and ask the lioness to come. I tell her I'm going to release Richard's soul part and I ask that she safeguard it and give it back to him. She agrees. I ask her to stay with him and give him courage. I release the soul part and blow out the candle. I feel a strong energy leave my body. It's done. Whatever happens now between us won't have that karma driving it.

I reflect on how drastically my life changes with each life transition. I don't think this time will be any different.

January 28, 2006

I visit Byrne regularly in the Garden, but it's hard not to question what I experience as real. I'd like some concrete validation.

I'm drifting between the awake and sleep state. I hear Byrne's voice say, "Darren." My heart sinks. He wants to tell me something. I think he wants me to make peace with Darren and I really don't want to do that. I journey to the Garden and ask Byrne what's up with Darren. He tells me Darren is in deep legal trouble and if he calls me asking for money, I'm not to give him any. I'm shocked. I expected something totally different. I assure Byrne I won't bail him out.

A week goes by and Brett calls me. He's calling to give me a head's up. He's deliberately vague about details, but tells me Darren is experiencing some problems and I may be hearing from him.

"Let me tell you what your father told me." I describe my experience.

After a few seconds of shocked silence, Brett says, "That's 100 percent correct."

I have my concrete validation. I'm ecstatic. Byrne and I are still communicating and looking out for each other, no barriers even in death.

I've spent nine years grieving since Byrne was diagnosed and I thought I didn't have any left, but I find I need more time to let go of Byrne. I'm visiting our Garden too often. I sob each time I see him. Byrne comforts me, tells me to hang in and I'll be happy again. Finally, he tells me he's leaving the Garden for a while because I need to move on and I won't if he's there every time I visit. He tells me I have to focus on the tasks at hand like finishing this book. I feel like I've lost Byrne again and it's wrenching. But I know he's right.

I've been sitting here at the intersection of my life for a long while waiting for the red light to turn green. Now that it has, I decide I need to linger. A haze of uncertainty clouds my vision. I don't want to move forward until I can see where I'm headed. There's no hurry.

When I look back on this life, I realize with gratitude that all went as planned, like a play in which we each performed our parts well, entering and exiting on cue with precision, the story unfolding as I the author intended, seamlessly.

Although my time with Bobby was relatively short—ten years—he played a critical role in my evolution. Bobby anchored me emotionally through those ten years when I needed him the most, comforting me through my dark times with Richard and nurturing and supporting me while I struggled in my relationship with Eddie. He never told me what to do or judged me. He asked nothing of me. He just loved me. My love and respect for him remains as strong now as it was when he died. I love that we are still connected.

When Eddie exited my life, Byrne entered at precisely the right time. I'm not sure

I would have been emotionally ready for him, or he me, until we experienced and fully acknowledged the pain of emotional deprivation from the two emotionally flawed people who were unable to love us. I'm grateful to Eddie and MJ for the roles they've played. The pain they caused us forged a strong bond between Byrne and me. It gave us the unwavering dedication to make our relationship as fulfilling as the others were empty. Our love benefited everyone in our lives.

Without Byrne's love, I don't think I ever would have been able to dig as deep into myself as I have, to have the courage to go to those painful places and put myself back together into a brave new form, to be the person I've come to be and fulfill my destiny. I owe him so much. I wish for everyone to know that kind of love.

Richard's implacable will weathered the assault of the heavy change planets. Their attempts to get him to heal the ancient wounds he's buried over the course of this and past lives were for naught. He is still the same person and I am not. It would never work. Our reason for being in each other's lives is done. I will always love that twenty-three year old I fell in love with. But I'm moving on and I intend to be happy again. Byrne loved me enough to last me the rest of this life.

Astrologically and psychologically, I'm back where I was in the summer of 1976. I'm tying up the loose ends of the 8th house energy, finishing my grieving for the life that's passing away and anticipating the new one waiting for me when Saturn moves into my 9th house in June. I look forward to the lighter energy. And for a while, it is.

May 18, 2007

It's funny how the planting of one tiny seed can blossom into a great adventure full of promise and potential.

A year ago I watched a special on the rain forests of South America and the role of plant medicines in the practices of the indigenous shamans. When researchers queried the shamans on how they learned to use the plants, they told them the plants spoke to them. That thought germinated over time and burst into life when I came upon a website from the rain forest in Peru offering the experience of working with the plant medicines Ayahuasca and Huachuma in a safe setting with two expert shamans. I want the plants to teach me and heal the pain and sadness that linger after Byrne's death.

Faces of Love, Death and Transformation:

Ayahuasca is a feminine energy, a powerful medicine said to purge you physically, emotionally, mentally and spiritually. The process is intense and challenging on all levels. Called La Purga, Ayahuasca often induces vomiting and diarrhea to clear debris from the energy field. I'd rather die than vomit, but I understand the necessity of clearing toxins. I'm desperate and ready to accept help and do anything.

There are seven of us: two women and five men. We sit in a circle in the thatch covered ceremony room deep in the jungle, passing the "talking stick" and sharing why we are here. I listen politely but inattentively. I'm exhausted emotionally and physically, mindful of only my own needs.

James is a casting director from Hollywood, a tall, dark and attractive 39-year-old. He's wired tightly as a suicide bomber with a vest full of explosives. "I am depressed and filled with rage and pain. I live in the most polluted city in the world and work with the most fucked up, corrupt, sleazy pieces of shit that ever walked the earth. I'm not married or even in a relationship. I'm not connected to anything. I'm not even connected to myself."

I am amazed at his candor. And Samhadi, the other woman in the group, drinks in James' litany of anger and pain like a thirsty vampire. The light in her eyes says she's not about to adhere to the agreement to not engage in tempting thoughts or actions of a sexual nature while here.

Samhadi, an acupuncturist from Colorado, speaks English with a thick German accent. She changed her name from Ursula to the East Indian name meaning self-realization. Recounting the break-up with a man she loved reduces her to tears. It's the last time she shows any emotion or shares herself in any way with the group.

Carl, the blond haired, blue-eyed psychologist from San Diego, seems sweet and vulnerable, yet has a reserved demeanor. He's depressed and suffers from chronic asthma and tinnitus, a constant ringing in his ears.

Debilitating depression and Post Traumatic Stress Syndrome plague Tom, a pony-tailed Vietnam vet from New Mexico. He's missing half of his right hand and tells us he was gut shot by an AK47 in Vietnam, his body full of shrapnel. His kind eyes gleam from his weathered, lined face, masking deep pain. He frequently punctuates his sentences with loud, raucous laughter. He's on total disability and spends his time traveling and studying shamanism.

Don is Tom's best friend, a tall, lean man with the air of a Southern gentlemen from another time. He shares Tom's interest in shamanism and other forms of alternative healing. I like them both. They remind me of the old cartoon characters Heckel and Jeckel, two magpies sitting on a fence watching and commenting on the world passing by. They never stop talking or smoking.

Dan moved to Peru from the States several months ago to apprentice with Howard. Spirit led him here to hone his shamanic skills and learn how to access that state of divine consciousness and communion critical to a shaman. Dan has a smile that says he loves life and blue eyes that sparkle with an inner joy you don't often see. He's friendly, approachable, funny and immensely kind.

I purposely keep my reasons for coming generic, citing the wish for a closer relationship with Spirit and my ongoing work with shamanism. I know if I get into the specifics I will end up sobbing. I'm not doing that. I'm having a hard time keeping myself together as it is.

Ayahuasca and SSRI antidepressants like Prozac don't mix and can be physically hazardous. I stopped taking my 5 milligrams a day three months ago. I've been taking Prozac since Byrne's Alzheimer's diagnosis ten years ago to keep from falling apart emotionally; without it I cry with the slightest provocation like a newly pregnant woman at the mercy of raging hormones. It's frustrating and exhausting.

Prozac anesthetizes my demons, allowing us to co-exist. I don't want that; I want them exorcised. My inappropriate crying plagues me because I haven't allowed myself to cry when it was appropriate. I harbor long-held tears of a lifetime. I'm terrified if I let them loose, they will drown me.

I've read Ayahuasca can rewire your brain so you don't need antidepressants. We're all here to banish depression. I want my brain rewired and my heart opened. I know I can't move on until that's done.

The two shamans couldn't be more different physically. Howard, American born, stands 6 feet 4 inches with a slim, strong body, a shock of white, curly hair and intense gray-green eyes. The natives call him Otorongo Blanco, the white jaguar. Howard reminds me of Byrne the way he sits and walks with easy grace and the confidence of a healer with strong intention and purpose. I find the resemblance distressing and comforting.

Don Rober, the Peruvian born shaman, is about 5 feet tall with a compact, muscular body and mischievous dark eyes. He wears a white tank type tee shirt and long pants, his hair coal black even at 62 years. Don Rober is a Banco Ayahuascero—a master shaman of Ayahuasca. He apprenticed himself to his uncle, a renowned Ayahuascero, at age eight.

It's Monday. We've been here at the Sanctuary since Saturday getting acclimated to our rustic surroundings and accommodations. The walls and floors of our rooms are wood planks, the beds standard Peruvian: wooden frame and slats with a two-inch mattress. Each room has a toilet and basin. We shower in stalls situated at the end of the two rows of dormitory like rooms. An unreliable solar system yields cold to tepid water.

Three Peruvian women cheerfully prepare our food in a primitive hut, turning out surprisingly good food in spite of the restriction on salt, sugar, fats, spices and pork, all things prohibited while "dieting" Ayahuasca. We dine on chicken, fish, rice, vegetables and local fruits. I'm addicted to the chicken soup with vegetables, requesting it even for breakfast.

As a group, we bonded over a 10-mile hike into the jungle on Sunday to attend a Harvest Festival given by the local Indians. We affectionately refer to the experience as the Bataan Death March. The highlight of the day for me was being peed on by Ruffa the resident monkey and dancing with a half naked shaman in a breechcloth with bells around his ankles.

Tonight is our first Ayahuasca ceremony. At 9 P.M., we sit in a circle in the large ceremony room decorated with tapestries made by the Shipibo Indians. We rest in rocking chairs made with plastic strips. Buckets with an inch of water sit at our feet. Flickering candles provide the only light. The Ayahuasca that Don Rober spent 12 hours brewing waits for us on the altar. Our anticipation and anxiety are palpable.

Someone asks Dan if he vomits every time he drinks Ayahuasca. He smiles widely, "Almost every time. I'm disappointed if I don't." He isn't kidding.

Don Rober and Howard enter dressed in their traditional shaman attire: round skullcaps with elaborate stitching around the band, white tunic and loose fitting white pants. The bond between the two men is a logical consequence of the love, trust and admiration they share for each other. We know we are in good hands.

Don Rober starts the ceremony, explaining in Spanish that there is only good medicine here, no black magic. He wishes us all well with our healing.

Howard tells us if we need to do any intestinal releasing to say the word, "baño" and one of the attendants will escort us to our room.

We each move to the altar when we are called and drink the Ayahuasca, legendary for its vile taste that we all agree is well deserved.

We settle into our rockers. Howard blows the candles out. We sit silently in complete darkness. Don Rober begins his icaro, the song that beckons the spirits of Ayahuasca to come and heal us. He chants in a mixture of Spanish and Quechua, an ancient language little used now. He moves to each one of us, tapping rhythmically on the tops of our heads with schacapa leaves, blowing the sacred tobacco smoke, mapacho, onto our crowns to open our energy field and protect us.

I keep my eyes closed and wait for visions. I feel the medicine move through my body. I'm nauseated and soon begin vomiting. This isn't polite puking, but gut wrenching, violent eruptions. I hear Carl next to me start vomiting and the sound of Don Rober sucking something out of Carl's ear. I figure he must be trying to heal Carl's tinnitus.

A movie screen showing Asian looking people smile at me. I sense these are past lives. A collage of images moves in slow motion; unfamiliar couples glide across the screen locked in various embraces. I think this denotes my outmoded concept of romantic love and that it needs to change, but I don't know how as yet. After numerous bouts, the visions and the vomiting cease. I ask the spirits if they're done and they say they are. I'm disappointed something more dramatic didn't happen. I console myself that this is physical cleansing and I didn't have that much to release. I'm in good shape.

Carl reports to the group that the ringing in his ears has lessened and now he can actually tell where sounds are coming from, impossible before. He's happy. Tom tells us he could see purple light shooting out of Carl's ears when Don Rober was sucking energy out.

The next night, we do the second ceremony to cleanse the toxins related to mental and emotional residue. This time I keep my eyes open and wait quietly. After a few minutes, I see bright colored blue fish swimming on the periphery of my vision. Suddenly, the room turns into the interior of a jet liner. Seats appear like magic on either side of me, and a row in front of me. A large black screen drops from nowhere. I'm entranced as objects float around the room. A thought form tells me to enjoy the flight and watch the movie. Now, I'm excited. I cross my legs, shift my position in my chair and get ready.

The first vision on the screen shows the five nuns who taught me in grammar school. I recognize each one. They disappear and I immediately vomit three or four times. At last I am rid of Sister Mary Christopher and the havoc she wreaked on my psyche.

The Ayahuasca gathers energy, reaches a crescendo and explodes inside me, racing to my brain like a runaway freight train, moving down the mid-hemisphere and bifurcating at the frontal lobes, the emotional center. I'm ecstatic. I've read Ayahuasca has a consciousness of its own; it knows where to go and what to do.

The sensations in my head feel like a brain orgasm. New neural pathways open on my right side. I feel reconstruction work being done on the left side.

The energy subsides; my brain appears on the screen healed and healthy. The color is blue—cross-culturally the symbol of wisdom and clarity. My request has been granted.

Spirits fill the room, gliding on air; their lighted bodies transparent and vibrating like neon signs. I realize these are not hallucinations. The Ayahuasca raised my vibratory rate, removing the veil between the dimensions. I'm dizzy with delight and awe.

I hear female voices chanting in unison with Don Rober. A woman with an elaborate headdress stands in back of the seat adjacent to me. As I turn to look at her, she steps out of my vision and points to the screen in gentle reprimand of my distraction. I return my attention to the screen to view scenes from this life. It seems important for me to acknowledge these connections to judgments, self-judgments and regrets before releasing them in another wave of vomiting. I hear calls of "baño" across the room. At least my intestines are behaving.

I notice with some amazement that each time I lean forward to vomit, the airline seat in front of me moves forward to give me more room. When I'm done, it moves back into position. This is just wild—equal parts of agony and ecstasy tangled together in a jumbled assault on all of my senses.

After three or four hours, I'm on overload, my head in my hands, leaning over the bucket. I'm reduced to vomiting bile. The noxious tasting combination of bile and Ayahuasca has me spitting into the bucket repeatedly. My throat is on fire. I'm begging for it to all stop and then countermanding that request with a plea to continue. I want it all out. It's what I came for.

An older woman with black hair now occupies the seat next to me. I'm seeing the spirit of Ayahuasca herself. I want to talk to her, but she turns to me and points to the screen. More vomiting. The chanting grows stronger and more intense.

I hear violent retching right next to me. I look and see a man on his knees vomiting into a bowl in Mother Ayahuasca's lap. She asks me if I recognize the man. His face morphs into Don Rober. I understand he's helping me clear by vomiting with me. I'm most grateful for his dedication and express my appreciation. I can't believe he's been doing this work for fifty years.

The next morning we gather as a group to share our experiences. Carl goes first. He tells us he was beset by demons, tearing at him, intent on killing him. He bursts into sobs, taking several minutes to compose himself. He fought the demons until angels came and rescued him. He cries again. His final words are, "There is nothing you can say that will ever get me to do that again." We understand—perfectly.

James is furious. "I am fucking pissed! It was terrible. You're all alone, no fucking support or comfort, just pain. Nothing but pain! Why does there have to be so much pain?"

I'm struck by the difference in our experiences. I saw spirits supporting everyone. For James, it was an expression of all the pain he's been harboring his whole life and the lack of support and comfort he feels in his life.

Samhadi informs us she does not suffer and talking about things does not help her. I'm tempted to ask her what does help her, but I really don't care.

We all agree we don't want to do this again; it's too hard.

The next day, James is a different person. His anger and angst have left. He's mellow, happy and upbeat. We are thrilled for him. He just needed time for the energy to settle and work its magic. Howard says Ayahuasca is the gift that keeps on giving.

This is the last ceremony. In spite of our protests, we are all present and ready to belly up to the bar. I've been apprehensive all day. My intestines tell me I'm going to see some action on that front tonight.

I huddle in my rocker in the ceremony room with my blanket wrapped around me squaw style. It's cold. A storm blew in earlier. The rain lashes the trees and soaks the ground. The wind blows fiercely in the unfriendly darkness as thunder shatters the usual quiet. I clutch my small flashlight like a protective totem in anticipation of a dash to the "baño."

The theme tonight is spiritual healing. I have no idea what awaits me, but I'm praying for mercy already.

The black screen reappears for me after profuse vomiting. The visions come in sepia tones of a late autumn at dusk dulled by dark clouds, grim and gray before the onset of rain. The scenes of my life with Byrne unfold in slow motion, punctuated by dead leaves falling from some unseen trees.

A man's voice calls to me in Spanish from far away, asking if I can hear him. I ignore his entreaty and turn my attention back to the screen. He keeps asking me the same question, turning up the volume each time as I ignore him. At last, he asks me in English at a volume I can't ignore. I answer in a decidedly irritated tone that I hear him and can't he see that I'm busy and please go away. I get the impression I'm being attuned in some way for further transmissions at a later time, but I have more pressing issues in front of me.

Byrne and I appear together on the screen hand-in-hand. I watch us doing all the things we used to love doing together. We are so happy and filled with love. The tears gather in my eyes. Now, we stand together holding hands, joyful and smiling. The focus moves to our clasped hands in a close-up. Byrne gently releases my hand and steps away, leaving me standing alone. The pain comes in waves, choking me. The vomiting racks me to my soul.

I'm deeply angry. I don't see anything spiritual about this; it's just more torture. I'm crying. Ayahuasca has stripped away the experiences of my whole life, everything that defined me both good and ill. I'm left with nothing but bare bones to start over. I feel alone and afraid.

The light dawns: I have just experienced what shamans call "the little death." I have died to myself to be reborn into a new form. At that moment, my intestines signal for release. I jump to my feet, flashlight in my hand and declare "baño." I'm dizzy and totally disoriented. I reach for the post I think is in front of me to steady myself; it isn't there but about three feet away. I'm falling. Don Rober's wife catches me, steadies me and leads me to my room, telling me "No tiene miedo, no miedo." Have no fear.

The intestinal release doesn't take long. I try to stand up, but I'm too dizzy. I sit on the toilet for what seems like hours, waiting for the Ayahuasca to wear off enough so I can at least get to my bed. I'm still crying and vomiting. Fortunately, the basin is conveniently close to the toilet so I can release from either direction simultaneously. I sit there observing various spirits sleeping on the spare bed, but have no interaction with them.

Samhadi has the room next to mine. The walls are thin. I hear her releasing from both ends. I ruminate with glee if she can still say she does not suffer, and then chide myself for being petty.

Out of nowhere, a hand appears in the doorway of the bathroom. I sense it's a male energy, possibly Don Rober. In his hand, he holds a white cocoon. It lights up as he blows on it, flies across the room and explodes on the wall. A white butterfly emerges and flies away. He does this three times with the same results. I understand the message: my transformation is complete. I'm too traumatized to be properly joyful, but I am appreciative.

At last I'm oriented enough to crawl to my bed, my pants around my ankles. I curl up on the bed in the fetal position. I'm shivering violently and cold to my bones. My blanket is in the ceremony room and I can't make it that far. I think about my shivering and liken it to the kind women experience right after they give birth. I realize in that instant that I've just given birth to myself. Now, I'm filled with a muted, exhausted joy.

It all makes sense: the three ceremonies were like the three stages of the birth process for me: early labor, active labor and finally birth. That's why each ceremony was more, not less, intense for me. I congratulate myself for surviving and overcoming my fears.

I walk cautiously back to the ceremony room, holding onto the railing. I don't want to miss Don Rober closing my energy field with the schacapa leaves and mapacho smoke. The room is empty except for Don Rober and Howard. The others, still in their bathrooms releasing, file back one by one to get their closing.

I think I'm home free, but I'm not.

May 27, 2007

Samhadi, James and Carl left yesterday. I give James credit for not succumbing to Samhadi's persistent efforts to seduce him. I'm glad she's gone. Her discordant energy was too distracting.

Today is our first Huachuma ceremony. I have no idea what to expect. All I know is Huachuma is a powerful male energy. Tom and Don are veteran mescaline users, and the newest addition to the group, Yuri, tells me it's like having an eight-hour orgasm. I brighten at the thought.

The ceremony begins at 2 P.M. so we have four hours of daylight and four hours of night while under the influence. Howard prepared an elaborate altar of sacred and ancient artifacts called a mesa. Shaped like a cross, it holds human and jaguar skulls, crystals, swords, a large, intricately carved stone lanzón and long-burning candles.

I come forward when Howard beckons. I take the Huachuma brew in my hands; it's filled to the brim of the cup. Howard's gaze and mine lock in unspoken understanding of what is to come. I know I'm in trouble. I gulp half the brackish liquid and gag uncontrollably. I breathe deeply and finish drinking, shivering violently from the taste I find more vile than the Ayahuasca. I eagerly accept a glass of limeade to kill the aftertaste.

Thirty minutes later I feel the first effects, a kind of dreamy, spacey detachment. My skin doesn't seem elastic enough to hold the mounting energy and it's uncomfortable. Everything is more intense: color, sound and feeling. I'm nauseated and concentrate on burping to relieve the pressure. For once, I wish I could vomit. Periodically, pleasant chills run through my body.

We are in the boat, going to visit the Santa Clara Indians who live some miles down the river from the Sanctuary. I feel out of control, physically ill and acutely anxious.

After docking, Tom and Don stay close to help me as we walk down a rickety bridge to the village. I cling to the railing for safety, walking slowly. At the end of the bridge, I stand and breathe deeply, trying to decide whether or not to stick my finger down my throat. I decide not and lie down on the concrete abutment. I curse Yuri and his promise of eight-hour orgasms. I wait for the others to finish their trading so we can go back to the Sanctuary. It's dark when we get back.

I've lost track of time. I don't know how long I've been in bed watching the wood walls breathe, rhythmically contracting and expanding. The mournful sounds of exotic birds punctuate the unearthly, bleak stillness I feel all around me. It's all very twilight zone and for the first time I'm afraid.

Howard comes to the door and instructs me to join everyone in the ceremony room so he can ground me. I hobble behind him like a wounded bird.

As I collapse in the rocking chair and pull my blanket around my shoulders, I'm bathed in sweat, my hair damp and plastered to my face. I'm sure I smell, but everything is so distorted I can't be sure.

Howard hands me a large crystal and tells me to hold it to my heart. I clutch it to my breast in desperation. Immediately, sobs well uncontrollably from a subterranean recess in my soul and envelope me. My head on my chest, I let the tears and pain wash over me. I don't really know why I'm crying, but I have to. Tears and snot mingle with sweat.

Howard sits next to me and takes my hand. "Feel your heart open."

Immediately, I feel a surge of powerful energy moving into my heart, filling it with love and compassion for everyone and everything, expanding with welcome warmth. I'm crying even harder and babbling incoherent words of gratitude for this extraordinary gift. My journey of the heart is complete at last. The male energy wounded my heart and now it heals it. Perfect synergy.

Howard smiles at me. "A new day is dawning for you."

And it has.

Faces of Love, Death and Transformation:

About The Author

For the first half of her life, Connie Marshall wanted the usual things: love and professional success. After several botched attempts to make Princes out of badly flawed frogs, she married Byrne, the love of her life, the sweet, funny, intelligent, romantic and handsome man she had dreamed of as a teen-ager. They successfully blended Connie's two daughters and his two sons into an enduring extended family.

Then came professional success: Connie earned a Master's degree in Nursing from UC San Francisco, moved into a high profile career where she taught, authored numerous articles and chapters in nursing textbooks and professional journals, spoke at national conferences and saw her consumer books From Here To Maternity and The Expectant Father published.

On turning forty, a hunger to connect with something greater than the self emerged, leading to world travel to sacred sites, astrology, meditation, past life regressions, and study of alternate forms of healing such as Reiki. Spiritual seeking became a passionate way of life.

Great love and great loss often go hand-in-hand. Byrne's terminal illness drove Connie even deeper into her heart, looking for ways to support him and cope with the immense challenges of day-to-day survival. She found inspiring, non-ordinary reality solutions to ordinary reality problems.

New teachers came to help: shamanism's connection to non-ordinary reality, opened the door to ways to transcend the inevitable crumbling of life structures and move to new levels of understanding. In the rain forests of northern Peru, studying with shamans, she completed her journey of the heart. This book is the story of that journey.

Faces of Love, Death and Transformation: